A —

TRADITION
THAT HAS
NO NAME

A

TRADITION
THAT HAS
NO NAME

*Nurturing
the Development
of People, Families,
and Communities*

Mary Field Belenky
Lynne A. Bond
Jacqueline S. Weinstock

BasicBooks
A Division of HarperCollins*Publishers*

Designed by Nancy Sabato

Library of Congress Cataloging-in-Publication Data

Belenky, Mary Field
    A tradition that has no name : nurturing the development of people, families, and
    communities / Mary Field Belenky, Lynne A. Bond, and Jacqueline S. Weinstock.
    —1st ed.
        p.   cm.
    Includes index.
    ISBN 0-465-02605-2
    1. Women—United States—Psychology.   2. Women—United States—Attitudes.
    3. Self-actualization (Psychology)   4. Leadership in women—United States.
    5. Women in community development—United States.   I. Bond, Lynne A., 1949– .
    II. Weinstock, Jacqueline S., 1961– .   III. Title.
    HQ1206.B345   1997
    155.6'33—dc21   96-53583
                                                                                CIP

97 98 99 00 01   10 9 8 7 6 5 4 3 2 1

To the memory of Ella Baker
1903 to 1986

Ella Baker was the adult advisor to the young people who created SNCC, the Student Nonviolent Coordinating Committee. This African American woman greatly intensified the quest for social justice in America. She sponsored a number of organizations—we call them public homeplaces—where silenced and excluded people meet, nurture each other's development, and emerge as leaders with a real say in the way their communities are run. They, in turn, go on to nurture the development of still others struggling to have a voice in society. Ella Baker was an outstanding example of a leader whose primary goal was bringing people from the margins into voice—an essential step in building a more inclusive, caring, and democratic society. Her story helped us see that many of the women we interviewed for this book were carrying on a long-standing tradition.

◈ CONTENTS ◈

◈ ACKNOWLEDGMENTS ◈

The Listening Partners (LP) program was supported by grants awarded to Lynne A. Bond and Mary Field Belenky from the Bureau of Maternal and Child Health of the Public Health Service, U.S. Department of Health and Human Services (#MCJ-500541, October 1, 1986, to June 1, 1991), the A. L. Mailman Family Foundation, and the Bendheim Foundation. We are indebted to all of the mothers who participated in this project. The group co-leaders—Jean Lathrop, Laura Latham Smith, and Ann Dunn—played key roles in the program design and implementation. The Lamoille Family Center in Morrisville, Vermont, sponsored and housed the program. Toni Cook, Ene Piirak, Patricia Burgmeier, Mary Sue Rowley, and David Howell helped with aspects of the research component. Ann Stanton spent a sabbatical year helping us analyze the data and think about the implications of our findings. Nevitt Sanford's support and encouragement led us to believe that a project like this was possible.

The Public Homeplace study was supported by the A. L. Mailman Family Foundation, the Green Mountain Fund for Popular Struggle, the Needmore Fund, and the late Virginia Stranahan. Elaine van der Stok was a dedicated transcriber of the interviews.

For an understanding of the Mothers' Center movement in the United States, we are indebted to the founder Patsy Turrini and Lorri Slepian, a leader of the organization for many years. Other founding members who helped us understand the early history include Phyllis Adler, Kathy Dolengewicz, Linda Itzkowtiz, Jane Maddalena-Barbieri, the late Joanne Magnus, Margaret Milch, and Wendy Wilson. Current members and staff who helped us understand the organization as it is today include: Ginni Allfrey, Maggie Cole, Suzanne Feingold, Brenda Kelly, Linda Landsman, Teresa Magee, Jeanette Mattar, Pam Mele, Mary Beth Merritt, Pam Reardon, Lynne Ritucci, Nancy Shaw, Michelle Todesca, and Sue Wald.

For an understanding of the German Mothers' Centers we thank the founders, Monika Jaeckel and Hildegard Schoos. We are also indebted to the many women who described their experiences with the Mothers' Center movement and the impact these have had on them and their lives. Angelika Blickauser, Eva Orth, and Hannelore Weskamp helped us understand the social context that gave rise to the Mothers' Center movement in Germany. These dialogues were greatly facilitated by the generosity of the Heinrich-Böll Foundation.

Our understanding of the National Congress of Neighborhood Women (NW) was facilitated by its founder Jan Peterson and a long list of past and present members or supporters. They include Katrin Adams, Lisel Burns, Elaine Carpinelli, Marie Cirillo, Maria Fava, Ronnie Feit, Angie Giglio, Ann Giordano, Ied Guiness, Mildred Johnson, Carol Judy, Brownie Ledbetter, Peggy Macintosh, Caroline Pezzullo, Lyn Pyle, Sangeetha Purushothaman, Susan Saegert, Sandy Schilen, Gwynn Smalls, the late Tessie Smith, Habiba Soudan, Elizabeth Speranza, Tillie Tarantino, and Zan White.

For an understanding of the Center for Cultural and Community Development (CCCD) we thank the founders Jane Sapp and Rose Sanders, as well as many groups of people who told us how their lives were touched by cultural work and CCCD. Former students at Miles College, in Birmingham, Alabama, and members of the African Ensemble include Lois Jennings, Valencia Power Bell, Nadine Smith, and Morgan Della Nettles. Those involved in cultural work projects at Miles College's satellite campus in Eutaw, Alabama, included Deborah Eatman, Etta Edwards, Elzora Fluker, Mollie Gaines, and Carol Zippert. Willie King and his group of musicians and supporters in Pickens County, Alabama, included Grayling Bantum, Azeline Prince, and Kennith Smith. Dean Elias, Gwendolyn Kaltoft, Suzanne Noble, David Osher, SuZanne Pharr, Nayo Watkins, and Alex Willingham gave us helpful feedback.

There are certain individuals who, for one or more of us, have contributed in diverse and the most fundamental ways to our understanding and experience of public homeplace: Robert Belenky, Anna Bond, Robert Bond, Lyn Mikel Brown, Dorothy Forsyth, William A. Gamson, Zelda Gamson, Nancy Goldberger, Betsy Hinden, Dana Jack, Josie Juhasz, Anita Landa, Lisa Peattie, Ann Rath, Sara Ruddick, and Jill

Mattuck Tarule. Blythe Clinchy's work on connected knowing enabled us to see an unnamed tradition, and gave us words to describe that legacy.

Each of us authors acknowledges one another among this group as well, as our collaboration over more than a decade has opened us to so many possibilities. We express our deepest gratitude for the vision, values, and new knowledge that have emerged from all of these relationships.

PART 1

OTHERNESS

INTRODUCTION:
OTHERNESS AND SILENCE

*We are presented as being subcultural, as if we are outside, the Other—
a tangent, a limb or something that if lost by the main body, life would
not be threatened. . . . The collective psyche of this society is based on
denying the existence of a society that is multi-cultural and composed of
many peoples and classes, existing in a world that is very small and
dominated by women, children, and peoples of color.*
                            BERNICE JOHNSON REAGON (1990, P. 4)
                            FOUNDER, SWEET HONEY IN THE ROCK

All too often girls and women are stigmatized as Other—different, deficient, unworthy of being full participants in society, their interests subordinated to those in power. Women living in poverty, immigrant women, and women of color are likely to face additional, more extreme forms of prejudice as well.

As a demeaned outsider, the Other can become an easy target, blamed for the problems that society cannot or will not solve (Allport, 1958; Gans, 1995; Katz, 1989). Increasingly the poor—especially mothers and people of color—are being scapegoated for causing poverty in the United States. More and more women from all walks of life are actually the victims of massive social and economic forces that are driving them and their children into poverty at unprecedented rates. Even before the recent dismantling of social programs that provided a safety net began, the percentage of mothers and children living in poverty in the United States was the highest among the developed nations of the world (Sherman, 1994; Sidel, 1996).

Many women accept the demeaning stereotypes, silently withdrawing from the social life of their community. Others ignore the degrading preconceptions, live full lives, and develop a full range of their powers. Some become community leaders who devote themselves to drawing out the voices of the silenced and making communities more nurturing places to live. Because this form of women's leadership runs counter to the conventional conceptions of both women and public leaders, these strong, powerful women remain largely invisible, their words unheard, and society fails to reap the full benefit of their contribution.

In this book we tell many versions of one story: how people help each other move out of the silence, claim the power of their minds, exercise their leadership, and come to have a real say in the way their lives, families, and communities are being run. This story grows out of a tale first told in *Women's Ways of Knowing: The Development of Self, Voice, and Mind* (Belenky, Clinchy, Goldberger, and Tarule, 1986/1997).

We start with Rachel's version of the story. Rachel was a participant in the Listening Partners project—one of several programs discussed in this book dedicated to bringing an excluded group into voice. The Listening Partners project focused on very isolated mothers of small children living in rural poverty in northern Vermont not far from the Canadian border. We developed the Listening Partners project to explore a basic question: Would being a member of a group where people listen to each other with the greatest of care enable isolated mothers to gain a voice, claim the power of their good minds, and break out of their seclusion? To assess the effects of the program we interviewed all of the participants (along with a matched group of nonparticipants) on three different occasions: at the beginning of the eight-month program, at the end, and almost a year after completing the program. This is how Rachel responded to some of our questions during the first round of interviews:[1]

CAN YOU THINK OF A TIME WHEN YOU HAD TO MAKE A DECISION, BUT YOU JUST WEREN'T SURE WHAT WAS RIGHT?

I don't know. *(long pause)*

A BIG DECISION. IT COULD BE RECENT; IT COULD BE ANYTIME IN THE PAST.

Hmmm, I don't know. *(long pause)*

DID LEAVING SCHOOL SEEM LIKE A BIG DECISION?

No, not really.

IT JUST SORT OF HAPPENED?

Yeah.

DID HAVING YOUR DAUGHTER SEEM LIKE A BIG DE-CISION?

No. *(laughs)* Because it wasn't a decision, it just happened.

WHAT ABOUT MOVING IN WITH YOUR BOYFRIEND?

Uh huh. We've been together for over three years; it will be four years.

WAS THAT A DECISION?

No. *(both laugh)*

WELL, THAT'S INTERESTING! WHAT'S YOUR LIFE GO-ING TO BE LIKE IN THE FUTURE, SAY A YEAR FROM NOW?

I don't know for sure. I don't like to think about things. I don't expect anything to change.

At the time of this first interview, Rachel did not believe she could think for herself even though she said she was a "really smart" person. This apparent anomaly occurred because Rachel had not even considered the possibility that people "think for themselves." She assumed that receiving knowledge from the authorities was *the way* everyone acquires ideas and information. ("How can you learn if the teacher isn't telling you?" Rachel asked us.) Rachel assumed she was smart because she had found it easy to remember what her teachers said and could answer their questions quickly, succinctly, and correctly.

Although Rachel believed she was really smart, she did not think she had a "right" to be smart. Conforming to the social norms of her rural community that presume females will subordinate themselves to males and that the poor are less able than the well-heeled, Rachel had done what she could to disconnect herself from the power of her very good mind. As a child she had been an outstanding student in her small rural school, but as she approached adolescence, she felt increasingly out of place as a really smart person. Mostly her accomplishments made her feel disloyal to her nonachieving friends—a problem common to children in urban ghettos as well (see, for instance, Fine, 1991; Ogbu, 1987). Rachel "solved" the problem of being "too smart" by dropping out of school when she was thirteen years old.

By the time Rachel finished the Listening Partners project three things were abundantly clear to her: (1) she was smart, (2) she had as much right as anyone else in the world to use the power of her good mind, and (3) listening to the words of authorities was only one way of gathering knowledge. Rachel reached these conclusions because she had been a full participant in a caring community of women who were constantly reflecting together on their experiences, defining problems, seeking solutions, comparing their emerging ideas, and building on each other's insights. In the process of developing bold new ideas for solving everyday problems, many of these women realized that they were capable, thinking people. The impact of this collaborative learning environment on Rachel is reflected in her second interview almost a year after she first spoke with us:

OKAY, RACHEL, HOW WOULD YOU DESCRIBE YOUR-SELF TO YOURSELF?

(laughs)

Ah, more ambitious. Very confident.

MORE CONFIDENT, MMM-HMMM.

More confident in when I'm speaking. Yeah. I speak up more than what I used to. I'm more open and tell what I feel and *(long pause)*. Like it has been nothing but a battle with my boyfriend.

DESCRIBE IT.

I tell him what I want from him, what I want and what I feel, and what I expect from him. Asking him to move out was an important decision for me. I had to make him realize that I wasn't going to live that kind of life with him if he kept up the drinking. I gained a lot of confidence in myself and was able to do something for myself, get something going so I could have a career. I have changed. I have a better outlook on life—knowing what I want out of life, what I want to do. I've made a lot of decisions and I'm going to go through with them. I had to figure out how I wanted to live my life.

Whenever one of the Listening Partners' women concluded that she *could* and *should* think for herself, her subsequent interviews were flooded with images of liberation, rebirth, agency, and self-direction—very much like those that pervade Rachel's revised self-description. Having decided they had the capacity *and* the right to have a say in running their own lives, these women, like Rachel, began solving many of the problems that had been buffeting them and their families at every turn.

By the time the Listening Partners project was completed, we had accumulated a good deal of evidence that it is growth producing to have opportunities to speak in settings where people listen to each other and work collaboratively to solve the problems they face. This was particularly true for those who had been the most silenced and excluded.

It was also clear that the metaphors of voice and silence that the women used were general indicators of their developmental status and sense of well-being. When a woman said she was "developing a voice," it was likely she was claiming the power of her mind and becoming more self-directed. When metaphors of voice were interlaced with images of listening, it was likely that the woman was becoming more aware of the collaborative nature of the construction of knowledge. Realizing that ideas develop in the give and take of conversation, these women are more likely to seek out the kinds of conversations that nurture their own thinking; they also ask the kinds of reflective questions that draw out the thinking of others, including the young children entrusted to their care. When people engage in this kind of mutual question posing and dialogue there is a good chance that they have entered into a developmental process that will perpetuate itself. As people are drawn out and empowered they are likely to draw out and uplift others, who in turn will reach out to still others. If all goes well the chain might remain unbroken for many generations to come.

Social psychologist Shulamit Reinharz (1994) says that people struggling to overcome oppression use voice metaphors (such as "gaining a voice") for good reasons. Voice metaphors are favored over visual images (such as Ralph Ellison's "invisible man") because they are proactive. Visual metaphors like the "invisible man" locate the problem in the one who is unseen and cast the powerless in an inactive role.

Understanding that the mind develops in the give and take of dialogue, people who struggle against oppression often link the development of voice with the development of mind as have many psychologists and educators (for example, Dewey, 1916/1966; Bakhtin, 1986; Tarule, 1996; Vygotsky, 1978). Typically, superordinates presume that the Other is incapable of independent thought. Subordinates are expected to listen and follow directions. If subordinates do speak out, they are seen as insubordinate. Although superordinates often see the Other— women, people of color, the poor, rural inhabitants—as capable of emotional power, they are not likely to think of them as well endowed with intellectual power.

If subordinates accept the idea that they cannot and should not develop the power of their minds, they are likely to remain powerless at the hands of the superordinates. If the excluded group rejects the demeaning stereotypes and begins a full-fledged dialogue with its members, they will begin to "feel," "see," and "hear" the power of minds gathering. Whenever many minds convene, people begin to move forward together with renewed clarity and vigor. *Voice* then becomes a metaphor for a community that is constructing and articulating its thoughts as well as exercising the right to seek justice.

Because metaphors of voice seemed so closely linked with significant aspects of women's development, we began to pay close attention whenever people talked with us about other projects and organizations created by women that were bringing people into voice. We were especially interested in projects involving people who had been cast to the side as Other. As we visited some of these groups, again and again we heard grassroots women talk about developing a voice in ways that were very similar to those described by the rural women in the Listening Partners project. These ongoing organizations also seemed to be learning environments that enabled people to cultivate more powerful ways of knowing, a greater sense of self, and a connectedness to others.

We believed that a study of ongoing organizations such as these could reveal important factors about the empowerment of people that could not be understood from an experimental design and a short-term project like the Listening Partners program. As a continuation of the work we began with Listening Partners, one of us (Mary Belenky) embarked on a study of four grassroots organizations. The new work could not have been achieved without the groundwork we did together on Listening Partners and our continuing collaboration.

Although the organizations we selected for study were similar to Listening Partners in many ways, there were also important differences. These organizations had been evolving for twenty-five years or more whereas Listening Partners was a time-limited demonstration project. These organizations also supported their members to develop a public voice, that is, to cultivate a commitment to the common good and to take a critical stance toward social arrangements that keep people silenced and isolated. Undoubtedly, the development of a public voice was possible because the women in these organizations had worked together on many projects to improve life in their local communities—something a very short-term effort like Listening Partners could scarcely attempt.

Organizations that sponsor the development of a public voice among their members seemed particularly important because people are withdrawing from civic life at an accelerating rate. We thought that a study of these organizations could help us begin imagining ways that a commitment to the common good and active involvement in reshaping public life might be kindled. (For incisive overviews of the problem, see Bellah, Madsen, Sullivan, Swidler, and Tipton, 1985; Daloz, Keen, Keen, and Parks, 1996; Elshtain, 1995; Lerner, 1996; McKnight, 1995; Oliner, 1995; Putnam, 1995.)

A study of these community organizations seemed auspicious for another reason. It would enable us to describe an important form of women's leadership that can arise in grassroots communities. While poor communities are recognized as having many isolated and silenced women like those we sought for the Listening Partners project, such communities are rarely thought of as having powerful, generative women leaders. Because society seldom looks to women as leaders, we probably know even less about them than we do about grassroots women silenced by depression and despair.

Research studies are now accumulating that show how poor communities cycle upward when grassroots women and their leaders are well supported (Hinsdale, Lewis, and Waller, 1995; Seitz, 1995; Sen and Grown, 1987). Such women are more likely to be deeply invested in seeing that the community meets the needs of all children and families; they have extensive experience promoting human development and many skills in community building. When women's leadership is supported, whole communities begin to thrive in ways that are not seen with modes of leadership that emphasize more hierarchical forms of decision making.

We decided to study four organizations that seemed highly effective in bringing an excluded group into voice. Two of them, the Mothers' Centers movements in the United States and Germany, had nearly identical goals, processes, and names even though they arose separately and independently. The National Congress of Neighborhood Women is a national network in the United States that supports the development of women's leadership in grassroots communities across the nation striving to make their communities more responsive to the needs of women and their families. The Center for Cultural and Community Development, also in the United States, grew out of the work of African American women who call themselves "cultural workers." They cultivate the arts and traditions of the African diaspora that draw out the voices of people and uplift the whole community. The center supports leaders from all oppressed communities who wish to reclaim their cultural traditions that enhance the development of people, families, and communities.

The people these four organizations have served are very different in terms of race, ethnicity, social class, and geographic area. Their short-term goals and approaches have also varied widely, although their general long-term goal has been the same: to bring a missing voice into a dialogue with the larger community.

We thought the diversity of organizations, leaders, and communities might be useful in several ways. Characteristics shared by vastly different programs and leaders could generate a better understanding of the kinds of practices that are truly important for propelling people and communities forward. The diversity might also help us get an inkling of how women's leadership develops under different cultural and social conditions. Additionally, we thought that an array of projects might be more likely to encourage a wider variety of people to think freshly about the problems facing their communities and the strengths they already have in place upon which to build. Furthermore, as white[2] urban women of relative privilege, working within disciplines that have centered largely on the study of the privileged, the inclusion in our project of women from diverse racial, cultural, and class backgrounds seemed critical.

We sought to develop a deeper understanding of women's lives and contributions by learning from and with women whose experiences differed from our own and, at the same time, by reflecting more deeply on our experiences as middle-class European American women.

A TRADITION THAT HAS NO NAME

As the study progressed it became clear to us that the National Congress of Neighborhood Women, the Center for Cultural and Community Development, and the Mothers' Center movements in Germany and the United States reflect many of the goals and practices found in highly nurturing, democratic families dedicated to sponsoring the fullest development of voice and mind in each and every member. It was also clear that the founders of these organizations had developed themselves as public leaders by extending and elaborating women's traditional roles and relational styles to an unusual degree. They were like mothers who had developed the most elaborate philosophy and set of practices for bringing people unequal in terms of power, status, and abilities into relationships of full equality. The inequality that mothers address, however, typically reflects the immaturity of the child, whereas the inequality that these community organizations confront arises from prejudice and discrimination as well as from immaturity.

In her book *The Rising Song of African American Women,* the African American educator, activist, and writer Barbara Omolade (1994) says women's leadership dedicated to drawing out the voices of the silenced has been essential to the survival of people throughout the African diaspora. This form of leadership, she says, is rooted in an ancient tradition, originating in African tribal societies organized around democratic/consensus-building processes.

Omolade points to Ella Baker, the adult advisor to the Student Nonviolent Coordinating Committee (SNCC; see the dedication in this book), as an outstanding example of a leader in this tradition. Under her guidance SNCC became a kind of laboratory where young people learned how to support some of the most severely oppressed people in the history of the nation to address the social problems they were facing. Omolade (1994, p. 165) writes:

> Bringing white and Black college students into SNCC enabled Ella Baker to influence and train leaders who became part of [many] national movements promoting changes [in and beyond the Black community]. . . . The white men she mothered brought the New Left Movement into being. The white women she mothered in the movement inspired others, creating second-wave feminism. . . . Her Black daughters combined and took from feminism, nationalism and the New Left, adding their own unique notions, to birth womanism.[3]

In short, Omolade says, contemporary feminism is rooted in the apprenticeships with Ella Baker that she and so many other women (black and white) held in the civil rights movement. They are all, she says, Ella's daughters. (For extensive discussion of the link between the civil rights movement and feminist movement, see Evans, 1979.)

Omolade goes on to say that this leadership tradition has no name. Surprised at the very notion of a tradition that has no name, we discussed the issue with the African American cultural workers we studied for this book and others from the black community. Everyone agreed with Omolade that there is an important ongoing tradition of black women's leadership devoted to promoting the development of people and communities. Most could describe many exemplars of the tradition whom they had known personally from the families and communities in which they grew up. Those they knew by reputation seemed countless. Our informants also agreed that this tradition has no name—or at least that it does not have a common name used by ordinary people in everyday conversations. No one had heard of the terms we found in the literature on African Americans, such as Patricia Hill Collins's (1991a) "community othermothers" or Charles Payne's (1995) "leaders in the developmental tradition" (see chapter 6 in this book).

One of the African American cultural workers we interviewed explained that when she was a child growing up in the segregated South, such women leaders were known by the title "Sister —." "If a woman was called 'Sister So-and-so,'"she said, "you knew she was the kind of leader who dealt with big issues, a leader who was always working to lift up the whole community." She went on to say that during the civil rights era everyone began calling each other "Sister So-and-so" and "Brother So-and-so" and the special term for designating this ilk of women's leadership was lost. She was not aware of a new term coming into the language to replace the one that was lost, even though she herself was devoting her life to the tradition.

We came to see that women of all colors often become community leaders who sponsor the development of the most marginal and vulnerable members of the community, even if this form of leadership goes unrecognized. Because black women come from a culture where the tradition of developmental leadership is more clearly established, they helped us see that there was a tradition to be studied even when the tradition had no name.

Because the public leaders we studied were so focused on nurturing the development of people, families, and communities, we decided to name their organizations "public homeplaces." A general definition of public homeplaces fits the four community organizations we studied: Public homeplaces are places where people support each other's development and where everyone is expected to participate in developing the homeplace. Using the homeplace as a model, the members go on working to make the whole society more inclusive, nurturing, and responsive to the developmental needs of all people—but most especially of those who have been excluded and silenced.

During the past century there has been a long line of educators who have created schools where the children of the excluded routinely develop their creative capacities to solve the problems of everyday life, to explore new challenges, and to become fuller participants in the social, economic, cultural, and political life of the society. In short, these schools are successful in supporting children often classified as being of low intelligence to become what psychologist Howard Gardner (1991) calls disciplinary thinkers—articulate, creative, and capable of solving the problems facing them and their communities. The educators include John Dewey (1916/1966), Reuven Feuerstein (Feuerstein, with Rand, Hoffman, and Miller, 1980), Paulo Freire (1970), Lawrence Kohlberg (Power, Higgins and Kohlberg, 1989), Loris Malaguzzi and his colleagues in Reggio Emilie, Italy (Edwards, Gandini, and Forman, 1995), Deborah Meier (1995), Maria Montessori (1917/1965), Lorenzo Milani (Schoolboys of Barbiana, 1970), as well as the teachers described by such researchers as Sara Lawrence Lightfoot (1983) and Mike Rose (1995). Lyn Brown's (in prep.) project with lower-class girls in rural Maine and Erich Fromm and Michael Maccoby's (1970) work with Mexican peasants are good examples of non-school programs expressly devoted to nurturing the development of voice and mind among the excluded. Francis Moore Lappe and Paul DuBois (1994) show the transformative power of civic organizations.

Leaders of public homeplaces, like all of the educators just cited, are intensely interested in the development of each individual, of the group as a whole, and of a more democratic society. These leaders want to know each person, what they care about, and where they are trying to go. They also work to articulate the goals that people in the group have in common. They look for each person's strong points, for the things already in place upon which the person could build. They also look for the strengths in the people's culture as a building foundation for the whole community. They ask good questions and draw out people's thinking. They listen with care. To better understand what they are hearing they try to step into the people's shoes and see the world through their eyes. Then they look for ways to mirror what they have seen, giving people a chance to take a new look at themselves and see the strengths that have not been well recognized or articulated. Because these leaders open themselves so fully to others, we think of them as connected leaders. We also talk about them as midwife leaders because they enable the community to give birth to fledgling ideas and nurture the ideas along until they have become powerful ways of knowing.

Connected, midwife leaders pull people into intense and continual discussions. They encourage everyone to question and construct views of how things *actually* do work. They also encourage people to develop a vision of how things *ought* to work. When that vision begins to come into focus, the energy level of the group often soars. The people find themselves posing more and more questions and searching, always searching, for better answers. The group becomes spongelike, soaking up ideas and information that might address the problems on which they are working. People work collaboratively—experimenting, testing, and refining their hunches through hands-on action projects and impassioned conversations. As the ideas develop coherence and clarity, the group becomes intensely committed to a common set of clearly defined goals and to each other. Because the vision has become so clear in everyone's minds and so vital to a better way of living, the people reach high, stretching themselves in ways they would not have dreamed possible. They find themselves going beyond the given, pushing each other's thinking into new territory, seeing beyond what others see, and giving names to things that have gone unnamed. As their projects unfold, the group often finds itself making such bold statements to the world that even those who once dismissed them as Other—alien, incompetent, nothing—begin to listen with new ears.

Because this tradition has no name it is difficult to realize that it is actually quite common. Once we began thinking of groups and leaders devoted to promoting human and community development as a well-defined organizational type, we found ourselves spotting new examples with surprising frequency. We can walk into a nursery school, a classroom in the poorest ghetto, or a graduate seminar in a great university and know that this is a kind of public homeplace. That is, it is a place where every voice is being heard, where the group's action projects are designed to address the members' most driving questions and concerns, and where all are supported to be the best they know how to be. We have discerned the form in families from all walks of life, in theater groups, in research collaboratives, and in all-women a cappella singing groups.

We now believe that both the civil rights movement and the women's movement flourished because public homeplaces devoted to bringing the excluded into voice sprang up in local communities all across the country and linked themselves together in national and even international networks. We suspect that these social movements would never have mushroomed in this way if there had not been large numbers of unrecognized leaders in both black and women's communities who already had a good deal of knowledge about the unnamed tradition. Not only could these leaders teach the philosophy and practices of their leadership approach to others, but there were multitudes eager to learn the methods for themselves. It was understood in both of these overlapping circles that this kind of leadership must become widespread if the dream of a more democratic society is to be realized.

We believe that this leadership approach has been invisible in much of our society because it is carried on outside of conventional ways of thinking. As becomes clear in chapter 10, this leadership tradition simply bypasses a whole range of dualistic notions that ordinarily shape the ways most people in our culture construe the world. Instead of perceiving a sharp division between private and public life, this tradition holds that all aspects of social life should be permeated with the values of home associated with nurturing the development of human beings. Instead of setting the individual apart from and above community life, this tradition understands that the growth of the individual is most fully realized when people work together nurturing the growth of the community.

Most centrally, this tradition rejects the notion of an Other—that there are inferior people incapable of becoming full participants in society. Instead, it holds that we are all members of one family—the human family. As such, everyone should be included; all should be supported to become the best they can be; all should be allowed to make their contribution to society.

This tradition rejects dualistic constructs that presume feelings and thoughts are separate and opposing processes. Instead, it envisions hearts and minds developing in tandem. It understands that emotions can spur the development of thought and that thought clarifies and nourishes emotional life. We focus more intently on the development of mind in an effort to right a grievous wrong—that people who are cast aside as "Other" are usually regarded as incapable of intelligence although they may be seen as full of heart.

This tradition rejects the notion that men and women are capable only of developing different and opposing capacities. It argues that men as well as women can develop the capacity for making nurturing connections, that women as well as men can become hard-nosed, creative, and powerful thinkers.

This tradition rejects the notion that science, public life, and market forces can be or should be "value-free." It argues that the world is always "value-full." Even the attempt to operate outside of a value system expresses a value—albeit one of the most dangerous and impoverishing sort. Indeed, the most central activity of this tradition is to develop a common set of goals and values to animate and guide the community.

This tradition also assumes that knowledge is best constructed in collaborative action projects where people work together to experiment, test, elaborate, and articulate goals, values, and ideas. Even experts and neophytes work together rather like coequals as it is understood that newcomers must have this kind of experience if they are to learn the skills of collaboration and become active, powerful constructors of knowledge. Once again, the stance is contrary to standard views that assume high levels of creativity are reached by autonomous individuals spurred onward by competition rather than collaboration, and that novices learn best by sitting at the feet of experts for many years.

In short, this tradition puts forth a model of public leadership dedicated to "drawing out," "raising up," and "lifting up" people and communities. As such, it is a leadership paradigm organized around values, metaphors, and activities generally associated with maternal thinking and maternal practice (Ruddick, 1994).

This mode provides a sharp contrast to public leaders who organize their leadership around paternal experiences and metaphors. Patriarchs see themselves as the "head" of their families; they "rule over," not "raise up." Indeed, the work of raising up is usually relegated to the least valued members of society, not to the leaders. In the past these were mothers, servants, and even slaves. Now much of the work is done by child-care workers, the lowest paid of all occupations (Bureau of the Census, 1995).

If you were to draw an organizational chart of the public homeplaces created by developmentally oriented leaders, you would find yourself placing the leaders in two different locations on a circle. Sometimes they would be found in the center of the circle; more often they would be in the array around the edge with everyone else. Because leaders devoted to the development of people and communities are interested in drawing out and bouncing ideas around, arrows indicating the flow of ideas would zigzag in all directions.

Because these organizations are always teaming up with similar groups, you would need to link the circle you have drawn with many other circles. The ultimate structure would look very much like a net or a web with many interconnections. Often you would even need to draw threads that encircle the globe.

Until recently standard organizational charts almost always depicted shapes that suggested a pyramid or a mountain. The leader stood at the apex while others were arranged on various descending levels below. Most of the arrows indicating the flow of ideas and decisions began at the top and pointed downward.

If a maternal developmentally oriented approach to leadership is more common among women than men, we believe it is only because women are more often engaged in the work of raising the young and caring for the vulnerable. A highly elaborated developmental approach can be realized by anyone—male or female—who engages in extensive practice, dialogue, and reflection on the processes involved. It is our hope that we have articulated the philosophy and practices that guide public homeplaces well enough that people new to the idea will come to value and cultivate the tradition for themselves and old-timers will feel confirmed and renewed.

CHAPTER 1

DUALISMS THAT DIVIDE AND DENY

[Because women were silenced] the world has had to limp along with the wobbling gait and the one-sided hesitancy of a man with one eye. Suddenly the bandage is removed from the other eye and the whole body is filled with light. It sees a circle where before it saw a segment. The darkened eye restored, every member rejoices with it.
ANNA JULIA COOPER, *A VOICE FROM THE SOUTH/BY A BLACK WOMAN OF THE SOUTH* (1892/1988, P. 122)

The mindset that pits We against Other divides a wide range of human experiences into dichotomies, that is, nonoverlapping categories of polar opposites. Culture vs. Nature, Thinking vs. Feeling, and Nature vs. Nurture are among the most divisive opposites common to Western thought. When we choose only one end of a polarity and avoid the other, we cultivate a limited part of what might be possible. For instance, when thinking and feeling are treated as mutually exclusive and opposing capacities we are encouraged to develop one and to deny the other. Those who cultivate their capacities for feeling but not thinking are likely to remain subordinated to all sorts of forces they do not even attempt to control. It is not by chance that those in power all too often attribute the ability for thinking to men and whites and the capacity for emotions to women and blacks.

The tendency to dichotomize human experience is persistent, powerful, and pernicious. Dualistic categories are such an organizing force because they provide a simple classification system that allows even the most complex and elusive qualities to be compared and contrasted in bold, clear terms. Things are either "black or white." In the starkness of this light, the blends and subtleties disappear (for discussions of dualistic thinking, see Bakan, 1966; Basseches, 1984; Bem, 1993; Haste, 1994; Keller, 1985; Labouvie-Vief, 1994; Merchant, 1980; Pagels, 1995).

★ ★ ★

Because dualisms seem to bring great clarity to the most ambiguous and elusive issues, people are particularly apt to use them to organize their thinking about morality, epistemology, and identity development—clearly among the most difficult and the most important subjects ordinary human beings try to ponder. Dualisms like Good/Evil and Right/Wrong have ordered human thinking about morality throughout recorded history. True/False, Mind/Body, and Thinking/Feeling have organized a good deal of human thinking about thinking. These dichotomies, in turn, have been associated with gender, interweaving and clustering characteristics from the domains of morality, epistemology, and gender identity. Culture/Nature, Public/Private, and Rights/Responsibilities are other examples of the kinds of dualisms associated with morality, epistemology, and gender that have been particularly powerful in shaping Western thought since the Enlightenment. Even Productive/Reproductive and its ideological twin Creative/Procreative have been construed as polar opposites.

Although these polarities may seem complementary, they are not. Most actually function as a hierarchy. One pole represents a value to be sought. The other represents its opposite, a negative to be avoided. The valued pole is regularly identified with maleness. It sets the standard and is affirmed by its feminine negation. When dualisms roll off the tips of our tongues, it is the value associated with maleness that we typically utter first. "Male and female" seems easy to say, but "female and male" is not. The same is true of "mind and body," "public and private," "productive and reproductive," "separate and connected," "big and little." Looking at the problem of evil from a woman's perspective, philosopher Nel Noddings (1989) traces the ways various polarities have been clustered in Western cultures. Right is coupled with Light, Up, Mind, Culture, Good, God, and Male. Wrong is joined by Dark, Down, Body, Nature, Evil, Witch, and Female.

When men are defined as Human and women as Other the consequences can be far-reaching. Psychologist Sandra Bem (1993) points to a telling example. Up through the 1970s the Supreme Court ruled that insurance companies did not have to provide pregnancy benefits under the equal protection clause of the Constitution because the exclusion did not involve "discrimination based on gender as such." The Court was able to reach such a decision because males had set the standard. All medical problems more prevalent in men (prostatectomies, circumcision, hemophilia, and the like) were fully covered by all the insurance companies whereas medical problems exclusive to females were seen as "additional" or "extra." Insurance companies were required to provide only the coverage that the "standard" human body would require. The standard human does not get pregnant. This is a prime example of how the social world organized from a male perspective routinely transforms biological and historical differences between men and women into male advantage and female disadvantage.

Bem (1993) draws on concepts developed by linguists to illuminate some of the processes involved in these sleights of hand. In dichotomies where the contrasting terms are asymmetrical (such as good/bad, tall/short, or happy/unhappy), linguists distinguish the terms as "unmarked" and "marked." The positive or unmarked term denotes the scale as a whole and the negative or marked term is only used to indicate the negative end of the continuum. Questions, Bem says, that use the unmarked terms, like "How tall is Chris?," do not imply anything about Chris's height. But if you were to ask, "How short is Chris?," it would be assumed that Chris was at the negative end of the pole. The questions "How good was the movie?" and "How bad was the movie?" or "How happy was the child?" and "How unhappy was the child?" operate in the same fashion.

Sociologist Barrie Thorne (1993) observed a related phenomenon while studying children at play that she calls "girl stain." Girls—regardless of their social rank—can contaminate any boy. A boy who joins the girls or does girl things is likely to be "stained" and moved to the bottom in terms of social status. Even objects associated with girls—such as valentines, dresses, and dolls—can be contaminating to boys. Girls, on the other hand, may well gain status when they join boys' games, wear boys' clothes, and play with boys' things.

Psychologist Helen Haste (1994) discusses "girl stain" more generally in her study of sexual metaphors. She says "metaphors of pollution" abound whenever hierarchical models cast qualities in terms of polarity, antithesis, and negation.

> The hierarchical model defines the masculine pole as the epitome of the human, and the feminine pole as its antithesis, a deficit or a support. . . . What could, in principle, be the free exchange of roles between persons, irrespective of gender, becomes instead contaminated with the metaphors of greater and lesser, and of pollution. (p. 18)

Girls' things must be clearly "marked" to distinguish them from boys' things if "girl stain" and other forms of "pollution" are to be avoided. Things associated with boys are "unmarked." They need not be avoided. Boys' things are labeled with terms that can be neutralized to include girls, but the negative "marked" term associated with girls never includes boys. Thus mankind includes women but womankind is too polluting to include men. It is for this reason researchers who study only men often feel free to say they study human beings and researchers who study only women do not.

A similar idea shapes the way many people conceptualize race. A single ancestor of color is seen as removing a person from the category of "white," whereas no amount of "white" blood affects the racial designation of a "black" person. An analogous phenomenon affects the way thinking and feeling are conceptualized. Whereas emotional involvement can easily disqualify an idea from the category of "thought," intense intellectual reflection does not remove an emotion from the category of "feeling" in the minds of many.

The New Zealand economist Marilyn Waring's analysis of the material consequences of these kinds of conceptual errors is most revealing. In her book, *If Women Counted,* Waring (1988) says that both women and nature are essentially left out of the economic accounting systems used worldwide for census taking and assessing national resources. Under the systems imposed by the United Nations as the international standard, activities are classified as "productive" when an exchange of money takes place. Women engaged in unpaid work in homes, farms, and communities are classified as "nonproductive" or "unoccupied" whereas the work of most men is classified as "productive." Even the unpaid work of a subsistence farmer is classified as "productive," whereas his wife performing identical activities is said to be engaged in "nonproductive" work.

The devastation caused by discounting women is more easily seen in the developing world. The United Nations' system lists women as "nonproductive" workers even when they spend most of their time gathering foodstuff, firewood, fibers, and building materials from a mixed forest for feeding, clothing, and housing themselves and their families. Their husbands who work for wages—no matter how minuscule—perhaps on a nearby plantation (that is, earth that once sustained a mixed forest, now cleared and replanted with a single crop for export), are counted as "productive." This way of construing reality leads to public policies that favor turning "nonproductive" lands over to "productive" profit-making endeavors. The women who engaged in all the "nonproductive" work in those "nonproductive" forests are excluded from the land when it is put into "production." When these transfers are made, the recorded wealth of a country is actually depicted as increasing while more and more of the nation's people go without food, clothing, and shelter. (See also Shiva, 1989.)

Waring argues that the classification system that makes women invisible is rooted in a view that women's caring work is an activity *of* nature, rather than an interaction of women *with* nature. In a study of early mothering, Amy Rossiter (1988, p. 19) says the assumption that it is nature, not women's agency, that counts is reflected in our daily language: "'No. I'm not working now'; 'Dr. Ross delivered the baby'; 'I didn't do anything today.'"

Waring goes on to argue that the international accounting systems fail to impute value to nature itself. A beautiful river flowing through a country, supplying the nation with safe drinking water, is not counted as having any value. However, the moment a government allocates funds to clean up a polluted river, it is classified as economically productive. Waring says that the environment being destroyed is seen as a free gift of nature to be exploited at will.

Whereas women's caring work and the natural environment are counted as nothing, the international accounting system considers war productive in spite of the fact that military spending allocates resources to unproductive and destructive endeavors. There are three facts on

Waring's long list that indicate a bias favoring war-making over human development:

1. The cost of a single new nuclear submarine equals the annual education budget of twenty-three developing countries with 160 million school-age children.
2. For every 100,000 people in the world, there are 556 soldiers and 85 doctors.
3. For every soldier, the average world military expenditure is $22,000. For every school-age child the average public expenditure for education is $380. (p. 172)

The United Nations' accounting system was originally devised by economists so that Western governments could better understand how to pay for World War I. If the United Nations had adopted an alternative system that helped governments understand how they could best support human development rather than war-making, the effects on social policies would be numerous. We would see much of unpaid work traditionally assigned to women being accorded the highest value. More people would invest their time in raising the young and caring for the most vulnerable. Society would invest in supporting human development at the same or higher levels than it now invests in industrial development. All sorts of public institutions would be reshaped so the development of people would become an important organizational goal. Schools on all levels would become more nurturing environments, sponsoring the development of whole persons as well as the acquisition of technical competence. Our great colleges and universities might even begin teaching the philosophy and practice of public leadership focused on promoting human development.

WOMEN IN TWO CULTURES

The way women and homemaking are discounted in a particular cultural context is more clearly revealed when we gaze at that context through a different cultural lens. The bizarreness of naming homemaking as nonproductive while war-making is called productive is more evident in the developing world, where most people live outside of a money economy—but it is a grotesque depiction of reality in any cultural context. Similarly, when we look through the lenses crafted by the African American women whom we interviewed, we get a better view of the ways European-based cultures discount, distort, and limit women and the work they do sponsoring the development of people, families, and communities.

Autonomy and Connection   Men in Western cultures began redefining themselves and their relationship to the world in an effort to free themselves from the Divine Rights of Kings, oppressive myths, and religions. They would be separate, autonomous individuals guided by reason alone. While the men went off seeking independence and autonomy for themselves, the women kept to the homeplace, weaving the connections that might salvage some semblance of family and community. Because males set the standard, maturity in the New World became equated with autonomy and independence. Human connections—being in relationships—became associated with dependence and immaturity (Chodorow, 1978; Gilligan, 1982/1993; Hirsch, 1989; Miller, 1976/1987).

Even with the extraordinary transformations in gender roles that have occurred in recent times, contemporary studies show that white adolescent girls coming of age in America are still trying to fit themselves into a notion of femininity that suggests the diminutive (American Association of University Women, 1991; Brown and Gilligan, 1992; Gilligan, 1982/1993; Orenstein, 1994; Sadker and Sadker, 1994). They go on starvation diets, curb their minds, and trim their assertive ways. These cutbacks are accompanied by a loss in the girls' intellectual performance and a decline in self-esteem. Apparently, white girls continue to believe that prowess, will, and command will destroy their capacity for care, connection, and community.

Black girls coming of age in America are more likely to collect rather than abandon their strengths and sense of self (Carothers, 1990; Greene, 1990; Ladner, 1971; Ladner and Gourdine, 1984). They gear themselves up to take on a strong family role as economically independent, resourceful, and hardworking women even if they resent the burden being placed so heavily on their shoulders. With the massive deterioration of economic and social conditions facing unskilled African Americans, this pattern may be weakening as more and more blacks—

male and female—become discouraged and stop trying. Yet even if passivity becomes more pervasive among African American girls and women, its increase would stem from the external difficulties of trying to survive in an increasingly hostile and unsupportive society, and not from pressures to live up to cultural mores that define women as passive, dependent, and selfless.

Some European Americans are confused by highly competent and powerful black girls and women. Because of their stereotypes, many have a difficult time associating such qualities with blacks (regardless of their gender) or with women (regardless of their color). Others see black women as powerful but blame their efficacy, in part, for the high rates of social disorganization in the black community. They believe that black men are emasculated by strong women, not by the discriminatory practices of a racist society (see Dill, 1987; Ryan, 1971; Wade-Gayles, 1980). Some African Americans (Wallace, 1979) have criticized the celebration of strong black superwomen. They worry that if black women are seen as providing ample care for those in need, all others else can excuse themselves from taking responsibility.

That many African Americans expect women to embody characteristics that European Americans assume to be opposing and contradictory no doubt causes much confusion. The ideal throughout the African diaspora is for women to be powerfully voiced, strong willed, and sometimes even cantankerous, while also being caring, warm, and nurturing. "She's a backbone," "she's a bridge," and "she's a fortress" are typical metaphors that black women writers use to characterize women who are also depicted as warmhearted and nurturing (for example, Bell-Scott, Guy-Sheftall, Royster, Sims-Wood, DeCosta-Willis, and Fultz, 1991; Collins, 1991a, 1991b). Toni Morrison (1983) sums it up this way:

> Black women seem able to combine the nest and the adventure. . . . They are both safe harbor and ship; they are both inn and trail. We, black women, do both. We don't find these places, these roles, mutually exclusive. (p. 122)

Bernice Reagon, a role model and mentor for the cultural workers we studied for this book, named her all-women a cappella singing group "Sweet Honey in the Rock," to mark the importance of embracing the full range for black women. She says,

Black women have had to have the standing power of rocks and of mountains—cold and hard, strong and stationary. That quality has often obscured the fact that inside the strength, partnering the sturdiness, we are as honey. If our world is warm, honey flows and so do we. If it is cold, stiff, and stays put—so do we. (Buffalo, 1993, p. 24)

African American women have many cultural heroes who are like sweet honey but also have the standing power of rocks. Harriet Tubman, a woman who guided many slaves along the "underground railroad," is a prime example. The Africanist scholar Molefi Kete Asante (1987, p. 110) says Harriet Tubman is a Great Mother who lives within the heart of every African American person. He links her with leaders down through the ages who would lift up their people:

It is from her that we get the numerous leaders who arise to deliver the people from bondage to salvation. She is not messianic in either the sense of Moses of the Old Testament or Jesus of the New; she is, rather, the spirit-mother, protecting, suckling, and leading her children. (p. 109)

This Great Mother is also seen as the Great Warrior. Tubman's ferocity is understood to be as limitless as her capacity for caring. Angela Davis (1981), the black activist/scholar, writes that Tubman is still the only woman in the United States ever to have led troops in war. In Tubman the capacity for rage against injustice and the capacity for love are fully joined.

Harriet Jacobs's (1861/1987) self-description in her autobiography, *Incidents in the Life of a Slave Girl,* first penned in 1857, presents an extreme example of the full range of maternal power common in descriptions of black women. Because the white intelligentsia could not imagine that a black female slave could have such will or write with such power and eloquence, the book was presumed for over a century to be a work of fiction. Only now have scholars (Yellin, 1987) come to accept that the narrative was actually written by a "slave girl [sic], herself."

Jacobs (1861/1987) wrote that the war of her life had begun when her owner told her, "I was made for his use, made to obey his command in *every* thing; that I was nothing but a slave, whose will must and should surrender to his" (p. 18). Jacobs thought otherwise. She said, "[T]hough one of God's most powerless creatures, I resolved never to be conquered" (p. 17). With the help of her grandmother, Jacobs countered the slave master's prerogatives with seemingly unlimited intelligence, absolute will, and the utmost of fortitude. When she believed she could no longer protect herself from her slave master's advances, Jacobs went into hiding. Although many encouraged her to escape to the North, she refused to leave while her children remained in bondage. She chose instead to confine herself to a windowless crawl space that served as an attic to a shed behind her grandmother's house. As the ceiling was too low to allow her to stand, Jacobs could only lie on her makeshift bed. She was able to bore several peepholes that allowed her to keep track of her children's comings and goings when they were below. After seven long years in the garret, safe passage to the North could finally be arranged for both her and her children. Only then did she agree to leave. Once Jacobs reached freedom with her children, she never ceased her efforts to bring an end to slavery and to ameliorate its effects.

Jacobs's search for freedom was not a hero's lonely journey but a family endeavor. She would assert her rights to independence but not at the expense of her children. She readily acknowledged the support and assistance she received from others. Valerie Smith (1990, p. 217) put it this way: "Jacobs's tale is not the classic story of the triumph of the individual will; rather, it is more a story of a triumphant self-in-relation."

By combining these two themes—the phenomenal assertion of self with the ability to remain steeped in caring relationships—Jacobs has given us a story that is seldom found in the literature by and about men and women from European-based cultures. In Europe, writing *A Doll's House* about the same time as Jacobs was penning her narrative, Henrik Ibsen (1879/1950) created Nora, a fictional mother who finds her life intolerable. Realizing that her husband will always infantilize her, Nora feels she must leave home to pursue her personal development. When she finally leaves the doll's house, she goes alone, abandoning her children as well as her husband.

Decades later, Kate Chopin (1899/1972) told a similar story in *The Awakening*. When Edna, another wife/mother, begins to feel a sense of self well up from within, she too finds the conflict between herself and her family unresolvable. As Edna readies herself to swim out to sea and her own death, "the children appeared before her like antagonists who had overcome her, who had overpowered and sought to drive her into the soul's slavery for the rest of her days" (p. 339).

Both Edna and Nora saw their own lives pitted against the lives of their children. Both were expected to raise the children, but they, themselves, were not allowed to rise. They saw no way to seek their own and their children's development at the same time. Nora could go off alone to elevate herself; Edna would simply eliminate herself.

Nora and Edna were struggling toward maturity in a culture where full adulthood was a status reserved solely for men. As such, adulthood and maturity were equated with becoming more separate and autonomous. As women like Nora and Edna were "squirrel wives" or pets for their husbands, the task of growing up was made impossible for them. They needed to remain children alongside their own children so that the uncertain patriarch might loom large and confident to himself and to the world at large (Woolf, 1929/1957). As Adrienne Rich put it, "Typically, under patriarchy, the mother's life is exchanged for the child's; her autonomy as a separate being seems fated to conflict with the infant she will bear" (1977, p. 161).

All social relationships are distorted when it is believed that maturity requires cutting ties to others, when the assertion of self is thought to be at the expense of others (Hirsch, 1989). A woman who holds the view that one advances alone at the expense of others will feel forced to choose between herself and others (Gilligan, 1982/1993). She can either assert herself and cause harm to others or she can stand in the background curtailing her own development so her children and husband might prosper. In contrast, those like Harriet Jacobs who assume they can advance themselves while lifting up others have a way of thinking that can empower everyone in the relationship (Debold, Wilson, and Malave, 1993).

When faced with the dilemma of choosing between self and other, few European American women commit suicide or abandon their children. Some say, "Nonsense! That is a bogus choice! I can be a fully mature person with a mind and a will of my own while remaining in loving relationships with others." Unfortunately, many others never confront the dilemma head on. Instead, they remain in relationships that promote the welfare of others while denying their own selfhood.

In her book, *Silencing the Self: Women and Depression,* psychologist Dana Jack (1991) traces the rise of depression—a kind of living death—in women who try to solve the dilemma through the denial of self.

Nora and Edna's quest for autonomy may or may not be emblematic of a woman's coming of age in European-based cultures. Be that as it may, many black women would agree that Jacobs's narrative sets a recognizable standard in their community. Mary Helen Washington (1984) says of Jacobs's narratives and those of other slave women:

> The historical mythology of the slave mother as a way of envisioning and defining motherhood maintains the importance of understanding motherhood in its political context. It challenges the fiction of mother–daughter hostility and the traditional way of seeing mothers as powerless in the world of men. (p. 160)

As a slave, Jacobs had no right either to her children or to her own self, but she chose both. Whereas Nora and Edna focused narrowly on their own personal freedom, Jacobs saw her individual liberation as only a beginning step in the liberation of her children and her people. She and her children would move toward freedom in tandem; together their footprints would help clear a path for others seeking the abolition of slavery.

Let us keep Jacobs's wondrous assertion and voice in perspective. From birth on, Jacobs had a variety of supports and privileges that were extremely uncommon for a slave to have. Of those who tried to exit from slavery, most were crushed in the attempt. Sethe, the slave mother in Toni Morrison's *Beloved,* succeeded in reaching the North with her children only to be apprehended by those who would see them all returned to bondage. Sethe takes the only option her love will entertain: she tries to kill her children. One dies before she is stopped. The discourse of mothers who bow before such choices, Marianne Hirsch (1990) writes, "is rooted in the body that shivers, hurts, bleeds, suffers, burns, rather than in the eyes, or in the voice, which can utter its cries of pain" (p. 426).

Procreation Versus Creativity   In African American communities, powerful mothers are also seen as fountainheads of intelligence and creativity (Bell-Scott, Guy-Sheftall, Royster, Sims-Wood, DeCosta-Willis, and Fultz, 1991; Collins, 1991a, 1991b; Walker, 1983). This perspective contrasts sharply with the dualisms central to Western thought that construe woman's capacities to feel and procreate as the polar opposite of man's capacities to think and create (Haste, 1994). This painful fact is reflected in much of the fiction created by women from Western cultures. Literary scholars Sandra Gilbert and Susan Gubar tell the story in *The Madwoman in the Attic,* a book first published in 1979. Their account helped open the field of literary criticism to feminist perspectives. When women first picked up their pens to write novels, Gilbert and Gubar say, all the mothers they portrayed were seen through the eyes of daughters. Fictional mothers seldom looked out at the world through their own eyes; they never spoke for themselves. The mothers these daughters portrayed were either mad or maddeningly trivial; only dead mothers were effective.

Gilbert and Gubar's newest work (1994) finds the voice of mothers increasingly gaining a presence in women's fiction written since the 1950s. The stories of mothers given us by such writers as Grace Paley (1994) and Tillie Olsen (1961/1978) bring an unnamed tradition into focus. Toni Morrison (1992) writes about the process:

> In these readings, a sense that the text has appeared to be wholly new, never before seen, is followed, almost immediately, by the sense that it was *always there*, that we, the readers, knew it was always there, and have *always known* it was as it was, though we have now for the first time recognized, become fully cognizant of, our knowledge. (pp. xi–xiii)

A remarkable number of European women who first emerged as creative, independent, and powerful writers had, in fact, lost their mothers early in life—very much like their fictional counterparts. Most ruled out motherhood for themselves as well. Marveling at the pattern, literary critic Carolyn Heilbrun (1988) says, "Think of George Eliot; think of Jane Austen; think of the Brontes" (p. 118).

To explore whether these patterns still persisted, Heilbrun reviewed two edited volumes (Ascher, DeSalvo, and Ruddick, 1984; Owen, 1985) of autobiographical writings of contemporary women engaged in highly creative work. Attending only to the essays contributed by European American women, Heilbrun (1988) found that highly creative white women still identified fathers but not mothers as a source of their creative awakenings. "Mothers may come to be recognized with a new, loving perception but . . . [t]hey leave their daughters as yet unawakened" (pp. 64–65).

In addition to the contributions by European American women in the two volumes that Heilbrun reviewed, there were essays written by three black women. When we looked at these essays we were impressed by the starkness of the contrast. All of these black women writers looked to their mothers and other women as a source of creativity, support, and inspiration—as did all of the creative black women about whom these essayists chose to write. None attributed their creativity to their fathers—nor, indeed, to any other men.

Gloria Hull (1984), a pioneer in the development of African American and feminist studies programs, contributed an essay on Alice Dunbar-Nelson. Dunbar-Nelson was an outstanding black writer known to the world only as the wife of Paul Laurence Dunbar—one of the first nationally recognized black poets in the United States. Hull (1984) depicts the sources of support and awakening that Dunbar-Nelson found in her life:

> Her mother, sister, and nieces in their inseparable, female centered household constituted a first line of resistance (sometimes in conjunction with her second husband). Then came other Black women of visible achievement . . . with whom she associated. In varying ways, they assured each other of their sanity and worth, and collectively validated their individual efforts to make the possible real. (p. 109)

Writing about the origins of her own creativity in this same essay, Hull names her mother but does not mention a father.

Elaine Stetson (1984), another of the black essayists, also centered the development of her own creativity in a community of black women. "Black women's history—from servitude and slavery to freedom," she writes, "tells me how to live, how to survive, and how to be. To survive, Black women had to invent themselves and did. They defined the terms of their existence" (p. 238). Stetson also links her own creative awakening specifically to her mother and fails to mention a father.

One of the two essays Alice Walker (1984) contributed to these volumes focused on Zora Neale Hurston. Born at the turn of the century, Hurston produced a prolific body of work as novelist, journalist, anthropologist/folklorist, and critic all through the 1930s and 1940s (for example, 1937/1991, 1979). Unprepared for the likes of Zora Neale Hurston, the critics dismissed her for her audacity and failed to give her work a fair reading. Although the familial roots of Hurston's creativity are not explored by Walker in this particular essay, Hurston (1979) has done significant thinking and writing on the subject elsewhere:

> Mama exhorted her [eight] children at every opportunity to "jump at de sun." We might not land on the sun, but at least we would get off the ground. Papa did not feel so hopeful. Let well enough alone. It did not do for Negroes to have too much spirit. He was always threatening to break mine or kill me in the attempt. My mother was always standing between us. She conceded that I was impudent and given to talking back, but she didn't want to "squinch my spirit" too much for fear that I would turn out to be a mealy-mouth rag doll by the time I got grown. Papa always flew hot when Mama said that. . . . He predicted dire things for me. The white folks were not going to stand for it. I was going to be hung before I got grown. Somebody was going to blow me down for my sassy tongue. Mama was going to suck sorrow for not beating my temper out of me before it was too late. . . . My older sister was meek and mild. [Papa said] she would always get along. Why wouldn't I be like her? Mama would keep right on with whatever she was doing and remark, "Zora is my young'un and Sarah is yours. I'll be bound mine will come out more than conquer. You leave her alone. I'll tend to her when I figure she needs it." (pp. 33–34)

The second of Walker's (1985) two essays was a sad lament about her own father. One of the last of eight children born to a sharecropper, Walker only knew her father as a man bowed by poverty, ill health, and overwork. While her older siblings gave her glimpses of a brilliant, engaged man who was a good father and moral leader of the community, that was not within Walker's experience.

Conversely, Walker traces a powerful link between her own and her mother's creativity in a collection of essays she titled *In Search of Our Mothers' Gardens*. To establish the existence of such a relationship, Walker (1983) begins by asking,

> What did it mean for a black woman to be an artist in our grand-mothers' time? In our great-grandmothers' day? It is a question with an answer cruel enough to stop the blood. How was the cre-ativity of the black woman kept alive, year after year and century after century, when for most of the years black people have been in America, it was a punishable crime for a black person to read or write? And the freedom to paint, to sculpt, to expand the mind with action did not exist. (pp. 233–234)

Walker found her answer by "think[ing] back through our moth-ers," to borrow a phrase from Virginia Woolf (1929/1957, p. 79). Walker writes:

> It is to my mother—and all of our mothers who were not fa-mous—that I went in search of the secret of what has fed that muzzled and often mutilated, but vibrant, creative spirit that the black woman has inherited, and that pops out in wild and unlikely places to this day. . . . [O]ur mothers and grandmothers have, more often than not anonymously, handed on the creative spark, the seed of the flower they themselves never hoped to see: or like a sealed letter they could not plainly read. (pp. 238–240)

Walker finds in her own mother a great artist. She writes:

> I notice that it is only when my mother is working in her flowers that she is radiant, almost to the point of being invisible—except as Creator: hand and eye. She is involved in work her soul must have. Ordering the universe in the image of her personal concep-tion of Beauty. (p. 241)

Tracing her legacy back through her mother and grandmother freed Walker to develop herself as an artist. She concludes:

> Guided by my heritage of a love of beauty and a respect for strength—in search of my mother's garden, I found my own. (p. 243)

Barbara Christian (1990), the black feminist literary critic, wrote,

> Walker turned the *idea* of Art on its head. Instead of looking high, she suggested, we should look low. On that low ground she found a multitude of artist-mothers—the women who'd transformed the material to which they'd had access into their conception of Beauty: cooking, gardening, quilting, storytelling. (p. 44)

Because art was woven into the fabric of daily life throughout the African diaspora, even the sons and daughters of the poorest sharecropper, like Alice Walker, might grow up amidst many great artists. Some, like Walker's mother, take on the responsibility of drawing out the creative talents of the children growing up around them.

Walker's essay is now a classic work, canonized by women everywhere. Women of all colors speak of this piece as they speak of Virginia Woolf's *A Room of One's Own,* where Woolf writes that "Poetry ought to have a mother as well as a father" (1929/1957, p. 107) and insists that "we think back through our mothers if we are women" (p. 79) for the roots of our creativity. Both Walker and Woolf cast lifelines to women, enabling us to link the artistry we seek in ourselves with that of our mothers.

The literary critic and black studies scholar Mary Helen Washington (1984) suggests that the creativity of mothers is an important source of unity, wholeness, and generativity that permeates African American culture:

> In assuming the voices of their mothers, these writers assure that character, culture, and creativity are interlocking systems in their worlds. This oneness with the community which these writers express is profoundly connected to creativity. No black writer has been able to reveal the black experience in all its range and complexity without that sense of unity—of oneness with his or her people. For black women writers, the mother is often the key to that unity. (p. 148)

When such women as Virginia Woolf and Alice Walker look back through their mothers to map out their genealogies, they provide touchstones for all of us who have ever stood in the shadows wondering,

"Can women write?" "Can blacks paint?" "Can women . . . ?" "Can I . . . ?"

The association of creativity with the maternal in black culture is further revealed by Andrea Rushing's (1987) study, "God's Divas." Rushing combed the works of black poets—male and female—for images of women, and found the most prevalent image was that of mother. This discovery is in sharp contrast to the focus of poets from European-based cultures on women's relationships with men while children are ignored.

The black poets' second most common theme portrayed women singers as having awesome powers whether they sang sacred music or secular blues. This was of great interest to us as the cultural workers we studied for this book fueled their work with the power of song. Rushing (1987) says that the number of poetic tributes to women singers and the terms with which these artists are celebrated suggest a resemblance between them and the female healers, priestesses, ancestors, and deities in precolonial African cultures.

> Women like Gertrude Rainey, Bessie Smith, Dinah Washington, Billie Holiday, Nina Simone, and Aretha Franklin . . . have been given by African American popular culture the titles, respectively, "Ma," "Empress of the Blues," "Queen of the Blues," "Lady Day," "High Priestess of Soul," and "Lady Soul." (p. 189)

The diva, the poets say, achieves immortality because her music is part of an "eternal song" that resounds long after the singer herself has died (Rushing, 1987, p. 192).

The Africanist scholar Donna Richards (1985) says it is hard for Westerners to imagine the mortals living among us as divine.

> In the African world view the human and the divine are not hopelessly separated, as they are in Western theology where the divine is defined as the negation of all that is human. It requires a miracle for them to interact. In Africa the human is divine, and the demonstration of this joining is the height of religious experience, as the spirits manifest themselves in us. To the African the sacred and the profane are close and can be experienced as unity. (p. 211)

Because great art is seen in African traditions as evolving out of a dialogue of the whole community, poets and composers are held more on a par with the rest. Everyone is encouraged to improvise with any given piece of music until it expresses what she or he has to say. Even after professionals were composing, publishing, copyrighting, and selling much of the music being produced in the black community, it was assumed that their compositions were only a beginning to be elaborated upon by anyone with something to add (Levine, 1978).

Among Eurocentric cultures great creativity is more often seen as an expression of an individual genius, not of a collaborative community dialogue. Practicing musicians and composers are as distanced from each other as are artists and audiences in the concert hall. Musicians often feel obligated to replicate a composer's work just as they imagine the creator intended it to be played. A creation is, in this view, the property of the creator. Copyright laws even make improvisers legally vulnerable (Ede and Lunsford, 1992).

As African musical forms spread out across the world they continue to have a transformative, often liberating effect. The educational philosopher Maxine Greene (1988) calls the jazz section of the Czech dissident movement resisting Soviet oppression "the live center of dissent" (p. 129). The music testifies, she says,

> to a power, not merely to embody and express the suffering of oppressed and constricted lives, but to name them somehow, to identify the gaps between what is and what is longed for, what (if the sphere of freedom is ever developed) will some day come to be. (p. 129)

Our explorations of the experiences of women in diverse cultures illuminate whole segments of women's lives that have been overshadowed by narrow conceptions of gender and what is possible for human beings. The whole society is impoverished when women are silenced and their homemaking is uncounted. Societies are likely to benefit—generation after generation—when women are supported to develop large hearts *and* powerful minds; to become powerfully voiced *and* careful listeners; to nurture themselves, as well as their families *and* communities (Thurer, 1994).

Women's mothering is not innate. Women cultivate the ability to nurture the development of human beings and homeplaces through continuous reflection on this work and the creation of a subculture where practitioners can experiment, discuss, value, and solidify their ideas, and teach their discipline to the next generation. Philosopher Sara Ruddick (1994) calls the body of reflections that women generate out of engaged practice "maternal thinking." Maternal thinking, she argues, is a discipline associated with a body of knowledge—just like the disciplines of law or medicine:

> The discipline of maternal thought, like other disciplines, estab-lishes criteria for determining failure and success, sets priorities, and identifies virtues that the discipline requires. . . . Maternal thinking is one kind of disciplined reflection among many, each with identifying questions, methods, and aims. (p. 24)

Ruddick says maternal thinking is "a revolutionary discourse" that has been silenced. It is, she says, a struggle for women to make their own viewpoint heard, even to each other and to themselves. It is for this reason that women who nurture the development of people and communities are carrying out an ancient tradition that has had no name. As a central discourse, Ruddick says, maternal thinking could transform the dominant, so-called normal ways of thinking. The chapters that follow tell of women who are deeply engaged in maternal thinking and maternal practice because they feel, as we do, that the more "normal ways of thinking" must be transformed.

CHAPTER 2

CONFRONTING OTHERNESS: PREVIOUS RESEARCH

Often when you come up in an oppressive culture, you question the importance of your very existence; you have to search for courage to express yourself. You have to talk to yourself so that when you speak with your voice, it is your heart, your mind, your eyes, your living, that supplies the text.   BERNICE JOHNSON REAGON (1993, P. 24)
                              FOUNDER, SWEET HONEY IN THE ROCK

When the first half of the twentieth century culminated in a Holocaust, many struggled to understand why one group of people declared another group as Other and believed its members to be the cause of all that was evil in the world. Studying great sweeps of human history, Simone de Beauvoir (1957) found the tendency of human beings to pit themselves against an Other recurring across many centuries and cultures. She concluded that people always view "the world under the sign of duality. . . . At the moment when man asserts himself as subject and free being, the idea of the Other arises" (pp. 69, 79). "Thus it is," she writes, "that no group ever sets itself up as the One without at once setting up the Other over against itself" (p. xvii).

De Beauvoir used this conceptual framework for examining the relations between men and women while her colleague and consort, Jean-Paul Sartre, pursued similar ideas in *Anti-Semite and Jew* (1948). In her book, *The Second Sex,* de Beauvoir described women's demeaned status as Other. Her powerful portrayal played a major role in unleashing this century's second wave of feminism in the United States as well as in Europe. De Beauvoir was, it is believed, the very first person to realize that conceptions of gender are shaped by rigid, dichotomous categories (Haste, 1994). She explains the core of her reasoning:

> The relations of the two sexes is not quite like that of two electric poles, for man represents both the positive and the neutral, as indicated by the common use of *man* to designate human beings in general; whereas woman represents only the negative, defined by limiting criteria, without reciprocity. . . . She is defined and differentiated with reference to man and not he with reference to her; she is the incidental, the inessential as opposed to the essential. He is the Subject, he is the Absolute—she is the Other. (p. xvi)

Men, de Beauvoir argued, claim for themselves the loftiest human attitudes—heroism, revolt, disinterestedness, imagination, creation— and relegate to women those capacities they do not want to acknowledge in themselves. They see themselves as active subjects, creating culture, reason, and individuated separateness. As a mirror image of man's "not self," women are seen as passively steeped in nature, emotions, and primordial oneness.

De Beauvoir was certain at the outset that the polarities setting Self against Other were impossible to transcend because of the underlying animosity that permeates all human relationships. She wrote,

> We find in consciousness itself a fundamental hostility toward every other consciousness; the subject can be posed only in being opposed—he sets himself up as the essential, as opposed to the other, the inessential, the object. (p. xvii)

She calls this attitude the imperialism of the human consciousness, seeking always to exercise its sovereignty.

De Beauvoir was only interested in women having the right to claim for themselves those human qualities men attributed solely to their own kind. Because she made no effort to reintegrate those aspects of humanity that men saw as inferior and relegated to women, she too needed a repository for basic but excluded human capacities. For de Beauvoir, the name of the Other became Mother instead of Woman. If women did not mother, they too could be freed from emotion; they too could be unburdened by their connection with nature and other human beings. She writes:

Ensnared by nature, the pregnant woman is plant and animal, a
stock-pile of colloids, an incubator, an egg; she scares children
proud of their young, straight bodies, and makes young people tit-
ter contemptuously because she is a human being, a conscious and
free individual, who has become life's passive instrument. (p. 495)

She goes on:

Gestation [in ordinary life] appears as creative; but that is a strange
kind of creation which is accomplished in a contingent and passive
manner. . . . Creative acts originating in liberty establish the object
as value and give it the quality of the essential; whereas the child in
the maternal body is not thus justified; it is still only a gratuitous
cellular growth, a brute fact of nature . . . she [the mother] engenders him [the child] as a product of her generalized body, not of
her individualized existence. (pp. 495–496)

In trying to see the new woman as having a fuller range of human
capacities, de Beauvoir ascribed to Mother all those characteristics that
men had found undesirable and projected onto Woman. In the mirror
de Beauvoir held up so that humanity might better see itself, Mother
reflected the New Woman's "not self," just as Woman had long held the
place for Man's "not self." It is curious that de Beauvoir's picture of
women who mother has raised so little comment during the last half
century, when feminists have been reading and discussing this work.
That women have not taken exception to such a characterization of
mothers suggests how disrespected women feel when they invest themselves in caring for the next generation. Reading de Beauvoir, many
mothers must have said, "Yes, she is right. I am a stock-pile of colloids."
Calling this phenomenon "matrophobia," the poet Adrienne Rich
wrote,

Matrophobia can be seen as a womanly splitting of the self, in the
desire to become purged once and for all of our mothers' bondage,
to become individuated and free. The mother stands for the victim
in ourselves, the unfree woman, the martyr. (1977, p. 238)

In visualizing a world where men and women might meet as
equals, de Beauvoir would have women cast by the molds that men had

designed for themselves. Not imagining anyone—male or female—choosing to develop their capacities for the most basic form of generativity, she argued that primary responsibility for raising children should fall on the state, not the parents.

De Beauvoir's work was of enormous importance to women's struggle against Otherness. Her polemic against motherhood was a much needed counterbalance to the sanctification that surrounded the institution. It helped women imagine that motherhood did not have to be compulsory; women could actually choose how they were going to pattern their lives. Nevertheless, it was a great tragedy that de Beauvoir continued to cast women caring for children as Other.

THE AUTHORITARIAN PERSONALITY

While de Beauvoir and Sartre worked on their respective books, a small number of social scientists gathered in the United States to grapple with the problem of Otherness. Their work was motivated by a passion for social justice, even though most social scientists of that day thought science-making should be detached, dispassionate, and value-free. These researchers also intended to study the thinking and values of their research subjects. This too flew in the face of accepted practice. In a time when most social scientists studied only concrete behaviors that could be measured with precision, these scientists conducted highly reflective interviews about complex issues that many people found too murky for clear articulation. To do this work, the social scientists had to develop the skills many had relegated to the artist. They had to enter into the perspectives of people who were often very dissimilar from themselves and find a way of narrating what they found. (For more on research methodology and narrative knowing, see Gardner, 1985; Bruner, 1986; Mishler, 1986; Polkinghorne, 1988; Sarbin, 1986; see Reinharz, 1992, for a review.)

Among the outstanding social scientists Professor Nevitt Sanford brought to the University of California at Berkeley to study these issues were two European refugees: T. W. Adorno and Else Frenkel-Brunswik. Having witnessed the rise of fascism and the genocide of their own people, they understood all too well the importance of comprehending the processes by which people divide Self from Other. With support from the

American Jewish Committee, the Berkeley group focused its attention on the nature of prejudice. The project was unprecedented in that it drew together specialists from such diverse fields as social theory, psychoanalysis, clinical psychology, and political sociology. The project also utilized an unusually wide array of research methods. The social scientists developed "objective" paper and pencil tests, but these were based on categories and knowledge gained from lengthy interviews and projective tests. Statistical analyses were combined with qualitative reports. All of the major findings were illustrated by compelling case studies. The studies were published in 1950 in a single volume entitled *The Authoritarian Personality*. To indicate their collaborative, nonhierarchical way of working, the authors listed their names in alphabetical order: T. W. Adorno, Else Frenkel-Brunswik, Daniel Levinson, and Nevitt Sanford. As it turned out, the name of the "primary investigator" came last.

The Berkeley group found that the tendency to divide the world between Good and Bad, projecting the Self's unwanted characteristics onto an Other, was characteristic of only a subsample of the population. De Beauvoir was clearly wrong when she declared that all human beings create an Other whenever they assert themselves as a Self.

The tendency to define people different from the self as Other was so intertwined with a specific configuration of personal characteristics that the Berkeley group declared it a specific personality type. People who held strong anti-Semitic views also held hostile and punitive feelings toward any and all groups that were seen as culturally different. Beyond that, people high in prejudice used rigid, dichotomous categories for thinking about all aspects of the self–world relationship, not just about the culturally different. Any sort of imaginative and ambiguous introspection, art, or discourse seemed to make highly prejudiced people feel uncomfortable. Things that could not easily be fitted into a simple binary framework were simply ignored or dismissed with disdain as "soft-headed."

Highly prejudiced people also demonstrated an obedient, unquestioning, and uncritical attitude toward authorities, construing everything in terms of power, status, dominance, and submission. Indeed, the association between prejudice and authoritarianism was so strong the researchers named their personality type "the authoritarian personality."

Because people who fit the authoritarian personality profile do not think about complexities and subtleties, they have no choice but to see themselves, their parents, and other authorities in idealized terms: they speak only of the positive and ignore the negative. In a masterful summary of the whole body of work stimulated by the Berkeley group, social psychologist Roger Brown succinctly described the relationship between prejudice and dualism: "The sins and weaknesses we miss in their self-descriptions and in their descriptions of their parents turn up in what they say about minority groups" (1965, p. 501).

An extraordinary amount of thinking, debate, and research was generated by *The Authoritarian Personality* in the decades following its publication. Almost all of the new studies avoided the more open-ended interviews the Berkeley group had developed and utilized only their paper and pencil tests. Assessing this massive body of research some thirty years later, Nevitt Sanford (1982) argued that this almost complete reliance on their easily scored "objective" paper and pencil tests had yielded remarkably little new knowledge from such a huge array of work. They themselves, he argued, had been able to develop such a comprehensive and compelling understanding of authoritarianism just because they used interview formats that invited people to share their thinking about the nature of authority and group differences in a more open and reflective way.

William Perry (1970) and Jane Loevinger (1976) were among the few social scientists of the day who shared Sanford's convictions about methodology. Thus when they sought to replicate and extend the findings of the Berkeley group, they too adopted open-ended questions that allowed respondents to express themselves in their own terms. Perry and Loevinger's research programs extended the original findings of the Berkeley group in such dramatically new directions that many contemporary observers do not realize that this work was rooted in the same soil.

EPISTEMOLOGICAL DEVELOPMENT

When *The Authoritarian Personality* was first published, William Perry and his associates were interviewing Harvard undergraduates each spring, tracing changes the students were experiencing in themselves as knowers and in their conceptions of the learning process as they progressed through the college. Early on, Perry identified a small number of students who construed the world as being sharply divided between "Authority/Right/We" and "Illegitimate/Wrong/Other." The match between his findings and the Berkeley group's was so close that Perry presumed he had located the authoritarian personality at Harvard University. Yet when Perry and his colleagues reinterviewed the same students over the next couple of years, they observed that this outlook receded and then disappeared altogether. They concluded that it would be more accurate to conceptualize authoritarianism as a developmental issue rather than as a personality type. Perry called the outlook "dualism" because rigid dichotomous thinking shaped the students' conceptions of knowledge and meaning-making in such powerful ways.

Perry maintained that people would abandon binary categories when they were supported to develop more complex ways of viewing the world. From then on the whole thrust of his work focused on tracing students' epistemological development—that is, how students' understandings about the construction of knowledge evolve over time. Perry and his staff selected interviews they had collected from male students and studied the patterns of change that appeared in this demanding academic environment. They found students who began as dualists (seeing truth as absolute and singular), traversing through multiplism (seeing truth as multiple but essentially unknowable except in personal terms) to contextual relativism (seeing truth as relative and contextual). They saw the relativist maturing with the understanding that even people with vastly different perspectives can comprehend each other if they work to develop good translations; that seeing something from many points of view can vastly expand one's understanding of "reality"; and that some perspectives yield more adequate views than others. Mature relativists had also constructed a reasoned basis for making firm ethical commitments even after abandoning all hope that universal and abiding Truths could serve as guides. The Perry scheme tracing epistemological development in college men was published in 1970 as *Forms of Intellectual and Ethical Development in the College Years: A Scheme.*

EGO DEVELOPMENT

At about the same time that Perry began interviewing students, Jane Loevinger (1976; Loevinger and Sweet, 1961) was constructing a projective test she called the Authoritarian Family Ideology (AFI) to tap the kinds of personality traits described by the Berkeley group. Her initial concern was to rectify some of the methodological flaws in the original studies, including the Berkeley group's (like Perry's) extensive reliance on male cases for theory building and illustrative examples. It wasn't long before Loevinger and her colleagues had used the AFI in a large number of studies of mothers looking at the way they conceptualize their parental responsibilities. Putting all of these studies together, Loevinger soon realized that authoritarian attitudes were less prominent among the mothers who were older, who had more education, and who had raised more children. She too concluded that authoritarianism was not a personality type but a function of development. From then on, Loevinger focused her professional career on tracing stages of ego development across the life span. In her scheme the immature end of the continuum is not marked by the extreme adherence to authorities described by the Berkeley group, but rather by a chaotic, impulsive, and extremely self-centered self-world organization. Deference to authorities was characteristic of her Conformist Stage, a midpoint in her continuum that culminates with a sequence of three stages she designated as Individualistic, Autonomous, and Integrated. The women who reached the end of the trajectory had developed the capacity to see themselves as self-governing and capable of taking a stance in the world independent of authorities. They viewed reality as complex and multifaceted, transcending the polarized thinking characteristic of earlier stages. She argued that it is these achievements, combined with courage, that enable people to deal directly with conflict and difference rather than ignoring them or projecting them onto others.

After the publication of *The Authoritarian Personality*, Nevitt Sanford also began following students' progress as they moved through college. He too observed that students' authoritarian attitudes declined over time. Like Perry and Loevinger, Sanford (1962) was forced to reconceptualize the issue. Construing authoritarianism as a developmental phenomenon rather than as a personality type clearly provided a much better fit for his new data, as it had for Loevinger's and Perry's. Other studies pointed to the role that social factors, such as socioeconomic class, played in the distribution of educational and work experiences that influence these developmental progressions (Kohn, 1977;

Kohn and Schooler, with Miller, Miller, Schoenback, and Schoenberg, 1983).

Other research (Allport, 1958) showed another phenomenon the Berkeley group had not captured adequately. People living in communities with a high degree of prejudice might adopt commonly held stereotypes but not necessarily exhibit any of the other characteristics typical of the authoritarian personality. It seems that these people accept the conventional stereotypes of their community without critical reflection. They are not, however, generally constrained by simple dichotomous categories, nor do they show excessive reverence for, and dependence on, authorities. In the introduction to the abridged edition (1982) of *The Authoritarian Personality,* released thirty-two years after its initial publication, Daniel Levinson and Nevitt Sanford point to these limitations in their earlier work:

> We now take pride in having shown the relative power of this paradigm, but we see the need for a broader approach. It is necessary to take sociocultural forces more into account, without neglecting the role of personality. Equally, it is necessary to take more account of individual change and development during the adult years. Developmental principles operate in adulthood as in childhood. Our personalities are not finished products by the end of adolescence; growth as well as decline occur throughout the life cycle. (p. vi)

The shift to a developmental stance was of the utmost importance. When authoritarianism is conceptualized as a personality structure it suggests something fixed and enduring. When it is cast as a developmental phenomenon it appears quite susceptible to change even in the adult years. De Beauvoir might have been less discouraged if she had had this insight along with the knowledge that the need to bifurcate the world between Self and Other is far from universal.

MORAL DEVELOPMENT

While the Berkeley group was conducting its original studies on authoritarianism, young Lawrence Kohlberg—just out of high school—was sailing the high seas as a merchant seaman. It was not long before he signed onto a ship running the blockade created by the British to keep Jews out of Palestine. With laws erected everywhere to prevent a tide of Jewish refugees from reaching Palestine, attempts to aid the exiles would involve the violation of one law or another. Kohlberg became a smuggler of human contraband. To protect the right to life of an endangered people, Kohlberg chose to violate the laws of many nations.

After the war, Kohlberg returned home to join those who were studying the questions raised by the Holocaust, but he framed the problem somewhat differently. Essentially he asked why some people say, "I was only following orders," or "I was only obeying the law," whereas others reject such explanations out of hand. Building on the work of John Dewey, Jean Piaget, and a host of others, Kohlberg (1981, 1984) began studying the development of moral reasoning in preadolescent and adolescent boys. He asked these boys to share their thinking about hypothetical moral dilemmas that pit the right to life against property rights and the law of the land. (An example of such a dilemma: Should Heinz steal some medicine to save the life of his dying wife? The druggist is charging an exorbitant price and will not let the husband defer payments.)

By reinterviewing these young men periodically over several decades, Kohlberg was able to delineate a series of qualitatively distinct and hierarchically arranged stages of moral reasoning that arise in an invariant sequence. Kohlberg's scheme focused on the development of conceptions of rules, law, social contracts, and, ultimately, the evolution of universal principles of justice. Each stage, according to Kohlberg, represents an increasingly adequate mode of resolving dilemmas posed by the competing claims and rights of individuals vis-à-vis each other and the society. Some kinds of environments are likely to stimulate fuller development than others. The sequence Kohlberg projected describes the path people take in developing universal principles of justice against which the orders of authorities and societal laws can be assessed. It is difficult to imagine a society capable of overthrowing authoritarian regimes and developing democratic traditions unless a substantial portion of the population could and would embrace such notions.

Like the Berkeley group's work on the authoritarian personality, Perry's research on epistemological development, and Loevinger's study of ego development, Kohlberg's theory of moral judgment stimulated much thought, research, and educational experimentation. Many were encouraged by this line of research to rethink educational and social arrangements so that subsequent generations might be better supported to meet the moral and intellectual challenges of their era.

GENDER DIFFERENCES

While research on the development and decline of authoritarianism was proceeding, many other social scientists were studying gender differences (for an overview of this research, see Kimball, 1995). Many of these researchers found minimal psychological differences between the sexes, with men and women often exhibiting characteristics commonly attributed to the other sex. These researchers also found evidence that the differences between the sexes were decreasing, no doubt in response to the enormous changes in social roles. Increasingly, they concluded that the stereotypes that held girls and women to be different and inferior to men were unwarranted.

Other social scientists concerned with gender began to think about an issue that had been almost completely ignored: nearly all of the psychological research that had generated contemporary theories about identity, epistemological, and moral development in humans had been conducted on samples of men. As with most (but not all) of the researchers we cited previously as our predecessors, there was a persistent tendency to study only men while generalizing findings to the whole of humanity. Noticing this rather extraordinary phenomenon, the new group of scholars essentially stopped asking the question, "Are women as good as men?" Instead they pondered, "Has anything been left out by studying only men?" "When men's experiences and values define our conceptions of human development, what aspects of our humanity might we be ignoring?"

Women's Identity Development Jean Baker Miller (1976/1987) brought these new questions to the public's attention with her groundbreaking book *Towards a New Psychology of Women*. She argued that theories of the self and identity development shaped by the study of men and male culture present models of "human" development that define health and maturity in terms of separation and autonomy. When women are judged against such models they are defined as deficient. More importantly, Miller maintained that this overwhelming emphasis on individuation shadows other aspects of human development that are also of great importance. She went on to argue that a careful study of women's conceptions of self makes it difficult to ignore the centrality of relationships and interconnections in human development. If we speak more of "differentiation" than "separation and autonomy," we might be better able to conceptualize how interdependent all human beings are—from the least to the most mature. If a theory of a self-in-relation were to replace the prevailing psychological theories of the autonomous self, our definitions of human maturity would have at the center notions of mutuality, connection, and dialogue. (See also Jordan, Kaplan, Miller, Stiver, and Surrey, 1991; Miller, 1988.)

Miller enabled us to see that the culture's conventional templates did not delineate women's experience very well. That was a great achievement because we have long equated the male view of the world with "the view." Even though the division of labor in modern society has encouraged men to place greater emphasis on autonomy and women to highlight the self-in-relation, not all studies of women have revealed the more connected way of conceptualizing the self-world relationship. Jane Loevinger's massive study of ego development began with women as her only informants, yet the language of connection enters into her descriptions of maturity with seeming reluctance. Loevinger writes of her penultimate stage: "The Autonomous person . . . typically recognizes the limitations to autonomy, that emotional interdependence is inevitable" (1976, p. 23). Although Loevinger calls the last stage of ego development "integrated," she does not use language that suggests a rich appreciation of the sense of connection that human beings can achieve. It is as if both Loevinger and her mature research subjects had discovered a cultural fault line but had not yet found a vantage point that would enable them to imagine bridging the rift.

In the struggle to become free of the commands of dictators as well as many constraining cultural and religious traditions, many men and women in the Western world celebrated notions of autonomy, freedom, and the individual. In the process they turned their backs on many other aspects of our humanity. The authors of *Habits of the Heart*

(Bellah, Madsen, Sullivan, Swidler, and Tipton, 1985) summarize the problem:

> If the entire social world is made up of individuals, each endowed with the right to be free of others' demands, it becomes hard to forge bonds of attachment to, or cooperation with, other people, since such bonds would imply obligations that necessarily impinge on one's freedom. (p. 23)

Miller's reading of women's experience provided many with a standing place that would open them to a broader vision of what human beings, men as well as women, should and could be reaching for.

Women's Moral Development   While Jean Baker Miller was writing on women's identity development, Carol Gilligan, a colleague of Lawrence Kohlberg's, began an interview study of women facing the crisis of an unwanted pregnancy. Gilligan selected this topic for study not out of concern for issues of gender but because she wanted to study people facing a serious moral crisis. She thought that interviews with people about the moral dilemmas they were actually facing in their lives would be more revealing than the kind of hypothetical dilemmas Kohlberg was utilizing in his research. The particular crisis of a woman's unwanted pregnancy was selected for study because it was a classic moral dilemma, with every decision or lack of decision having serious and irreversible consequences.

Gilligan, with the collaboration of Mary Belenky, interviewed a number of women twice: in the first trimester of pregnancy, prior to any irreversible action, and again a year later. The issue of gender became increasingly salient as Gilligan tried to place the women's thinking about their abortion dilemma on Kohlberg's map of moral development. She often found the map Kohlberg had drawn from male data deficient for making sense of the women's responses. Sometimes the women were expressing ideas that were completely absent from the Kohlberg scoring manual; more often the idea was there but the women seemed to conceptualize the issues in far more complex terms than those delineated by Kohlberg. Gilligan began drawing a new map to reflect the ideas she was hearing in the voices of the women she had interviewed. In the end Gilligan traced aspects of moral thought that were not well articulated in

Kohlberg's work. She named the themes she heard while listening to women "the ethic of care" or "the response orientation" to moral conflicts. She called Kohlberg's scheme "the ethic of justice" or "the rights orientation." (See Belenky, 1978; Brown and Gilligan, 1992; Gilligan, 1977, 1982/1993, 1990; Gilligan and Belenky, 1990; Gilligan, Lyons, and Hanmer, 1990; Gilligan, Ward, and Taylor, 1988; Lyons, 1983.)

As Carol Gilligan describes Kohlberg's rights orientation, conflicts are resolved through the lone individual's impartial application of rules and principles whose hierarchy can be determined logically. (An example we have contrived: Yes, it would be right for a man to steal the outrageously priced medicine if stealing was the only way he could save the life of his wife—or indeed, the life of anyone, including a stranger. Logically the right to life must take precedence over property rights. Property can have no value unless human life is protected.)

In the rights orientation the ideal is to treat everyone equally. Because all the rules and procedures are geared to the ideal of equality, every effort is made to create a level playing field for those who in actuality might be quite unequal on a huge range of relevant issues. To achieve fairness in the midst of any inequalities, everyone is to assume an impersonal and impartial stance when making moral decisions. The key metaphor for suggesting justice is an image of a blindfolded woman with a scale in one hand and a sword in the other (Hirsch, Kett, and Trefil, 1993). The ethic of justice holds that we should blindfold ourselves, as philosopher John Rawls (1971) suggests, "by donning a veil of ignorance." In other words, one is to resolve moral conflicts without considering who the people actually are or what roles they might occupy in reality. In this way decisions will not be swayed by inequalities, self-interest, emotions, and/or personal relationships that might give any one person undue advantage over another.

Whereas the ethic of justice approach prescribes a profound distance between the actors in any moral drama, the response mode as described by Gilligan takes a different tack. Here conflicts are resolved through dialogue. It is not an impersonal and logical ordering of hierarchical rules and principles that leads to an understanding of what would be the best resolution. It is, rather, a listening mode where the effort to understand and respond to everyone's concerns is seen as the way to bring about lasting and satisfying solutions to moral predicaments. (An example: It is hard to know if a husband should steal the medicine to save his dying wife. Maybe he could talk with the druggist who is charging so much; they might be able to work something out. Besides, why is the druggist charging such an outrageous amount? Maybe his wife is also dying. It is hard to know what the husband should do. He should talk with his wife. What are her wishes? What is her condition? Who would take care of the children if she were to die and he was in jail?)

In the rights mode the individual is more likely to work in isolation, thinking everything out in his or her own head. In the response mode resolutions are reached through conversation, storytelling, and perspective sharing. To those used to thinking in the rights mode, the response mode seems wishy-washy because it is tentative and vacillating. It is questioning rather than assertive. Decisions are always changing because people and circumstances keep changing. Rather than distance and impersonality, the response mode demands empathy, openness, and connection. By contrast, the moral decisions of individuals operating out of the rights mode appear clear and certain.

Gilligan cited Lever's (1976) research on children's play, showing boys from an early age being drawn into play where their combativeness is curbed by intricate rules of the game, whereas little girls shun rule-bound games and instead play out dramas of care and relationships. Gilligan goes on to show how women struggle with moral conventions that dictate how a woman should be—selfless, listening, and preoccupied with drawing out the thinking of others when confronted with moral conflicts. The same conventions dictate that she, herself, should shy away from voicing her own concerns and taking her own perspective. In Gilligan's scheme moral maturity is achieved with the understanding that the flaw in the conventional arrangements is *not* in the extending of care to others as de Beauvoir would have it. Rather, it is in the expectation that women should do most of the caring work by themselves and that they should exclude themselves as people worthy of equal consideration when weighing moral claims. This "flaw" points to a central contradiction in our cultural heritage that has had tragic consequences for men as well as women, for children, for families, and for the society as a whole—that those who do the caring work do not require, or warrant, care.

Two notions central to Kohlberg's rights or justice orientation undoubtedly mark some of humanity's most important achievements: that all persons are of equal worth, and that the rules of the game, societal laws, social contracts, democratic practices, and moral principles can be used to level the playing field so everyone will be treated with greater fairness. Still, although the ethic of justice lays out elaborate procedures for establishing principles that minimize the potential impact of differences between people, it does not address well the question that drives our work: How do you actually "uplift" people who enter a situation from positions of great inequality (whether because of age, social position, or other factors)? In essence, the rights orientation seeks to overcome inequalities and avoid personal bias by having decision makers blindfold themselves to all the particulars when making moral choices. To ensure fairness, they make choices without taking into consideration who the specific individuals are or who actually occupies which positions in the situation.

The response mode or the ethic of care Gilligan described is not so focused on overcoming inequalities in the decision-making process. Its concern is with maintaining nurturing relationships that sponsor human development of people, most especially that of the young and the least advantaged. While the rights mode provides principles for treating people as if they were equals, the responsibility mode outlines the principles for supporting the people's development so they might become capable of participating in society on an equal basis. Sponsoring the development of a subordinated people and illuminating what has been ignored requires a profound openness to dialogue and connection, rather than blindfolds, monologue, and distance.

The ethic of justice does not wrestle well with another set of questions we believe to be of great importance. When the ethic holds that everyone should be treated equally it does not ask: Equal to whom? Who sets the standard? Who decides what is deviant? How could fairer standards be developed?

Any society that aspires to be more just and democratic must learn how to honor the values cultivated by people standing in the shadows. In short, it must learn how to construct a shared vision of the human person we are all trying to become. That too requires an openness to dialogue and connection.

Gilligan (Gilligan, 1982/1993; Gilligan and Wiggins, 1988) made an argument many readers found difficult to hear (see, for example, Broughton, 1983). The ethics of justice and care delineate different but interconnected aspects of morality. Each has distinctive aims that deal with issues not well covered by the other. The two are not polarized opposites—one better than the other—nor is one cultivated by men and the other by women. Both are important. Both can and should be cultivated by all human beings—female and male. If one set of ethics is subsumed by the other, many essential elements of the subordinated view will become invisible and the interconnections will be lost. Even if these two perspectives never fully converge, people will have fewer moral blind spots if they are able to move freely back and forth between the two—as one might do, Gilligan suggests, with a reversing figure-ground picture (see also Kegan, 1982).

Women's Epistemological Development   Many were influenced by Gilligan's work because it seemed to open up contemporary thinking about moral development in both men and women, just as Miller's work had expanded conceptions of identity development. Among those influenced were Mary Belenky, Blythe Clinchy, Nancy Goldberger, and Jill Tarule, the authors of *Women's Ways of Knowing (WWK)* (1986/1997; see also Goldberger, Tarule, Clinchy, and Belenky, 1996). We summarize this work in detail because it provided much of the foundation for the two projects discussed in this book.

Following Gilligan and Miller's lead, the *WWK* collaborative interviewed women to explore whether there were certain conceptions of knowing that were more easily heard in the voices of women. The collaborative believed that the inclusion of the women's experience might expand the scheme Perry had constructed from male data to illuminate a broader range of human experience. (Although Perry did interview female students, these interviews were set aside when he constructed his scheme. Only later did the researchers analyze the interviews they had collected from the women. They found that the females conformed to the patterns they had observed in the male data; however, the researchers did not ask if there were other patterns that might be easier to see in female data that males might also adopt.)

One hundred and thirty-five women from all walks of life were interviewed about their development as knowers. Many of the women were enrolled in a variety of colleges. The range included a community college serving inner-city residents and a highly selective private women's college—one of the seven sisters. Other women came into the study sample through one of the three social agencies serving mothers of young children living in rural poverty. One of the programs paired teenage mothers with a volunteer—another mother close in age—who would serve as a mentor. The second was a local chapter of a national self-help network for parents working to overcome a history of child abuse and family violence. A children's health program that viewed the support of mothers as central to the health care of children was the third program. These programs were called "invisible colleges" to distinguish them from regular degree-granting institutions. The invisible colleges were included in the study because they were, for the most part, women-led organizations designed for women by women. It was thought that the study of institutions that held the perspectives and values of women in the highest regard might provide another window into ways of functioning in our culture that had been ignored and poorly understood. The invisible colleges were also included because they were reaching out to poor mothers—one of the more isolated, unsupported, and demeaned groups in contemporary society.

Each woman interviewed was asked to describe her own personal theory of knowledge: How does she actually go about making meaning in a variety of different circumstances? What had helped her develop the powers of mind and what had held her back? The research collaborative then tried to place what the women said on the map Perry had drawn from male data. Like Gilligan, members of the collaborative tried to be particularly aware when they had to push and shove to make the women's data fit, or when the women expressed ideas that had not been well articulated in Perry's work.

Early on, members of the *WWK* collaborative noticed that many of the women equated the growth of mind with "gaining a voice." Because this theme was so striking they made a special point to attend to each woman's experience of voice. They also documented how the experience of voice changed as the women developed more complex ways of knowing. Attending to notions of speaking and listening, the researchers focused their attention on the women's conceptions of the source(s) of knowledge. As they read and reread a woman's interview, the researchers asked such questions as: Does this woman see truth and knowledge as something that can be discussed and passed down from one person to another? Does she listen to her own inner voice, understanding that insight and truth can spring from her own mind? What role does she see dialogue playing in the development of ideas? Does she have to choose between listening to others and listening to her own thoughts? Or can she attend carefully to the voices of others while also marshalling her own ideas? Switching metaphors, can she achieve a kind of double vision that allows her to hold on to her own perspective while also seeing the world from another's point of view? Does she understand that people must work hard at constructing knowledge? If so, how does she describe the procedures she actually uses for understanding, developing, and testing ideas? Does she see the construction of knowledge as a collaborative or a competitive process?

After reading and rereading the women's interviews it became clearer that there were places on Perry's map that did not capture women's experiences well. To remedy this shortcoming, the research collaborative began sketching in the missing details. The revised scheme grouped women's perspectives on knowing into five major epistemological categories or frameworks people use for meaning-making.

These ways of knowing were not presented as representing fixed, universal stages of epistemological development. It was presumed that different approaches to knowing, their order of appearance, and their end points would vary under different social contexts and cultural conditions (Goldberger, 1996; Harding, 1996; Rogoff, 1990; Shweder, 1991). It was also assumed that similar categories could be found in men's thinking, and that other researchers might organize similar observations differently.

The scheme described the ways that people think they think— their theories of knowledge-making—not necessarily the ways they actually think. People often use more complex approaches to generating knowledge than they are able to describe. It is also the case that people sometimes articulate more sophisticated ways of knowing than they regularly use. Nevertheless, if a person is able to articulate a way of knowing very clearly—with convincing examples of actual practice—it is quite likely that the person has used that way of knowing enough to get a good grasp of its shape, assumptions, and processes. A person's theory of mind is of the utmost importance. People who are aware of the intellectual tools that they have at their disposal are likely to cultivate and use those tools much more effectively and consistently than are people who have not yet articulated the existence and function of a tool (Flavell, 1988).

Indeed, the central issue we try to address in this book is the tragedy of well-endowed people who have been led to believe that they have little or no intellectual power to develop. We spell out the ways of knowing scheme in detail because it provides us with a "road map" of the routes people take when the powers of mind are being developed.

Silenced[1] describes an outlook unlike anything Perry reported among the Harvard students he studied. Whereas the silenced women might believe they learn from their own concrete actions, they do not believe they are capable of learning from experiences mediated by language. They think of themselves as "voiceless" because they feel unable to give words to what they know. They also find it difficult to acquire new understandings by listening to what others might have to say.

Most of the women interviewed who held this outlook described themselves as having been raised in social isolation with few mediated learning experiences. Some grew up "on the wrong side of the tracks" in families muted by demeaning stereotypes and excluded from the broader community; some came from families that had been well integrated into the ongoing social life of their locality, but for one reason or another, the women had been excluded from participation in family life by their own relations. Most described childhoods full of violence. They seemed to have closed themselves off to language because the isolation and violence had led them to see words more as weapons than as a means for passing meanings back and forth between people. Without the give and take of dialogue with others, the silenced do not develop their capacities for thinking, which is largely an interior dialogue with one's own self (see, for instance, Feuerstein, Rand, and Rynders, 1988). Because the silenced do not think they can think, they are often impulsive and chaotic, very much like the women Loevinger (1976) described at the earliest stages of ego development.

Silenced as an outlook on knowing should not be seen as a step in any normal sequence of epistemological development. Rather, it should be taken as a reflection of social disintegration. The phenomenon may well be on the increase as the social factors that numb people into silence are rising rapidly. These most certainly include the escalating levels of violence; the decline of all sorts of social institutions that support the development and well-being of people (families, schools, health systems); the ever-increasing disparities in access to resources; the exclusion of more and more people from full participation in social life; and the increased blaming of the excluded for causing the problems that society cannot or will not solve.

Received knowers see themselves as capable of receiving knowledge by listening to authorities, but not as able to give voice to their own ideas. Received knowers assume that any problem has only one right answer and that one learns to tell "right" from "wrong" by listening to authorities. Not imagining that the authorities (or anyone else) ever actually construct knowledge, received knowers assume that authorities learn by listening to other authorities. Received knowers are not likely to take a critical stance toward knowledge because they automatically presume the authorities speak truth. To question an authority is disrespectful and implies one does not know one's proper place in life. This way of knowing has much in common with the Berkeley group's authoritarian personality, Perry's dualists, and Loevinger's conformists, but the men in the earlier studies usually identified themselves with authorities. That is, they expected they could—and would—pass knowledge and directions down to others who knew less than them. The women who were received knowers seldom expressed such expectations (see also Baxter Magolda, 1992).

Dependence on authority for knowledge and direction can be a severe handicap for anyone in a modern society driven by rapidly evolving technologies as a premium is placed on independent, creative thinking. Unquestioning conformity to authorities and the norms of one's community can be particularly problematic for people presumed to be Other. If they are to move beyond their situation, it is necessary that they question the authorities and traditions that have defined them as subordinate, submissive, and without the capacity for intelligence.

Subjective knowledge is a perspective held by women who hear an inner voice and feel ideas emerging from their own minds. They listen to their inner voice, express their own thoughts, and criticize their former dependence on authorities for knowledge and direction. Locating the source of knowledge, standards, and authority in the self is liberating for everyone who makes this discovery. For those who have been subjected to distorting stereotypes, demeaning cultural norms, and abusive authorities, this discovery can feel life-saving. Typically images of liberation, rebirth, agency, and self-direction flood the interviews of women who have recently achieved this outlook.

Subjectivists believe that one's personal point of view is unique and thus cannot and should not be compared, judged, or communicated. They know from their own experience how silencing criticism can be and worry that negative evaluations will constrain people from listening to their own inner voice. They worry that language and thought will diminish rather than develop their insights and intuitions. They listen politely to others but do not actively struggle to enter into their viewpoints. The subjective knowers' distrust of language, evaluation, and sustained thinking can leave them isolated and floating on the surface of things. No longer subject to the judgments and directives of others, subjectivists can be quite self-absorbed, withdrawn into an inner world unfettered by any sense of consensually validated truths or standards. This sense of personal freedom leads many to put aside commitments to their community and the mores of their culture. Many contemporary observers see this kind of rootlessness as one of the great dangers of modern life (Bellah, Madsen, Sullivan, Swidler, and Tipton, 1985; Daloz, Keen, Keen, and Parks, 1996; Gergen, 1991; Greene, 1988; Kegan, 1994; Taylor, 1992).

Procedural knowledge is a perspective that has one core belief: ideas can be developed, analyzed, tested, and communicated if people are careful to curb their subjectivity with the use of procedures. The claims of authorities can and should be subjected to such procedures as well. The *WWK* collaborative observed two markedly different sets of procedures: "separate" and "connected" modes of knowing (see also Clinchy, 1993, 1996, in press; Clinchy and Zimmerman, 1982; Ruddick, 1996). The separate approach was well delineated by Perry and many other psychologists who studied human cognition; the connected approach heard in the women's interviews has seldom been described by social scientists. These two approaches parallel the moral orientations of justice and care as described by Carol Gilligan (1982/1993).

At the heart of separate knowing is detachment. Separate knowers hold themselves aloof from the object they are trying to analyze. Like those operating out of the justice ethic, they seek objectivity by taking an impersonal stance—following predetermined standards so that judgments will not be swayed by emotion and personal bias. Separate knowers play what Peter Elbow (1973, 1986) calls the "doubting game." The worth of an idea is best tested and proved in an unimpassioned debate among adversaries. An argument that survives many attacks and counterattacks is seen as more "defensible" or more likely to be correct than one that does not. (See also Moulton, 1983.)

The connected approach is personal, with an emphasis on dialogue, empathic role-taking, and contextual analyses. Connected knowers seek understanding rather than proof. They *enter into* the perspectives of others through empathic role-taking processes that draw on feelings, narratives, and the particulars of personal experience. Connected knowers play the "believing game," sharing, encouraging, asking good questions and drawing out each other's thoughts, looking for the person's strengths, and building on each other's insights. Connected knowers focus on what is coming into being. They listen for hunches, revelations, and dreams even as these are being born. They find ways to document fledgling ideas, hopes, and visions so people can see where they are trying to go. They also encourage people's confidence by documenting their abilities, strengths, and steps already taken. When connected knowers mirror a person's progress with care and accuracy they enable people to journey out from the place where they happen to be at the moment—which is always the best starting place. The more connected knowers might disagree with another person, the harder they will listen and try to understand how another could imagine such a thing. Even though connected knowers understand full well that a person's point of view is partial, they refrain from judgment. They worry that marshalling judgments and counterarguments will impair their ability to understand what the other person is really trying to say. They also find it difficult to embrace another's perspective while dismantling it. Listening to and hearing another person in his or her own terms has particularly deep ethical overtones for connected knowers:

understanding engenders caring whereas misunderstanding can breed self-doubt and silence.

Constructed knowledge is a perspective held by women who see themselves and everyone else—even the smallest child—as active constructors of knowledge. They understand that knowledge is constructed by the mind and not by procedures, however useful procedures might be. Because the knower is such an integral part of the known, people who operate from this perspective do a lot of metathinking: they evaluate, choose, and integrate the wide range of procedures and processes they bring to the meaning-making process.

Constructivists understand that the most important form of learning comes about when people are actually actively engaged in wrestling with problems they see as significant. They themselves are always grappling, questioning, and coming up with new problems to work on. They encourage others to do the same. As soon as an answer begins to become clear, they see new questions arising. It does not bother them that things are never settled. They never will be.

Abandoning the belief in a universal unchanging truth is one of the many signs that constructed knowers have overcome the last vestiges of dualism to appreciate the dialectical nature of knowledge. They have also forsaken the notion that there is one "right" way of knowing. They cultivate the whole range of approaches: learning from concrete experience as with the silenced; learning from listening to others as with received knowers; learning from one's own experience, intuition, feelings, and insights as with subjective knowers; and learning from strategies cultivated by procedural knowers in both the separate and connected modes. With this integration, constructivists can stand back, question, take apart, speak out, and criticize. They can also move inward, see the whole, listen, understand, integrate, and build up.

The dethroning of dualism can also be seen in the ways authorities are conceptualized by constructivists. Received knowers think of an authority as superior (the master) while they are inferior (the subservients). The inequality and distance between authorities and nonauthorities is vast and unbridgeable. Subjective knowers stand this notion on its head. By casting themselves as the only relevant authority needing consideration, they place themselves above and beyond people with expertise. Procedural knowing is the first position where the knowers see themselves and authorities as equals capable of carrying on a dia-logue. The separate knower stands back, looks for flaws in the author-ity's logic, and presents alternative arguments. The connected knower steps forward, enters into the authority's perspective, and tries to see the world through his or her eyes. Both procedures require the knower and the authority to situate themselves on the same level. It is, we believe, the capacity for connected knowing that enables the construc-tivist knower to draw out and appreciate everyone's potential for authorship, including the very young and those who have been silenced. Constructivists seem comfortable locating themselves wher-ever they must be to step into another's shoes and see the world from a different perspective.

Although the original *WWK* sample contained only a few women thought to be constructivists, the outlook is common among the developmental leaders we discuss in Part III of this book. They enable us to round out the description of this outlook, especially of a form of constructed knowing that relies heavily (but not exclusively) on the more connected approaches to meaning-making. These women are always questioning, evaluating, and criticizing points of view they see as partial, unfair, and destructive. Even so, they are more likely to invest more in the construction of new ways of thinking than in the destruction of the old ways. The language they use to describe the knowing process utilizes metaphors that suggest openness, growth, development, expanding, building, and embracing rather than the war metaphors that Lakoff and Johnson (1980) say are so common in this culture. The constructivists speak of seeing with new eyes, getting a bigger picture, seeing the world through the eyes of others, expanding one's own point of view, and seeing beyond what others see. And always, they speak of the importance of voice: hearing someone's story, bringing the silenced into voice, and finding words for the things that are known but seldom named.

Because the constructivists understand that knowledge is always in the making and is always situated, they see the development of ideas as a highly collaborative and open endeavor. Everyone has a contribution to make. Even the youngest and the most inexperienced can stimulate the thinking of the more seasoned, enabling them to see with "new eyes." Constructivists are also more likely to understand that art-making in all of its various guises (including music, dance, theater, painting, poetry, literature, architecture) can be as powerful a medium as science-making for developing, testing, and communicating our deepest insights about the human condition. Art frees the imagination, enabling the knower to envision things as if they were otherwise, the first step to be taken if one is to go beyond the given. When insights are explored, refined, and verified through art-making, knowers are able to name more of those experiences that sit at the edge of conscious, articulated knowledge. This imagining, thinking, rethinking, and testing can be playful as well as earnest. It can occur in an endless variety of places: the artist's studio, juke joints, and jazz clubs, and over the course of many hours that singing groups, theater troupes, and dance groups rehearse together. Constructivists seek dialogue with audiences. They realize that the work will continue to grow when it becomes part of a public conversation where more and more people can build on the ideas that are coming into being (see especially Greene, 1988, 1995).

The Women's Ways of Knowing collaborative made several informal observations about the invisible colleges they studied that we explored more systematically in the projects described in this book. Most of the women who did not think they could think (that is, the silenced and received knowers, women who had no idea they could develop knowledge by reflecting on their own experiences) came into the *WWK* study sample through one or another of the invisible colleges. These agencies seemed to be enabling the women to gain a voice and claim the powers of their minds.

It seemed that the invisible colleges were making a difference because they provided a context in which the women regularly drew each other out and listened to each other with care and respect. According to the women's descriptions, many of the "faculty" of the invisible colleges seemed to be good examples of connected teachers. That is, they used the skills of connected knowing so they might view the world through the student's eyes, with the hope of understanding each student in her own terms. Like midwives, these connected teachers worked to draw out their students' fledgling thoughts and foster the growth of their ideas. They focused their attentions on a person's strengths and affirmed what they saw. By naming and celebrating the strong points, they helped the women become more aware of what was already in place upon which they might build. Because the "faculty" of these invisible colleges were so skilled at drawing out the abilities of these women, the *WWK* collaborative named them "midwife teachers."

The invisible colleges also stressed other practices common to most self-help or mutual aid groups. Individuals were supported in their personal development *and* they were expected to support the development of others. Helping others was clearly an empowering experience for women with a long history of feeling dependent and helpless.

All of the invisible colleges sponsored ongoing discussion groups where the women could talk with each other as equals about the problems facing them and their families. Being one among equals seemed to be a watershed experience for most of the women. All too often they had been confined to the bottommost rungs of the social hierarchy. In these discussion groups the women helped each other develop an analysis of their situation, solve problems, and imagine alternative ways to live. They often spoke of their amazement that others were coping with similar problems, which was of the greatest importance, since it suggested that many of the women's problems were a function of the social arrangements that devalued and excluded women (especially mothers and the poor). Previously, the women assumed the difficulties they faced were due to their personal inadequacies—a paralyzing assumption that left most without a sense of hope.

There was another informal observation we thought important to document more systematically. Women who had a better sense of the power of their own minds seemed more likely to think of their children as active, thinking people who struggle to make better meaning of their experience in the world and better life choices. These women influenced their children's behavior by engaging them in reflective dialogue, drawing out their problem-solving abilities. By contrast, the women who did not see themselves as thinkers seemed much less aware of their children's thinking processes. They relied almost exclusively on authoritarian, power-oriented child-rearing techniques. Many of these women were in relationships with men who used similar techniques on them.

If these observations were correct—that invisible colleges and connected midwife teachers do empower women to gain a voice and claim the powers of mind—these programs might well lead to more democratic families. The ripple effect might be felt across communities as well as through the generations. With all of this in mind, we embarked on the Listening Partners project.

PART 2

THE DEVELOPMENT OF VOICE IN PRIVATE LIFE

CHAPTER 3

THE LISTENING PARTNERS PROJECT

My high school was a big scary school. Our little country elementary school never prepared us for a big school like that. There were cliques. If you weren't smart you were separated out. It was awful. I almost quit.

SALLY[1]

My parents made me feel that I wasn't smart enough to think for myself. They thought I needed a husband because I wasn't smart enough to do anything by myself. So if I was going out with a guy I always let him think for me, talk for me. CAROL

As a kid I didn't feel smart because of school. I felt like shit in school. The other kids thought they were high and mighty jus' 'cause their parents had money. . . . The things they used to do to me on the school bus, ya know? . . . None of the teachers ever stood up for me. Finally I got sick of that. I quit school. I ain't been back. I was fifteen years old. LIL

While they were growing up, Sally, Carol, and Lil were subjected to the assault of prejudices that caused them to doubt themselves and their intelligence—a phenomenon all too common among the very poor who live in declining rural areas. As young adults, they were participants in Listening Partners, an "action research" project whose goal was to promote the development of voice and mind so as to enable women to name, question, and overcome the stereotypes that had left them feeling so diminished. With generous funding and significant encouragement from the A. L. Mailman Family Foundation,[2] we had the opportunity to conduct pilot work exploring preliminary hunches about the kinds of experiences that would achieve such goals. Subsequently, with very generous financial support and guidance from the federal Maternal and Child Health Bureau,[3] we were able to implement a comprehensive and systematically designed program as well as to assess the effectiveness of the program in achieving our stated goals, and to explore the influence of the women's conceptions of themselves as knowers on their relationships with children and friends, as we describe in the following chapters.

This well-funded experimental context introduced a wealth of opportunities but also certain constraints. On the one hand, it provided us with extraordinary time and resources for program implementation and evaluation, as well as opportunities to ask carefully constructed, detailed, and pointed questions. These luxuries are rarely available to community agencies that serve the most isolated and impoverished constituents. On the other hand, our commitment to conduct a systematic program of research, one whose protocol had received prior review and approval from professionals and funding agencies, reduced some of our flexibility to modify the program in an ongoing fashion during its implementation and evaluation as we identified better ways of doing things. In addition, the relatively short time frame allotted for the program (eight months of three-hour, weekly meetings, as we later describe in greater detail) contrasts with the long-term and ongoing promise of sponsorship that is provided by the kinds of supportive community projects we describe in Part III of this book.

In this chapter we describe the substance of the Listening Partners intervention program—its goals, participants, and program activities. In the subsequent two chapters we describe the research context and protocol of this intervention program and summarize some of the major knowledge we gained from implementing and evaluating the program.

THE GOALS OF THE LISTENING PARTNERS PROJECT

The Listening Partners project was designed to bring together socially and often geographically isolated, poor, rural mothers of preschool-aged children to work collaboratively in developing their powers of mind and voice and their skills in fostering the development of others. We invited the participation of those women who were most likely to think of themselves as unable to learn from words or as unable to generate knowledge for themselves even when they were comfortable receiving and understanding the words of others. Guided by the Ways of Knowing scheme and the teaching procedures for knowing rooted in the connected approach for constructing knowledge, that is, the empowering tools of "midwife teaching," we hoped to support the women through their own epistemological development and as they supported such development among their peer participants and children.

Originally, we had hoped to accomplish the Listening Partners program goals within a preventive/promotive intervention framework that literally brought women together as partners for listening and speaking. In our pilot project, the women were paired by geographic proximity and similarity in age, number and age of children, and other demographics; each pair met in one or the other's home or at a nearby diner or community center as neighbors might do. We were drawn to this approach because of its ecological validity within rural communities; it seemed to offer greater promise for the program activities to become fully integrated into the daily lives of community members. Through intermittent visits from the project staff, we had hoped to encourage conversations around particular topics such as children and family; these were subjects that we felt presented both struggles and opportunities for establishing shared experience, common stories, and collaborative problem solving. Our goal was to structure opportunities and guidance for the women to engage in high-quality dialogue with their listening partner, which would foster both skills and a relationship that could then continue to flourish on their own and generalize to others.

In that pilot project, however, dialogue did not come easily to the participants, and the meetings often failed to occur. Women felt inadequately prepared, guided, and supported to work as a part of a team of only two individuals; the sense of exposure and responsibility of being a member of a pair often proved to be extreme and debilitating. In fact, we had grossly underestimated what a difficult and demanding situation this presented to the partners. We had asked women who felt voiceless and often mindless, distrustful of words and conversation, and unfamiliar with collaborative thinking to talk freely with each other, reflect and articulate their deep understandings, trust each other, and help each other to be confident thinkers, all with relative independence and minimal guidance.

Because we hoped to speak with the most marginalized individuals—those who had had the least opportunity to develop a sense of voice and to discover the powers of their own minds—we originally sought women who identified themselves as single, that is, having no adult "partner" in their lives. Meanwhile, as we began to meet and speak with community women, it became clear that both mothers with and without partners were raising children with extremely limited social supports. Although mothers with partners sometimes have more adult support within the home, as well as more access to certain social networks outside the home, these "partners" can also contribute tremendous stress to home life, especially in the face of extreme poverty and accompanying frustration. Moreover, women with partners frequently have fewer formal supports offered to them from outside the home. Local, state, and federal agencies commonly operate on the premise that a spouse in the home, for example, will be a source of financial, social, and psychological support and, therefore, restrict the services they offer to those without such adult "assistance." In the end, therefore, we chose to speak with marginalized women without regard to their marital status as we developed our program.

Through talking and working with the participants in our pilot project, we came to envision a modified Listening Partners—women coming together as a "circle of learners," sharing experiences, analyzing problems, working together to change their own lives, and eventually developing the skills of "midwife teaching." In the revised Listening Partners, women would gather weekly in small groups with staff support, relieving inordinate pressure from any one individual to perform, yet having the support, attention, and space for each to explore her way into the activity at a pace and in a form that she chose. Each of the weekly group participant sessions would conclude with group reflection on what had transpired during the gathering, what did and did not feel productive, and where the subsequent sessions should move. The staff would also meet weekly in a Listening Partners session of its own, to talk through the most recent group sessions and participants' insights, and firm up plans for the subsequent week's activities.

Figure 3.1 provides a schematic diagram of the program's components and hypothesized effects. The solid arrows symbolize some rather simple, general relationships that we expect exist. The broken arrows

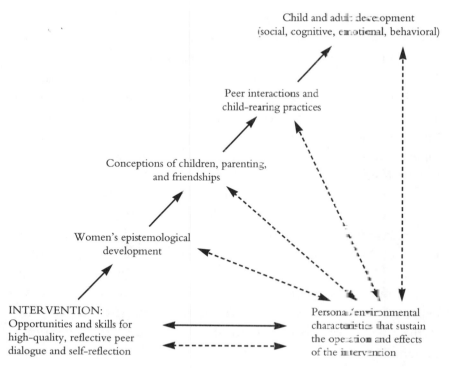

Child and adult development
(social, cognitive, emotional, behavioral)

Peer interactions and
child-rearing practices

Conceptions of children, parenting,
and friendships

Women's epistemological
development

INTERVENTION:
Opportunities and skills for
high-quality, reflective peer
dialogue and self-reflection

Personal/environmental
characteristics that sustain
the operation and effects
of the intervention

FIGURE 3.1

symbolize some more complex interactions where cause and effect flow in multiple directions and, in fact, overlie and complicate any of the simple relationships suggested by the solid arrows; together they establish an interactive system in which each and every one of the variables ultimately influences the others.

Following the solid arrows, the program was designed as a multi-level preventive/promotive intervention. The intervention activities, focusing on opportunities and skills for high-quality, reflective peer dialogue, were designed specifically to sponsor women who have had little confidence in themselves as knowers to gain a voice and develop the powers of their minds, that is, to realize epistemological gains. We expected that the mothers, in turn, would become more able to conceptualize their children as active knowers and, therefore, to more fully draw out their children's intellectual, social, and emotional capacities, promoting healthy child development and decreasing the likelihood of child developmental problems. At the same time we expected that participants would become more able to recognize, cultivate, and prosper from constructive peer relationships, supporting their own and their peers' development. With greater understanding of the forces that have marginalized their own voices, participants would be drawn to examine and acknowledge those forces in the lives of their neighbors; with an increased sense of mind and voice themselves, participants could increasingly come to appreciate similar power and potential among their community peers.

As the broken arrows in Figure 3.1 illustrate, we expected that each level of program effect (from the intervention activities through the enhanced developmental status of the child and adult peer) would feed back into promoting an environment that nurtures and sustains the operation and effects of the intervention. For example, the promotion of more effective strategies for relating to children and peers was expected to provide a context that ultimately nurtures the development of the child or adult peer *and* provides the mother, herself, with more opportunities to engage in collaborative problem solving, reflect on her reasoning skills, and augment her competence and confidence with the tools of mind and voice.

In other words, each of the levels of program effects was expected to contribute to self-confidence, motivation, collaborative problem solving, high-quality dialogue, reflective thinking, and social support systems that, in turn, sustain the experiences incorporated in the intervention and their associated outcomes.

At the core of this model then is the assumption that individuals' epistemologies or ways of knowing provide a framework for imagining the nature of relationships with others, including friends and children. A person's vision of the nature, role, and function of her relationships with others will simultaneously shape and be shaped by her own epistemological outlook and the interactions themselves. In Table 3.1 we summarize our understanding of the links between epistemological perspectives of oneself and relations with one's peers and children. The Listening Partners project was designed with the premise that these connections evolve in a dynamic and bidirectional way; that is, a woman's emerging epistemological outlooks encourage her to consider her relationships in more generative ways while her experiences relating with others in contexts of greater reciprocity and mutuality contribute to nurturing new epistemological perspectives.

Jacqueline Weinstock (1993) has gathered considerable evidence that documents the relationship between epistemological perspectives and friendships as portrayed in Table 3.1. Chapter 5 of this book presents a variety of illustrations of the links between epistemological outlooks and mother–child relationships (see also Bond, Belenky, Weinstock, and Cook, 1996).

Although the Listening Partners project involved exclusively poor, rural women, we hoped that this example would encourage educators, social service providers, and grassroots and other community leaders to create programs and curricula for and with a diversity of individuals who have had limited opportunities to cultivate the capacities for dialogue and mind. The model may also prove particularly useful when adapted to meet the needs of those who have been encouraged to cultivate autonomy, individuation, and competition at the expense of connection, community, and collaboration.

THE PARTICIPANTS

Each year for two years a new group of thirty socially isolated, low-income, rural mothers of preschool-aged children joined the Listening Partners project. The women (aged 17–34 years) and their families live in a mountainous, rural area of great beauty and extremes of great wealth and great poverty. The small family farms that once were the backbone of the area's economy have been either abandoned or consolidated into large, highly technical enterprises often owned by out-of-state investors. While many community members sought opportunities elsewhere, those who remained without getting extensive education now tend to work in service industries or as farmhands with low pay and little security. Along with the high level of poverty and unemployment, the counties from which Listening Partners participants were drawn had the highest indices in Vermont of teen pregnancies, reported incidents of child abuse and neglect, wife battering, and indictments for driving while intoxicated (Vermont State Office of Economic Opportunity, 1983).

We sought women who were particularly isolated because loneliness is one of the most chronic and serious complaints of mothers

Table 3.1

Epistemological Perspectives of Self and Relations with Peers and Children

Epistemological Perspective	Mother's View of Her Mind and Voice	Mother's View of Friendship	Mother's View of Child's Mind and Voice	Mother's View of Child Rearing
Silenced	Feels stupid, mindless, and voiceless; feels she can't teach others; words are weapons	Distant and guarded; fears betrayal; can't learn from peer dialogue; talk, even about similarities, is dangerous	Child is mindless and voiceless; child can't learn; child's feelings are dangerous, and not understood	Uses raw power to influence child; neither listens nor explains; much yelling; no dialogue; enforces absolute rules
Received knower	Goal is to receive, store, and transmit without modifying information; learns through memorization and recitation	Friends give/receive help and advice, share expertise; have similar right beliefs, behaviors, ideas; judge differences as wrong and to be avoided	Child learns by listening to elders; should be seen but not heard; child needs to be molded and filled with information	Informs child through lectures; teaches right and wrong using rules, rewards, and punishments; emphasis on training and modeling

Subjective knower	Inner voice discovered; truth comes from inner voice and experience, not authorities; values individuality	Friends exchange stories; accept individualities and differences; view experience as personal, not generalizable; nonjudgmental	Child has own inner voice; each child is unique; delights in child's spontaneity	Lets child think and speak for her/himself; laissez-faire; nonjudgmental
Procedural knower	Goal is to articulate and examine thoughts and feelings; uses procedures to evaluate and guide thinking	Friends explore stories; understand one another's views; help each other articulate, examine, and support one's perspectives	Child has thoughts and feelings to be developed; child can learn procedures for finding good answers	Asks for and provides reasoning and explanations; both share processes behind each other's thinking
Constructed knower	Can collaborate in construction of knowledge through dialogue with self and others; creates new synthesis, not merely uncovering information	Friends collaborate to share, evaluate, and create new perspectives; ask challenging questions; draw out and build upon one another's best thinking to create ideas and a relationship greater than the sum of its parts	Child has ability and responsibility to think through and make choices; can and should listen to heart and mind of self and others; in-ventor; little scientist	Draws out child's thoughts and feelings; asks questions and provides feedback; takes and evaluates child's perspective; they share and talk through views; challenge, think, and plan together

raising very small children in our society and because prolonged social isolation is found repeatedly to be associated with many forms of distress and family dysfunction (see, for example, Brown and Harris, 1978). Further, Belenky, Clinchy, Goldberger, and Tarule (1986/1997) found that most women who were extremely unaware of their intellectual powers had had lifelong histories of social isolation.

The Listening Partners project had the aim and the resources necessary to recruit the poorest and most isolated women in the area. We could travel vast distances on poor roads, making arrangements with women who had no phone and home visiting when necessary. We and the participants who had cars could transport those without cars to and from meetings. Several social agencies and community members worked with us to identify isolated families. Public Health workers were particularly helpful; at that time the Women, Infants and Children (WIC) program was reaching 97 percent of eligible families in Vermont compared to a national average of 12 percent. WIC's staff seemed to be on good terms with every poor family with preschool-aged children, no matter how far off the road they lived. Thus we were able to find and contact many of the most isolated women in these communities.

Between 80 and 85 percent of those we invited to participate in the program agreed to do so. Some of the mothers we approached felt they neither were isolated nor had time for the project. Others who turned us down outright appeared extremely shy or had a partner who opposed their participation. Sometimes we had to make many visits before a woman (and/or her partner) was willing to develop sufficient trust or strength to commit to the program. Worrying that we were imposing ourselves on women who might be having a hard time saying no, we would always ask if they would like us to return again for more talk or not, leaving the decision in their hands. Later, some of the women told us how grateful they were that we were so persistent.

The degree of social isolation experienced by many of the women often astonished us. Some had never shared a meal or even talked on the phone with another person who was not a member of their own family. A number had never held paid jobs of any sort, not even babysitting or odd jobs for neighbors, although their families were dreadfully poor.

We enrolled sixty Listening Partners participants and an additional sixty women who were "nonparticipant matched controls," in the jargon of research design. These additional women were similar to the Listening Partners participants in age, family status, numbers and ages of children, living conditions, sources and amount of income, race, religion, employment status, and education (as we describe in the next chapter). This "control" group did not participate in the LP intervention but completed the same program evaluation measures, allowing us to understand the effects of program participation by comparing the assessments of participants and nonparticipants over time. (See Appendix A for the protocols and measures that were utilized.)

Each program participant and matched control was interviewed extensively at her home at three different times: upon joining the Listening Partners program, eight months later when the intervention groups ended, and then again nine or ten months after the conclusion of the intervention. At each point, interviews focused on the women's epistemological development and were audiotaped and subsequently transcribed. Their Ways of Knowing interviews revealed that our recruiting goals were accomplished: Approximately 75 percent of the participants were predominantly silenced or received knowers when they joined the project; the remaining 25 percent were predominantly subjectivists. None were predominantly procedural or constructivist at the beginning of the program.

As a part of the assessments we also examined the women's parent-child communication strategies, self-esteem and social support (described more fully in Chapters 4 and 5), and their children's problem-solving skills and self-competence. Each mother was also videotaped teaching and playing with her child (see Appendix A). In the subsequent chapter we will focus on what we garnered from our interviews, assessments, and analyses. At this time, we describe the heart of the intervention program activities.

THE LISTENING PARTNERS PROGRAM

Dialogue as Key

When people talk and listen to each other with care, trying to understand each person in the person's own terms, they tend to develop caring relationships. Dialogue sponsors the growth of family ties, friendships, and community. As Parker Palmer (1983, p. 8) said:

> The mind motivated by compassion reaches out to know as the heart reaches out to love. Here, the act of knowing *is* an act of love, the act of entering and embracing the reality of the other, of allowing the other to enter and embrace our own.

Besides sponsoring the growth of kinships, friendships, and community, dialogue also empowers individuals. In drawing out everyone's best thinking and helping people experience their own thoughts as they are being created, dialogue sponsors the growth of self, voice, and mind in the participants. Therefore, our primary tool for sponsoring both the growth of community and the growth of individuals was participation in highly reflective conversations.

Listening Partners was not the first parent program to look to high-quality dialogue for empowering mothers and their children. The Child Study Association of America (see, for example, Auerbach, 1968; Badger, 1971, 1973) developed a model program for parents' groups centered around reflective open-ended discussions. Utilizing Loevinger's (1976) measure of ego development, Diana Slaughter (1983) found that mothers who attended discussion groups using the Child Study Association model showed higher levels of ego development than did participants who attended parenting programs with other emphases. The children of mothers participating in programs with the discussion group format showed greater cognitive gains as well. Many other programs that effectively promote intellectual and ethical development are centered expressly around open-ended reflective discussions (for example, Berkowitz, 1985; Damon and Killen, 1982; Fromm and Maccoby, 1970; Kohlberg, 1984; Sprinthall, 1980); consciousness-raising groups also rely heavily on this process for supporting development.

The importance that dialogue has for an individual will vary with the framework for meaning-making that a person brings to the conversation. For the silenced knowers, participating in dialogue provides opportunities to learn to be comfortable listening and speaking—to find meaning in others' words, find words to articulate one's own meanings, and discover that trading stories and ideas can be useful. Participation in the very same dialogue can help a received knower develop an awareness of the interpretive and creative powers of the mind—her own as well as others'. After achieving a clear understanding that ideas can and do emerge from one's own mind, a person is more likely to begin consciously to develop, use, articulate, and integrate procedures for constructing knowledge and ideas. Because most of the participants we recruited for the Listening Partners project viewed the world through the lenses of the silenced and received knowers, the focus of our activities was on becoming more comfortable listening and speaking, and on hearing one's own emerging thoughts. We concentrated on drawing out each other's voices and thoughts by asking each other the questions of a good interviewer, for example, "What do you mean?" and "Can you say more?" Such questions encourage the speaker to re-create and "re-say" in different words what it is that she thinks or feels. In the process, a person expands her capacity for self-reflection and thinks more about what it is that she could mean.

Conceptions of relationships in which dialogues are usually embedded also vary with epistemology (see, for example, Weinstock, 1993). Dialogue may mean different things to women with varying experiences of relationships just as it means different things to women with varying frameworks for meaning-making. For example, those of us who have grown up where words were used as weapons and where betrayal was more common than trust are likely to envision dialogue as threatening and trust as precarious. Remembrances of betrayal by friends—in the past and in the present—make it difficult to feel safe opening up to others; for many, such honesty does not seem worth the risk. Communication is tied to trust, and fostering another requires attending to the other. Thus, recognizing the interconnections between developing capacities for conversations and developing trusting relationships—between ways of knowing and ways of relating—Listening Partners focused not only on promoting dialogue but also on creating a context of reciprocal care and mutual respect in which the women could experience trust and being trusted, speaking and being heard, raising up and feeling raised by others.

Creating a Safe Space for Conversation

The first task was to make the meetings feel safe enough that the women could risk expressing themselves. We put the issue on the top of the agenda by focusing our first group meetings on it. We encouraged the women themselves to think about the problem in a "round robin." We went around the room, taking turns completing the sentence, "Groups are scary because . . .". Starting with such a topic was empowering as all the women were experts on the subject. Following this exercise, we worked together to develop a series of rules that would help all the participants feel safe and allow them to move at their own pace. Among the rules generated were agreements about maintaining confidentiality and "passing." By passing we meant skipping a turn if someone was not yet ready to speak.

Another important aspect of creating an atmosphere that would encourage relationships characterized by mutuality and reciprocity involved minimizing the social distance between staff and participants. While it is neither possible nor desirable to ignore real differences between staff and participants with respect to life circumstances and experiences with privilege, it is possible for people to engage with each other in mutually respectful and reciprocal relationships even in the midst of great inequalities. Recognizing that many of the women were accustomed to authorities who wield unilateral power, demand conformity, and discourage independent thought, the staff took care to demonstrate a different way of being authoritative. First, the intervention staff, themselves, were women who had long histories of active participation in grassroots efforts in neighboring rural counties. Thus, they shared a deep understanding of the lives and circumstances of these families and communities. We used first names and wore simple clothing. Whenever we could, we arranged the chairs in a circle. Sometimes the staff sat on the floor looking up to the women. Above all, we tried to make it clear that we might teach some of the tools involved in talking and thinking problems through collaboratively, but we would not—nor could we—teach answers. We, as staff, also shared our own stories and presented our issues for problem solving along with everyone else, although we tried to remain sensitive to our special role and were concerned not to occupy too much group time with our personal concerns.

While we as staff took great pains to limit aspects of our personal power, we heightened the use of our own intellectual powers. Thinking everything through freshly, trying not to rely on received solutions, was intellectually demanding. Developing a dialogue with a whole group of women was also challenging. We were constantly striving to understand where each woman was coming from and where she was trying to go. To enter another's frame takes a great leap of imagination even when the other person is very articulate. Since the words were not readily available for many of the participants, we had to keep searching for questions that could help to draw out a woman's fledgling ideas and the words to communicate their shape and substance. Working hard to draw each other out and to listen to and speak our own stories often reminded us of the way friends gather around the kitchen table: talking, sharing stories, laughing, and sometimes sitting lost in thought, pondering meanings and alternatives. These are the conversations—the talk of "The Poets in the Kitchen"—that author Paule Marshall (1983) points to as the origin of her own development as a storyteller and writer. Marshall, a black American writer of Bajan descent, describes the many hours that she, as a young girl, spent in the kitchen of her home in Brooklyn listening to her mother and other Bajan women fill the room with talk.

Re-presenting the Women's Words

Not only did we want the women to experience being deeply heard by others, but we hoped that they would begin to listen to themselves with care. To help the women hear themselves thinking, we tried to capture and re-present many of the women's own words. Because many of the women had limited literacy skills, we made audiotapes of all conversations. Each woman was given a tape recorder so that she could, for example, listen again to the group discussions and maintain an audiotaped journal at her own convenience.

When we discovered that almost all of the participants even those with very limited reading abilities, could read words that they themselves had generated, we began creating a written record of our dialogues. Someone often wrote down participants' ideas on newsprint as they were being generated. As a conversation progressed, more and more newsprint would be posted around the room.

The text from the newsprint was typed, photocopied, and returned to the group for everyone's reconsideration. All of the participants were given a sturdy portfolio folder for storing the photocopies, along with materials such as journal entries or letters that the women might generate at home on their own. Periodically reviewing the portfolios enabled the women and the staff to trace long-term changes in their thinking—a good exercise for seeing the power and developmental course of one's mind unfold.

The process of writing down the ideas generated in our meetings was undoubtedly helpful in other ways. It slowed the discussion and provided us with time to reflect on our thoughts and find the words that might communicate our meanings to others. The process also helped us all become more comfortable with silences.

The staff began transcribing and editing some of the most interesting group discussions, particularly conversations that the participants identified as especially helpful or intriguing; these were distributed and read at the following group meeting. The women were often astonished when they first heard their own words read aloud—this was a novel experience for most. Sometimes they fled the room, as if overwhelmed by hearing their own words, needing distance to regain their composure. Mostly, the astonishment seemed to come from realizing the extent of one's own thoughtfulness.

We edited the tapes mostly by removing the extra verbiage so the main ideas might be heard more clearly—oral language does not read well. Because we wanted to encourage the women's strong, distinctive language, we seldom corrected their grammar or removed colloquial expressions. Selecting and editing the participants' best thinking, however, still required a high level of interpretation. Consequently, we often provided participants with the original transcripts and our edited versions of their words, inviting them to assess our interpretations and to continue revising the text until it adequately reflected their thoughts.

Re-presenting the women's words in these ways was undoubtedly worth the effort. It allowed people to discover, refine, critique, and build on their own and others' ideas. The process also provided an opportunity to observe one's ideas unfolding and gaining in power, making it clear that one really does "get smarter" when talking and thinking problems through with care.

Thinking About Thinking

We tried, in particular, to draw out participants' thinking about themselves as thinkers. To focus the conversation on epistemological issues, we designed a series of "round robins" where we took turns responding to such questions as, "Why do so many smart women feel so dumb?" and "Why do so many women feel so voiceless?" Other round robins posed questions that encouraged us to think about our accomplishments and our own intelligence. We struggled to finish such sentences as:

- The most clever thing I did this week was . . .
- I worked hard to . . .
- I spoke up when . . .
- One thing I have done that makes me feel pretty smart is . . .
- What I have come to appreciate about myself is . . .

At first it was extremely difficult for most of the women to conceptualize their intellectual strengths. We would laugh together and discuss why it is so difficult for women to think of themselves as competent persons. When an individual member could not think of any personal achievements, one of the coleaders would take the lead in interviewing her. We asked questions that would encourage the person to sift through her memories of a whole day, systematically looking for incidents that reflected her achievements and intelligence. We often discovered that the woman had been working successfully on problems and goals that were of the utmost importance, but that she had not thought of her actions either as successful or as involving problem solving—for example, figuring out how to pay a series of long overdue bills, managing to help a hyperactive child to be more focused, or getting a spouse to be more supportive and less authoritarian with the children. Again, these discoveries were written up and reflected upon. As the weeks went by, nearly everyone found it easier to discuss her accomplishments.

Besides articulating the women's intellectual achievements, we were concerned to develop and preserve any analysis that illuminated the processes by which very smart people are led to believe that they have nothing to say and cannot think for themselves. With permission, copies of the women's transcribed words were also circulated among the concurrent groups, so other women could build on these ideas. Examples from one group's morning conversation are as follows:

How I Am Manipulated into Thinking I Am Stupid

- I don't understand how he does it. He just makes me feel like a complete idiot. I can't stop him. If I do say "no" to him, he just talks his way around it.
- My husband makes me feel like I can't have a thought of my own. He has run my life ever since I met him. He made all of my decisions for me. I sat back and let it happen. I thought that was what you were supposed to do.
- Every time I open my mouth he finishes my sentences for me. If I had a thought, he would say it before I did.
- You start going, "Yeah, that is right." You start believing what he says. You're so afraid of disagreeing with him, you make yourself start feeling the way he said you were feeling. I finally said to my husband, "Is that the way you want me to feel?" Do you know what he said to me? "We have to have the same thoughts and feelings!" I am not supposed to have any ideas that are different from his!

A deep chord was struck when these excerpts were shared with the other Listening Partners groups. Realizing that being manipulated into feeling stupid was at the root of feeling dependent, one of these groups framed the following questions for themselves to address: "Why do you feel so overly dependent?" and, "Why do you stay that way?" Some of their answers were the following:

- He finishes your sentences for you.
- You are afraid if you stand up for yourself he will be mad.
- It is easier. It's too frightening to be on my own.
- He doesn't want to admit that he might be wrong.
- Because my dad ran everyone's life, I want a man to run mine.
- No phone.
- They do anything to keep you home and from doing anything for yourself.
- You feel like you can't do it on your own.
- He wants you to be just like Beaver's mother.

These were just some of the many occasions we felt words were being given to the unspoken and the unspeakable. Such occasions were invariably peppered with laughter and outbursts such as, "Aha!," "Yes, that *is* how it is!," and "You too?" Those who had felt very much alone found that they were keeping very good company, indeed. Insoluble problems experienced as personal faults came to be seen as understandable—and sometimes solvable—social problems.

Women's Growth Stories

We drew out, transcribed, and circulated Listening Partners participants' personal stories of aspiration and realization—that is, growth stories. Attending to the growing edge contrasts with the practices of many educators and clinicians who tend to focus on mistakes deficiencies, and/or pathology. It also contrasts with the habits of many women and people with low expectations for achievement. All too often, the successes of these individuals are more likely to be attributed to external and/or unstable characteristics (e.g., luck) with little credit given to their skills or abilities in contrast, their failures are attributed to internal and/or stable personal factors such as skill (see, for example, Hansen and O'Leary, 1985). Thus, a focus on strengths may be particularly important when working with people who have experienced the level of criticism, violence, and trauma that is common to poor women in this society.

A painful story contrasting a participant's response to two different rapes provides a dramatic illustration of the sort of growth we worked to highlight—the author came to understand that the crucial ideas had been developed by her, in her own head, out of her own hard labor. This is emphasized in the title that was chosen from a line embedded in the story, as was our practice.

I Sat and Figured It Out on My Own:
It Took a Lot of Understanding

Then I was raped again, by another man. Again I couldn't talk to anybody. I felt like I was used. Like a piece of trash that was thrown away. But I had really changed. This time I went back and faced him. One day I went down there to ask him why he done it He told me that I had asked for it. I said, "Don't tell me this bullshit! I was sound asleep!" I didn't have a counselor that told me how to do this. I sat and figured it out on my own. I went and did it on my own. The way I faced it myself was that I sat alone in a room with no one around. I listened to music. The only one that was there was my dog. She was always a comfort to me. It took a lot of facing. It took a lot of understanding to understand what had happened to me and why it happened. I didn't ask for it. It was nothing that should have ever happened. He never touched me again. He put me down, but he didn't win. He respects me to this day as a person.

This young woman considered at length the mistreatment she had suffered from a person who held considerable power over her. She determined in her own mind that he was wrong and that she herself had done nothing to cause the behavior. She presented him with her judgment and asked him to account for himself. When he tried to put the blame back on her, she backed up her arguments with facts he could not dispute. The man accepted her judgment and altered his subsequent behavior.

While stories like this one arose spontaneously in group conversations, we also designed sessions where women took turns telling their life story, as narrative is the primary tool we have for making sense out of our experience in the world. Stories also draw people into each other's lives. They compel listening—even for those who previously have had little experience or skill in listening. Together we discovered that when people listen carefully to each other's stories not only do they come to understand each other, but they come to appreciate each other as well. Upon hearing each other's stories, the women said again and again, "Oh, I can see that I am not alone!" Even when the stories reflected different, unfamiliar experiences, the group was often moved by the commonality of human emotion and aspirations underlying the experiences.

When collecting the life stories, the whole group often took turns focusing on one person, drawing out her story. Other times we divided into pairs and the partners would take turns interviewing and being interviewed. There were advantages and disadvantages to each approach. When the dyads were successful the participants seemed to feel particularly empowered and intensely close to one another. As we had learned from the pilot study, however, working in pairs is not always successful. If both partners did not have fairly well-developed interviewing skills, the work was likely to remain on the surface, sponsoring little in the way of self-reflection. It was also difficult to divide the larger group into pairs as everyone wanted to hear everyone else's stories. Overall, the stories collected by the group as a whole ended to be more consistently fruitful. When all the members of a group worked together, the more experienced interviewers were better able to structure the interview and model the process, stretching the less experienced members' understandings of the process and promoting their use of more exploratory, open-ended questions.

To prepare for collecting the life stories we first listed a number of the possible turning points that people's lives might take; turning points help organize the story line. We also listed good questions for drawing out another's story. As usual, everything was printed and posted on newsprint around the room. We discussed the difference between closed questions that demand short, specific, and sometimes superficial replies, and open-ended questions that invite the speaker to dig deeper and deeper. We examined the questions we had gathered to see which were more open and which were more closed. We starred those that seemed most likely to draw out a thoughtful story. Although gathering and evaluating questions before beginning the interview process was very helpful, we learned that it was not useful for participants to walk into the interview itself carrying the list of questions. The script served only to keep the interviewer's attention riveted to the next question rather than on what the interviewee was trying to say.

Returning to our original model utilizing dyads, participants who were becoming skilled interviewers went out to collect the stories of women who were missing the weekly meetings. Lil and Carol, two of the three women whose quotes open this chapter, were such a pair. Lil seldom came to meetings. When she did, she arrived late and left early. We think she worried that her and her family's reputation in the community would make her unacceptable to the group. She said everyone in her family had always been treated like "scum in these parts." We could not help but notice that Carol, a woman with a similar history of stigma, was becoming a wonderful interviewer. Carol began visiting Lil regularly. In collecting her story, Carol drew Lil into the Listening Partners process, although Lil never did attend the meetings regularly. Just as we originally envisioned, confidantes develop mutually supportive and empowering relationships. Carol began to see her own potential as a leader, helper, and friend. Lil, perhaps for the first time, had a friend who would talk with her about matters of substance.

After being interviewed, some of the women took the audiotapes and notes home and wrote up their stories themselves. Others preferred that the staff transcribe and edit the interview, returning a working draft to the interviewee. Either way, the women often worked together on revising early drafts in pairs or small groups. When the author read her story aloud, others were encouraged to say what it was that they liked about the story and what they wanted to know more about. Such questions focus on the author's successes and on further drawing out her ideas. Some members worked through several drafts whereas others were satisfied with the original versions. For those who engaged in the revision process, self-reflection seemed to deepen. When a person tells her story she has to define herself as a person, linking the present with the past and with her deepest aspirations for the future. As McAdams said:

> The story is the person's *identity*. The story provides the person with a sense of unity and purpose in life—a sense that one is a whole being moving forward in a particular direction. From the standpoint of personal identity, therefore, the person is both historian and history—a storyteller who creates the self in the telling. (1990, p. 151)

Shaping the history to fit the life seemed to encourage some of the women to shape their lives to fit their visions. Sharing common stories often led to a broader analysis of conditions once thought to be created by one's own personal ineptitude. Sharing stories helps one stand back, gain perspective, and imagine new choices.

The final drafts were beautifully typed, photocopied, and distributed to everyone in the group. When we thought someone might be particularly interested in a story, we sought permission to share the stories with members of the other Listening Partners groups. Some of the stories about teenage parenting were made available to other agencies and schools so they might integrate them into their curricula. Still others were shared with a shelter for battered women and with students in adult literacy classes. "Publishing" and finding an audience can be a very empowering experience It forces the author to see herself from a broadened perspective.

Children's Growth Stories

We also looked for and returned the stories the mothers told about their own children's growth and achievements, hoping the women would become even more conscious of each child's "growing edge" when these stories were re-presented to them. To encourage the women to bring their own children's growth stories into focus, we asked the mothers to observe and record their children's accomplishments and successes. At first, many of the women found it as difficult to think about their children's achievements as it had been for them to think about their own. Again, the group would patiently interview each woman until she could begin to imagine and articulate her child's gifts, strengths, and accomplishments. Our stock of questions included: "Tell us the story of a time your child accomplished something special, or when your child was particularly courageous, or creative, smart, etc."

These stories were transcribed and edited. Small segments of the text were printed in large type at the bottom of heavy stock paper. The mothers illustrated the pages. If a mother did not have adequate reading skills, we would read the text to her and she would draw the pictures she deemed appropriate. Later she could retell the story to her child by "reading" the illustrations she had created. The pages were then laminated in plastic, bound together into a beautiful book, and presented to the child as a gift. The following "growth story" was told by Sally, the first woman we quote in the epigraphs to this chapter. She tells of her son's courage in criticizing his father for "picking" on a younger sister:

It Took a Lot of Courage

One morning Bill was hollering at the baby and my son Jim said, "Don't holler at her like that." And then Jim said, "I will be glad when I get to school and can get away from all of this." I was shocked when Jim spoke up to his dad. It took a lot of courage for him to do that. Bill never dared to speak up to his own father. To this day Bill is afraid to ask his father for anything. [*Note:* Bill works as a farmhand on the farm where his father is the head herdsman.] I do not want my children to be afraid to say things to their father. That night Bill patted Jim on the head [after he had fallen asleep]. Jim got to Bill's heart.

As often happens, the achievements Sally recounted of her child reflected goals that she was working on herself. She too was working hard at becoming more outspoken. Indeed, she had "disobeyed" her husband when she joined Listening Partners. When Sally supports her child in speaking his mind, her own struggle for the right to be heard gains strength as well.

Sally's story is also a story of her husband's growth. She intimates that he too praised the child for speaking out, even if he did give the praise after the child had fallen asleep. Within the next two years Sally came to tell us stories first about how her husband was listening more and hollering less, then about how he was becoming more outspoken with his own parents, and finally about how he quit working under his father to become a head herdsman on one of the other farms owned by the absent investor.

The Problem–Solving Approach

Another major activity of Listening Partners centered on developing interviewing techniques that would promote collaborative problem solving. People who rely on others for ready-made answers and direction seldom think of themselves as problem solvers. They do not develop specific procedures and tools for dealing with the problems that they and their family members face day in and day out. Not only does collaborative problem solving draw out and integrate a wide range of human capacities in the participants, including thinking, feeling, and action, but it draws together people of similar circumstances (see, for example, Rogoff, 1990).

To encourage collaborative problem solving we drew heavily from the work of Myrna Shure and George Spivack (1974, 1978), who trained teachers and parents to use a series of open-ended interview questions for drawing out the children's thinking about the problems they faced. Children whose parents or teachers have routinely used this approach are less likely to act impulsively and are more apt to develop cognitive skills for interpersonal problem solving than are children of teachers or parents who have not had this training.

The interview questions for collaborative problem solving encourage participants to move from defining the problem and articulating goals, to brainstorming or "idea gathering" (as we called it) as many solutions as possible, to evaluating the consequences of different options, and finally to making a choice and acting. The sequence evokes capacities that range from problem posing, to divergent thinking about alternatives, to consequential and valuative thought, and, finally, to commitment and action. In our groups, we focused on each step of the process, guided by a printed work sheet we created that provided spaces for us to write our ideas. These steps, briefly described as follows, were both discussed and modeled in the group meetings:

1: *Posing the problem.* At first the staff took a great deal of responsibility for defining and posing problems. For many of the women it was difficult to ask questions. When someone complained or ruminated about a worry, we would ask her to frame it as a problem that might be solved. For example, early on when we were just beginning to get to know each other, a woman said, "I am worried that I will feel really let down when this group is over." One of the coleaders asked her how she might state the worry as a problem to be solved. After much discussion, "How can we deal with feeling that we're being abandoned when the project is over?" was written across the top of a large sheet of newsprint and the problem-solving process began.

2: *Idea gathering.* After at least one clear statement of the problem had been recorded, we turned to "brainstorming" or "idea gathering," writing down as many different possible solutions to the problem as came to mind. We taught two basic rules for encouraging idea gathering:

- Think up as many ideas as possible—even silly or impossible ones; be playful; toss them all in.
- Do not censor or evaluate the ideas; just let the ideas bubble up.

Ruling out all the "nos," "ifs," and "buts" is particularly helpful for people who routinely think up objections to their own ideas even before they begin to spell them out. Because idea gathering enables people to see ideas spring up, it may be particularly useful for people who have not yet begun to imagine that ideas can be created. When we pooled our ideas in this fashion we noted a heightened sense of collaboration and that our work was not as stormy as the term *brainstorming* might suggest. It was this insight that caused us to change the name of the exercise from "brainstorming" to "idea gathering."

3: *Considering the consequences of choice.* When the stream of ideas diminished to a trickle we would begin the evaluation process. The problem poser was asked to read through the list of possible solutions, to star those ideas that seemed particularly worth pursuing, and then to list some of the possible consequences for choosing the starred options. Upon observing a tendency to associate any given solution with either a negative or a positive outcome, we encouraged the women to consider both kinds of consequences, trying to push beyond dualistic notions. We found that this expanded and engaged our thinking greatly.

4: *Resolution and action.* We then turned our attention to bringing about a resolution of the problem. Although committing one's self to action is the logical step for concluding the problem-solving sequence, we learned to take this step very gingerly. Many of the women expected single answers that would be "right" and unerring while the problems we were working on were all too often complicated, longstanding, and rooted in powerful family and societal forces. We learned to encourage the women to delay action or to try many alternatives, and to keep reconsidering and revising the choices as we worked on the problems from one week to the next.

Lucy provides an example of how the group guided each woman through the problem-solving process. Because Lucy was unusually reluctant to speak, we told her a week in advance that her turn would be next in order to give her time to prepare her thoughts. With much coaxing, Lucy did pose a problem:

> My kids fighting. . . . It goes on twenty-four hours a day. . . . I worry I'll end up hanging them. . . . The problem is they are jealous of each other. Maybe they don't get enough attention from their father.

The first three possible solutions that Lucy contributed to the idea gathering were facetious and indicative of her underlying anger: "I could tie them up"; "I could hurt them"; "I could leave them." After other women had contributed many ideas to the process, Lucy went on to suggest that the children's father could take them away for a weekend. After evaluating the possible consequences of that idea, Lucy decided to evaluate a suggestion offered by another woman: "Let the child express his feelings and then together try to solve the problem." At first Lucy doubted that her child would "sit there and talk," but then she said that if she were to do that, "He could get whatever is bugging him off his mind. . . . If he could express his feelings, then he might stop bugging his brother and I would be less ugly." A coleader of the group wrote in her weekly report: "I think this was a most amazing experience for Lucy. I would guess that she never had a hundredth of the attention and interest given to her feelings and thoughts before. When she went out for her smoking break, she was back in about two minutes—the shortest I've seen." Having had the opportunity to express her own feelings, Lucy began to imagine offering her child such an opportunity, as well.

Problem Solving Outside of the Group   We encouraged the women to take copies of the problem-solving work sheet home with them because most of the problems they posed in the groups were deeply rooted in relationships with other people—particularly husbands or boyfriends—whose responses were central to any resolution. Many women reported that they and their partners came to use the work sheets and that they were beginning to talk and think their problems through in a new way. Both parties were getting better at articulating their own needs and ideas; both were getting better at listening and imagining their partner's points of view. Many of the women thought that they and their partners were becoming less dependent on power-oriented techniques for resolving their differences. This lesson was important for the staff, as we had not anticipated having the opportunity to witness such constructive change in the short-term life of the program; we had expected, instead, reports of increasing tensions between participants and spouses or partners as the Listening Partners women dared to use their voices in situations where they had not before. Although such struggles did emerge, it is striking that there were no differences between the participants and matched controls in rates of divorce or separation following entry into the program. We imagine this situation reflects the fact that Listening Partners drew participants into the hard work that fosters nurturing relationships, and the women appeared to bring these developing skills and accomplishments to bear on their lives at home (as the women, themselves, describe for us in subsequent chapters).

Many of the problems the women were struggling with were political as well as personal. We tried to identify them as such and to connect the women with special-interest groups that were working on their concerns. We helped some of the women pass their stories and issues on to newspapers, the state legislature, and other agencies. Newspaper reporters, legislators, and educators used some of the women's stories to educate the public on little-known facts about living in poverty and rural isolation.

Because the duration of the program meetings was only eight months, and because the isolated women who were involved found working on a political level so difficult to imagine, activities dealing with the public domain were explored on a piecemeal basis. Long-term efforts at empowering people who have been excluded and silenced should include a systematic attempt at finding political as well as personal responses to problems that are primarily rooted in the social structure.

Problem Solving with the Children   After the women were fairly proficient at problem solving among themselves, we focused on how they, as mothers, could adapt these open-ended questions to support their children in talking and thinking through the problems they faced. The following activities were designed to help the mothers teach the problem-solving approach to their children. First, we conducted "idea gatherings" of those experiences that had made us, as small children, feel empowered and disempowered as thinkers. Using the same four-step format described earlier, we modeled and role-played teaching the problem-solving approach to children. After everyone got the feel of it, we encouraged each mother to try it out at home and to report back to the group.

Although many of the women had begun to use the problem-solving approach with each other and some were problem solving with their partners, most had difficulty adopting the process for use with their children, finding it difficult both to imagine their children capable of thinking through problems in a systematic manner and to envision themselves able to draw out such capacities in their children. It had been difficult for the women to imagine themselves and their peers as capable of these tasks in the context of working with other adults. To do so with children appeared more daunting and required the women to challenge a culture that expects parents to dictate to their children and to reinforce their dictates with punishments and rewards. Moreover, focusing on their own problems was such a luxury that many of these women found it difficult to shift their attention to the children's problems. And yet, slowly but surely, some of the women began to tell stories of small successes in problem solving with their children.

Problem Solving Among the Staff   To better understand the problem-solving approach, we decided to use the process in systematically framing and solving problems during our weekly staff meetings. This was productive—we became more knowledgeable about the process and gained insights on how to teach it. Not only did the process help us think about our goals with more precision, but the playful idea gatherings led us to many interesting tacks that probably would not have emerged otherwise. For example, we problem solved on ways of dealing with "overtalkers" and "undertalkers," a chronic problem for most ongoing groups. The following were among the ideas we gathered for dealing with the problem that we eventually included as part of our process:

- Invite (but don't pressure) quieter people to speak in the group.
- Work on helping both over- and undertalkers feel really heard.
- Give both time to collect their thoughts with round robins, by making appointments for their turn a week ahead and/or warning them about the time frame they have to work with
- Suggest they make notes so they will be surer to say what they really want to say when their turn comes.
- Suggest they practice talking into a tape recorder
- Idea gather with the group on how everyone can get their share of airtime.

- Idea gather on the roots of overtalking and undertalking.
- Idea gather on what makes talking easy and what makes it difficult.

We came to understand that often excessive talkers blurt out cascades of words because they have little confidence in their ability to think through what they want to say. It is our impression that the speech of both the over- and the undertalkers got more organized, coherent, and concise when they gained faith in their own intellectual powers. A link between the tongue and the mind seemed to be forged with that confidence.

GRADUATION CEREMONIES

Our original insight was confirmed. Trying to understand each person in her own terms—trying to enter and embrace each participant's reality—did create a caring community. Just before the meetings were to come to an end, the groups took turns focusing on each member, asking what it was that we had come to appreciate about that person—why we had come to value her so much. Each person herself was also asked what it was that she had come to value about herself. All of these thoughts were duly recorded on newsprint. These conversations were highly reflective and very interesting. The ideas we pooled indicated just how much we had learned about ourselves and each other. Each set of descriptions was printed on quality paper, then rolled up like a diploma, and presented on our last day together. Like all people who listen and talk together with care, we had grown closer as well as more knowledgeable and appreciative of each other. It was also clear that we had grown more knowledgeable and appreciative of our own selves.

CHAPTER 4

WHAT WAS LEARNED

I think things through more than I used to. It's like before I used to just jump and do it, but it's like now I, I'll think it through. . . . In Listening Partners I've learned to speak out for what I believe without screaming.

RUTH

It's a place where you can talk your feelings through; you can meet new friends and really get to know yourself and some others; you work through some problems and learn how to stand up for yourself.

MAUREEN

In Listening Partners you share ideas, and make new ideas . . . Now I'm trying to put more trust into what I think and feel.

DAWN

For many who grew up in relatively supportive and affirming environments, a host of experiences has nurtured the development of mind and voice. Common everyday experiences have built upon each other to nurture the developing sense of mind, voice, and reason. Family members who are concerned with how we are feeling, friends who share or even question our joy or concern, neighbors who seek our advice, teachers who encourage us to arrive at our own opinions, a store clerk who is interested and responsive to our needs, a child who is grateful for our guidance—these experiences, day by day, cultivate our skills and our sense of power of mind and voice.

But the most marginalized in our society report that such experiences have been rare. Many tell of isolation—feeling some combination of physical, social, emotional, and intellectual exclusion. As Maureen describes:

I feel isolated, away from everything, because I don't have a phone and I don't have a car during the day. Even though my family is

around it's like nobody ever has time to come to the house because everybody else works.

Many also recollect childhoods associated with a lack of mutuality
and reciprocity in relationships—experiencing a paucity of friends,
ideas, or control over life, and a sense of being stuck at the depths of
powerful hierarchies. Tales are told of lives dominated by feedback that
one's thoughts and feelings have little consequence or value, leading to
overwhelming expectations of powerlessness that even blur and transform any evidence to the contrary. Examining these sobering recollec-
tions of lives that denied growth of mind and voice, we wondered
whether the Listening Partners intervention could support the transition from silence to voice by cultivating high-quality dialiogue, reflection, and experiences of mutuality, reciprocity, collaborative problem
solving, and feeling deeply heard—the foundations of the Listening
Partners program.

The Listening Partners Program was planned and implemented as
an "action research program" to support the development of voice in a
rural, isolated, and impoverished setting. As such, the program was designed to systematically gather information regarding a set of interrelated research questions at the same time that it served as an agent of
community service and change. While the previous chapter described
the substance of the intervention program—the principle agent of service and change—this chapter and the next both focus on the *research*
framework and the knowledge that it generated.[1]

THE RESEARCH FRAMEWORK

Our Questions

Working together with the Listening Partners participants—each of
whom was living in rural impoverishment and isolation—we hoped to
develop a greater understanding of a set of interrelated issues. The project posed a series of research questions that focused specifically on involvement in the Listening Partners intervention, which we will explore in this chapter.

- Is it possible to recruit and engage the most silenced and marginalized women into a peer-focused group such as Listening Partners?

- Could participation in a weekly peer-group program such as Listening Partners be sustained over time despite the many competing practical and emotional tugs and pulls in the lives of the participants?
- Within the constraints of a time-limited intervention, could we structure a set of experiences that would truly promote women's understanding and development of their sense of mind and voice as well as their appreciation of relationships as a context for supporting these transitions?
- To the extent to which transitions of mind and voice arise, could they be sustained and, ideally, serve to fuel ongoing growth, even after program participation ended?
- What sorts of experiences are most useful for supporting silenced, marginalized women to gain a voice and claim the powers of mind—and to develop capacities to help others accomplish the same?
- How do women's understandings of their own mind and voice grow from and contribute to their peer relationships?

Our Research Strategies

In selecting our research strategies and design, we were guided by several goals. First, we wanted to evaluate the Listening Partners program in a way that would allow a comparison of our procedures and findings with related work—past, present, and future. We felt it was important to be able to relate our work to a broader body of literature—a process central to the greater construction of knowledge. Therefore, we were diligent in reviewing existing models, programs, and their evaluations; we considered their theoretical frameworks, the kinds of questions they posed, the measures they employed, and the ways in which they interpreted their patterns of responses; and we tried to draw upon those that had proven most constructive in relevant settings.

A second guiding aim was that of enabling replication of our work. We wanted to be certain that both the Listening Partners intervention and its outcomes were documented in a way that would allow them to be replicated in other settings, with and by other groups of people. This approach not only permits the use of a program in varied contexts but also provides the foundation necessary for the process of translating, refining, and improving procedures and programs—again, processes fundamental to the course of constructing new knowledge and understanding. For these reasons, we took great pains to maintain consistency in our practices even when it meant that we had to sacrifice a certain degree of flexibility and spontaneity. In addition, we conscientiously monitored and recorded ongoing practices and events in the program and its evaluation.

Third, we wanted to draw upon diverse techniques and to include both quantitative and qualitative analyses of the project in order to construct a more complete, inclusive, and refined understanding of the issues. While passionate debate continues between advocates of qualitative and quantitative research across a number of disciplines and scholarly circles, we hoped to benefit by weaving together and drawing upon the strengths of both approaches—reflecting upon their distinct as well as converging outcomes—to relate our work to past and present research, to shape our questions for the future, and to strengthen or temper the convictions that would ultimately emerge from our analyses.

Finally, we were committed to adopting research strategies that were true to the theoretical framework and the goals of the Listening Partners program—research strategies that support the expression and development of mind and voice by promoting true dialogue and assuring that people's thoughts and words are listened to most carefully. Nevitt Sanford's (1982) article had alerted us to the power of highly reflective interviews for promoting the development of both individuals and organizations. We wanted the research and research experience to enlighten the investigators and participants alike. We worked to incorporate strategies that would promote constructive, dynamic exchanges, pulling for the "growing edge" of images and understanding. We hoped that the research experience would lead us all—researchers and participants—to a deeper appreciation and understanding of mind and voice. In fact, we hoped and anticipated that the very process of engaging in many of the portions of the research endeavor would support women's sense of voice and mind, whether or not they eventually participated in the intervention program itself. We expected that the research interviews and assessments themselves would provide a powerful experience for women who had felt unable to think for themselves and who had histories of feeling unheard, dismissed, and incapable of expressing their own perspectives. We imagined this would be especially true for those who lacked relationships and opportunities in their lives that might otherwise provide such experiences.

Our Research Design

One hundred and twenty women participated in the Listening Partners project, all of whom resided in two contiguous and similar rural, impoverished counties in northern Vermont. Each of the participants was seventeen to thirty-four years of age and had at least one child who was six years old or younger. The families were living near or below the federally defined poverty level, in social and rural isolation, and were identified by agencies or individuals in the community as having little family support and as being at risk for abuse or neglect of the children or under unusual stress. In an effort to recruit the most isolated of women into the project, we sought only those who had no history of previous involvement in peer support groups. In fact, many of the women who came to participate in Listening Partners had actively resisted invitations to be involved in such organized activities in the past.

In an effort to chart particular dimensions of the women's development and perspectives over the course of the project and beyond, each of the women engaged in two half-days of interviews and assessments with the program staff at three different points in time:

1. "Preintervention": before the Listening Partners intervention began.
2. "Postintervention": nine months later, immediately following the conclusion of the weekly peer-group sessions.
3. "Follow-up": nine to ten months following the completion of the intervention.

Only half of the women actually participated in the weekly peer-group intervention sessions (between the pre- and postintervention interviews). The others, our "control group," completed only the interviews and assessments. Because we recruited the intervention and control groups of women so that they would be comparable in other ways,[2] we could compare their reflections and assessments at postintervention and follow-up to explore the effects of participation in the Listening Partners intervention.

To use our resources most effectively, we conducted two separate waves of intervention groups. During the first year of the program, three groups of ten women and two staff facilitators met for eight months; several months after those groups concluded, we began the second set of three groups. In terms of research design, this system enabled us to examine whether the participant and staff experiences with the program were similar across the first and second waves (or cohorts). Consistent findings did emerge across these two cohorts supporting the reliability (versus idiosyncrasy) of the program's activities and outcomes.

The research evaluation included a variety of measures of characteristics—thoughts and behaviors that we envisioned were particularly important in supporting and reflecting movement from silence to voice and the capacity to nurture these transitions in others. The assessments examined experiences of social support; self-esteem; understanding of the nature of knowledge and truth and conceptions of oneself as a knowe r (epistemological perspectives); beliefs about the nature and role of friendships; conceptions of child development, children as knowers, and effective child-rearing strategies; and behaviors that acknowledge and encourage the active minds and voices of children. In addition, we gathered a considerable amount of information about each woman's present and past living situation, including her parents, family, and household members; educational and training experiences; income and employment history; health and health care; housing; access to transportation and communication (for example, telephone); involvement with community support agencies; religious affiliation; and sense of those people who have been important in her life and development.

We posed our research questions in diverse ways in an effort to construct a broad understanding of the issues and provide opportunities for the women to communicate to us in whatever ways they found most useful and effective. Thus we used some widely accepted standardized "pencil-and-paper" measures that are common to the social and behavioral sciences, and some rather traditional as well as more innovative structured and unstructured interviews that, to varying degrees, encouraged the women to chart the direction and content of our discussions. In addition, we observed and videotaped the women in their homes as they played with their children and taught them particular tasks we put forth (described in the next chapter).

We also gathered information weekly over the course of the intervention sessions. The staff who acted as group facilitators maintained a weekly log of each group session, recording the group's activities and dynamics as well as important individual contributions and transitions of group members. We audiotaped each weekly group session and transcribed those portions that highlighted and illustrated the participants' thinking, feeling, and development. This helped us all—the participants and the staff—to reflect upon and document the course of each person's thinking and development throughout the eight-month intervention period. Collaboration in this process—reviewing weekly contributions, idea gathering, and life stories—proved to be an incredibly powerful experience for many of the participants. It was clear that the research evaluation was, in fact, an important dimension of the intervention.

In planning the analysis of our research evaluation, we considered the advantages of a holistic, case study approach to coding interviews and assessments. By sitting with the entire collection of each person's assessments and examining her comments from start to finish, a rich narrative can be reconstructed that more accurately simulates and reflects the experience and story of the teller. In contrast, when we examine individual excerpts (or components) of the respondent's story, we can lose meaning, referents, and assumptions—just as the storyteller speaks from a holistic mind frame, feeling no need to make each sentence, paragraph, or even page stand on its own, the research respondent is communicating from a holistic perspective; we lose some of this perspective when we break her commentary into fragments.

On the other hand, there is value in analyses that are "blind" to information beyond the measure in question. From a separate knowing perspective, the most accurate and fair assessment requires the elimination of potential for bias or distortion that can be created by seeing things in context. One's hopes and expectations clearly shape one's perceptions—this holds true for researchers, as well. Therefore, scientists usually try to code and analyze their research data in ways that will minimize the potential that their interpretation will be influenced by the research expectations or other so-called extraneous factors.

Given the goals of the Listening Partners project, which included testing certain hypotheses at the same time we were exploring new dimensions of development and relationships, we decided to take advantage of both of these approaches to data analysis by employing them sequentially. We began with blind coding of each of our measures and instruments. All interviews were transcribed by a typist who was independent of the project and unfamiliar with its goals and assumptions; then a research assistant removed identifying information from the transcripts and subdivided them into their individual component measures. Different teams of trained researchers coded each of these component measures; the coders were unaware of respondents' individual identities and intervention status, and unaware of whether the assessment was from the pre-, post-, or follow-up evaluation. This procedure generated the scores that were examined in our quantitative analyses.

Upon completing this process, we carefully reviewed the entire collection of material that was provided by each respondent, examining it in the sequence in which it was generated from the preintervention, postintervention, and follow-up periods. This procedure allowed us to build a richer understanding and interpretation of individual and group themes and transitions—findings we point to as an integral part of our qualitative analyses.

THE OUTCOMES

Recruiting Women to the Listening Partners Program

When we first proposed the Listening Partners program to federal funding agencies in the hopes of soliciting their support, they responded to our ideas with great interest accompanied by considerable skepticism. "How will you ever be able to recruit the participants you hope for?" they asked. Our goal was to involve the most isolated, marginalized, voiceless women from impoverished rural communities of northern Vermont; in particular, we hoped to engage those very women who had been pursued by social service agencies in the region but had refused participation with organized groups in the past. Before funding agencies would commit support to our proposed program, they felt they needed evidence that we could identify and engage these participants.

Spirited support from the A. L. Mailman Family Foundation funded a pilot project for twenty Listening Partners participants that enabled us to demonstrate to others (as well as ourselves) that we could bring isolated, marginalized women into such a program. Next, with support from the Maternal and Child Health Bureau for the full-scale Listening Partners program, we found we were able to recruit the full complement of 120 participants. In fact, over 80 percent of the eligible women we invited to participate in the project agreed to do so.

As we explained earlier, some women needed a great deal of encouragement and a number of home visits to discuss the program before they were ready to agree to participate. The concept of Listening Partners was quite frightening to those who lived with the assumption that they had little to offer and much to hide from others. Many also had to contend with the fears and anger of family members who appeared very threatened by the possible "intrusion" of the program into their lives. As Maureen explained,

> My husband was always scared I would do something if I joined Listening Partners—afraid they were going to talk me into something.

We are convinced that the women's ultimate willingness to participate in the program, despite many fears and obstacles, resulted from the fact that so many found the program's description and preliminary interviews quite compelling. We had explained that we were interested in learning more about the lives of rural women and the experience of raising children in rural isolation—that we wanted to disseminate this story. We had said that some of the women would have the opportunity to participate in groups that were designed to help women break through social isolation, gain a voice, feel the power of their minds, and support each other and their children in talking and thinking through their problems.[3]

The first two portions of our interviews—the Self-Description and Background Information and the Epistemological Development Interview: Ways of Knowing—were designed to draw each woman into a thoughtful conversation about her perceptions of herself, her life, and her children. We began the first section—the Self-Description and Background—by asking each woman, "Thinking back over your life for the past year or so, what stands out for you? What kinds of things have been important?"[4] We also asked her to "Tell me something of what your life is like right now." Drawing from the work of Gilligan (1982/1993), we asked, "How do you describe yourself to your self?" and "How do you see yourself differently now compared to the past?" And we inquired about her relationships with her children, family, and friends—who was important to her and why, and how that had changed over time. The Ways of Knowing Interview (adapted from Belenky, Clinchy, Goldberger, and Tarule, 1986/1997) encouraged the women to think through their notions of truth, knowledge, authority, and themselves as thinkers. We talked with each woman regarding how she went about learning new things, and about people and experiences that had been powerful in guiding her approach to learning and understanding. Building on questions developed by Gilligan and colleagues (for example, see Brown, Argyris, Attanucci, Bardige, Gilligan, Johnston, Miller, Osborne, Tappan, Ward, Wiggins, and Wilcox, 1988; Gilligan, 1982/1993; see also Weinstock, 1989), we developed questions to explore the women's conceptions of conflicts and disagreements and how their approaches to conflict had changed over time.

Both of these interview sections and the description of Listening Partners struck a deep chord with many of the women we met. While they often seemed anxious and intimidated by the whole notion of Listening Partners and had difficulty imagining themselves able to contribute to such an effort, they certainly resonated with the problem voicelessness and marginalization. Although their first interviews, in some ways, were sometimes rather painful, this strenuous activity generated some amazement and deep-seated satisfaction upon their discovery that they *did,* in fact, have some thoughtful ideas and that we took care to listen intently, record, and reflect upon their words. This was a dramatically new experience for many—one that encouraged them to venture further in Listening Partners.

Appendix B summarizes the characteristics of women who agreed to participate in the Listening Partners program and demonstrates the similarity between the intervention participants and the control group. We were pleased to discover that we had managed to recruit to the program precisely those women we had hoped to involve— those feeling on the fringes of society with little appreciation of the potential of their own minds.

Approximately 60 percent of the women we recruited were sup-

ported by public welfare monies and more than half were single mothers. On average they had less than a high school education (ranging between six and fifteen years of formal education); their parents typically
had less than a high school education as well (with four to sixteen years
of formal education). Standard measures of socioeconomic status
(Hollingshead, 1975) indicated that 82 percent of the women[5] were
raised by parents defined as either "semiskilled" or "unskilled" workers
(using the terminology of the classification systems). Eighty-eight percent of the women were presently heads or coheads of households that
were similarly classified as comprised of "semiskilled" or "unskilled"
workers. In other words, the women who chose to join the Listening
Partners program were representative of many who are currently at the
center of ongoing welfare debates in our nation, enabling us to learn
more about the plight of mothers on welfare.

As one strategy for exploring the women's feelings of social isolation versus social support, we used the Family Social Support Scale
(Dunst, Jenkins, and Trivette, 1984). This questionnaire asks the respondent to rate the extent to which various formal and informal sources of
family support (for example, social agencies, physicians, relatives,
friends) have been available and helpful to her and her family over the
recent past. Responses to this questionnaire confirmed that the Listening Partners women joined the project with an extreme sense of social
isolation. In fact, of the seventeen traditional sorts of social supports assessed by this scale and typically found available to diverse groups of
people, the Listening Partners women reported, on average, that more
than 20 percent of these supports were totally unavailable to them. Furthermore, they reported that approximately 60 percent of those supports that were available were not adequately accessible.

Reviewing the Ways of Knowing interviews, it also became clear
that we had succeeded in recruiting participants for Listening Partners
who had very little sense of themselves as active knowers or thinkers.
Seventeen percent of the women expressed silenced as a predominant
view of themselves as knowers, 67 percent were predominantly received knowers, and 16 percent revealed predominantly subjective perspectives—fewer than a third of whom expressed varying degrees of
procedural knowing as well. Thus, we had identified, for the most part,
women who saw themselves at the mercy of others for knowledge and

direction—feeling unable to generate ideas or evaluate the ideas of others, let alone facilitate the growth of mind and voice. Even some of the most silenced women on the fringes of the community appeared willing to take the risk of venturing into the Listening Partners program as it promised to provide a safe and supportive environment for confronting experiences well known or felt by them.[6]

Sustaining Participation in the Program

While attracting women to the Listening Partners program was challenging but doable, attaining regular involvement in the weekly meetings was more demanding, as we had anticipated. Many of the Listening Partners women had extremely complex and demanding lives. Some lived in very isolated settings and had no personal means of transportation, leaving them to rely on neighbors' schedules to hitch rides for grocery shopping, visits to the doctor, and the like; some lived in relationships with abusive partners or other family members whose whims, moods, and drinking activities determined the schedules and opportunities of household members; some had to work around regular or irregular visits from affiliates of various government agencies, community groups, and schools; and almost all had to deal with the multiple ongoing stresses in the lives of women who are struggling with inadequate food, housing, health care, and general support.

Therefore, as we foresaw, weekly participation in the intervention was somewhat erratic. Sixty percent of the program participants attended at least a third of the group sessions; another 10 percent attended at least five to ten of the thirty-four weekly meetings. Approximately half of the eighteen women who attended fewer than five meetings did so because of family moves, family illnesses, new jobs, and the like; the other half appeared unable to overcome their shyness and discomfort in their group. Perhaps most surprising to us was the significant proportion of women who *did* remain committed to the group, despite—or perhaps, in part, because of—the competing distractions and tensions that were so often presented by their poverty, child-care responsibilities, social isolation, and volatile households. We were particularly impressed because we had sought out participants who were living in social isolation with little prior experience with peer groups and social service agencies.

We wondered whether there were some distinctions between the women who regularly came to the intervention sessions and those who did not. Perhaps those with the youngest children would find it most difficult to get away (although we provided free child care at a nearby site), or perhaps the intervention was more attractive to women with a particular level of education, child-rearing strategy, epistemological perspective, or the like. To ask these questions in a systematic way, we conducted statistical analyses to identify which characteristics, if any, distinguished women who regularly attended the weekly sessions from those who did not.

We found the results quite interesting. Through a series of analyses that examined various characteristics of the participants,[7] we found that feelings of social support were the best predictor of whether or not an individual would regularly attend the intervention. Those women who regularly attended the intervention groups had reported fewer social supports available to them before the intervention began, especially fewer formal social supports. Formal social supports refer to agencies, organizations, and individuals (for example, social service providers, physicians, and teachers) who have a formal role in society to support community members—in contrast to friends, relatives, neighbors, and the like whose roles are not "formally" defined.

Meanwhile, attendance at the weekly sessions does not tell the entire story of participation in the intervention. Occasionally, when a particular woman was having difficulty coming to the meetings, one of the other group members would travel to see and speak with her between sessions. This provided a powerful message to the absent member about her importance and value in the eyes of her group. Moreover, it was an opportunity for the traveling member of the group to be featured in the role of midwife teacher. In light of our rural setting where women live at great distances from each other, these visits enacted certain dimensions of our original vision of what Listening Partners could and should be—women gathering in twosomes and threesomes in their own homes, much as friends might do, talking and thinking together, supporting each other as they work through questions, issues, and concerns. While our pilot work had revealed that this task was too overwhelming in the context of most participants' lives, there were a few Listening Partners who grew into this demanding role over the course of the eight-month intervention. It became clear that their efforts to reach out and raise up their absent peers both reflected and promoted their own growing sense of mind and voice.

The Effects of the Intervention Program

Perhaps our most pressing question had been whether or not it was possible to structure a set of experiences within the constraints of this time-limited intervention that could promote women's understanding and development of mind and voice and their skills for fostering environments that support the continued development of mind and voice in themselves and others. Three hours per week for a mere eight months was such a small portion of time, especially amidst the innumerable life demands upon these young, impoverished mothers of small children. Were we overly optimistic to hope that this brief and confined Listening Partners experience would have sufficient power to begin to redress what was, in many instances, a lifetime of feedback that contradicted the messages we hoped to convey? And yet, because we cannot relive our lives or those of others, it seemed critical to understand whether or not such time-limited intervention had the potential for supporting further development—particularly development that could take on some life of its own, not only sustaining but building upon itself.

We had hoped and anticipated that those who participated in the Listening Partners intervention would show greater epistemological gains than nonparticipants as a result of their program experience. We also hoped that they would develop a greater appreciation of relationships as a context for supporting these transitions. Moreover, we expected that participants' increased capacity for self-reflection and social interaction would empower them to contribute to more healthy interactive environments for themselves, their peers, and their children—environments that, in turn, would support ongoing growth of mind and voice even after the program had ended. In other words, we were asking not only about the short-term effects of the program but two additional questions: "Would program outcomes be sustained when participants were no longer actively involved in the groups?" and, "Would these effects not only be self-sustaining but also self-nourishing so that they would actually continue to *increase* over time, even after the program had ended?"

Such goals present quite a challenge for those who work with social programs. There is a long history of interventions that lead to short-term gains only to find that these gains dissipate once the participants are no longer actively involved in the program. Such a finding does not suggest that the program is of no value, but only that ongoing program participation is necessary to maintain the program benefits. Yet within the typical constraints of insufficient and time-limited resources, ongoing program participation often is not an option.

We began our analyses of the program's effects by asking the participants and nonparticipants how things had changed for them since we last interviewed them (over the course of the eight-month intervention or follow-up period). In an effort to be as accurate as we could in surmising the effects of participation in the program, we considered women as "program participants" only if they had attended five or more of the weekly group meetings. We then compared the postintervention and follow-up changes in their interviews and assessments to those of the "control" group—the women who had not had the opportunity to participate in the weekly intervention. We were struck by the finding that our quantitative analyses of questionnaires and standardized assessments and our qualitative analyses of interviews and participants' commentaries converged on a set of interrelated and anticipated results. This was the case despite the fact that the analyses were conducted independently of each other and by coders who were unaware of respondents' membership in the intervention or control group, and responses to other measures.

During our interviews with intervention participants at postintervention and follow-up women often told us, "I feel better about myself now," "I'm getting some control over my life," "I can look out for myself better," "I stick up for myself better." Analyses of the questionnaires supported these commentaries. Each woman had completed a Checklist of Changes (see Appendix A) at the postintervention and follow-up periods that inquired about a variety of potential changes in status of housing, communication, transportation, health, education, and the like. Intervention participants reported lifestyle changes over the course of both the intervention and the follow-up period that suggested they were taking more control over their lives and making strides in reaching out into the community. Whereas the participants and nonparticipants had not differed from each other before the intervention began, ten months after the program had ended intervention participants were more likely to report that their housing situations had improved or held steady rather than deteriorated, they were less likely to be smoking, and they were more likely to have a driver's license than nonparticipants.

In addition, at follow-up, every one of the four intervention participants who was still without a driver's license reported that she was currently working on obtaining one; in contrast, only eight of the seventeen nonparticipants who were still without licenses indicated that they were working on that situation. These driver's license findings are striking because even in this very isolated rural setting, women frequently do not drive; tradition holds that men rather than women should be in the driver's seat. Furthermore, taking the written driver's test can be quite problematic and traumatic for individuals with poor literacy skills or a history of school failure.

Analyses of the standardized social support measure (Dunst, Jenkins, and Trivette, 1984) revealed that program participants experienced an increase in the number of formal supports available to them between the posttest and follow-up interviews;[8] during this same period, the nonparticipants actually reported a *decrease* in formal supports. This result suggests that program participants became better able to reach out to formal resources in the community for assistance. As the participants reflected upon their lives in the community many months after the program had ended (during follow-up interviews), they expressed certain themes again and again that revealed this sense of accomplishment:

- "Now it's easier for me to figure out what I need and ask for it."
- "I'm not so worried about asking for help."
- "I can take care of myself better and look after what me and my kids need."
- "I've learned to say what's on my mind when I need to."
- "I figure, now, if other people can get things, I can get them too."

These sorts of convictions underlie the strength and courage it takes to venture into the maze of community support systems.

Perhaps most exciting and encouraging was the evidence we gathered that women who participated in the Listening Partners intervention made greater gains in appreciating and developing the power of their minds and voices compared to nonparticipants. Like our other measures, the Ways of Knowing interviews had been coded without awareness of respondents' status in the intervention or their responses on other measures and at other periods of time. Yet when the scores were statistically analyzed and compared across time, we found that intervention participants who began the program as silenced and received knowers had made greater gains than comparable nonparticipants by the conclusion of the weekly sessions; moreover, as we had hoped, this difference between the two groups was even greater at the follow-up period—nine to ten months after the intervention had concluded![9]

Eager to examine these changes more thoroughly, we wanted to understand whether the intervention was more effective in promoting development of mind and voice for certain groups of individuals rather than others. For example, would a woman's age, level of education, social support, or epistemological perspective at the onset of the project prepare her to make greater gains? We conducted a series of statistical analyses to determine whether these gains could have been predicted from the women's characteristics or background at the beginning of the project.[10] Focusing on the intervention participants (who had attended at least five of the intervention sessions), we discovered that the number of intervention sessions the women attended did not predict the gains they achieved; however, those women who began the project with the least appreciation of themselves as thinkers and knowers showed the most development over time. We imagine that this outcome reflects, in part, the fact that we had designed the Listening Partners program to address the needs of these most silenced and voiceless women. Most of the activities during the group sessions focused on early struggles in establishing mind and voice.

Thus we found that many of the women who began the program as silenced and received knowers made impressive transitions over the course of the intervention and follow-up periods. Consider Leslie, for example, who entered Listening Partners as a silenced knower, with little sense of who she was, what she thought, or that she thought. In her initial interview, images of change and transition were absent from her descriptions of her life. She was literally unable to describe herself, appearing puzzled by the very notion of having a self.

What do you mean by that? Describe myself? [*laugh*] Um [*laugh*] I don't know. I got no ideas for that one [*laugh*].

Leslie could scarcely begin to imagine how she would go about learning or understanding something new.

Like?

ANYTHING. WELL, LIKE IN YOUR PERSONAL LIFE, SAY WITH FRIENDS OR FAMILY, HOW DO YOU GO ABOUT LEARNING OR UNDERSTANDING?

Well, what I think I do mostly is just like sit there and listen to them, and if they come up with something, I know I can always try it, and if they don't, then I don't.

Change and transition were absent from Leslie's images of her life; she was clear that she had not changed over the years as a learner: "No, I do the same. Just sit there and listen to them."

Leslie could not fathom that someone could learn on her own or make choices about what to learn. Asked to react to another woman's statement that "I LIKE IT WHEN TEACHERS AREN'T ABOVE US—AREN'T BEING THE BOSS. I LIKE MAKING MY OWN DECISIONS ABOUT WHAT I'M GOING TO LEARN," Leslie says,

No, in that case you would have to kind of listen to the teacher before you could learn anything.

Not only are Leslie's images passive, but she sees herself as empty and unable to contain and hold onto thoughts—she can do what others say, but even so, she cannot absorb or hold onto their knowledge. She feels amazingly void of *any* ideas or opinions, let alone those she can call her own; asked how she would figure out what is true when there are differences of opinion—when her opinion differs from someone else's—she responds:

What I would do is just go over and ask if it is true or not.

UH HUH. ASK?

Ask the other person.

Speaking with Leslie a year and a half later, her epistemological perspectives remain relatively limited, but a new sense of self and voice are evident throughout our conversations. Reflecting on how she had changed over the past year and a half, Leslie explains,

> I don't have so much problems as I did before. I don't care who it is, whatever I have to say I'll just come out and say it now. Before I never did. . .

SO WHY DO YOU THINK YOU CHANGED LIKE THAT?

> I think, now let's see. I used to keep quiet and let them say things to me. I never said nothing to them. But it just got to me after a while and I figured if they can do it, I can too. . . . I figure I've got my own life to live.

Leslie has not only achieved an identity, voice, and a set of opinions, but she sees herself as someone with whom others must contend. She now understands the potential for her voice to influence others in various ways. She explains that sometimes people "get ugly" when she speaks her mind, but sometimes others agree with her as well.

> If we disagree, we have to just really sit there and keep talking until, you know, we do agree.

Having identified a self and a voice, she can now imagine learning new things, and even doing so on her own in some limited ways.

> By just listening and looking at things, I can pretty well learn on my own. I'm an easy person to learn things to.

Meanwhile, the notion of carefully thinking things through continues to feel far removed from her life; she has found an assertive voice, but one that feels guided by impulse more than thought:

> I really don't sit there and think. Nope. I mean, if I have something to say, it just comes out. I don't sit there and think of what I'm gonna say. Whatever comes out, comes out.

WHAT HAPPENS, WHAT GOES ON IN YOUR HEAD?

> There ain't much that goes on up there.

Still, while Leslie's voice is impulsive, she has identified a self and voice that is distinct from others—that can influence as well as be influenced by the behaviors and even ideas of those around her. Thus Leslie is now positioned to imagine herself within a social network where there is give and take and the potential for change. She has come to recognize talking as a vehicle for achieving agreement as well as disagreement, opening up avenues through which she might gather and share ideas and eventually even consider their development and refinement.

While Leslie struggled for some time to identify any voice, others had started Listening Partners where Leslie left off—projecting a voice but one with a life of its own—impulsive and not associated with a sense of thinking. These women experienced, in their words, an "eruption" of emotion and behavior: "It just comes out. I don't really think about anything beforehand. I don't think about what'll happen." For many of these women, Listening Partners provided an opportunity to focus on merging thought with voice and action. Says Ruth, whose words opened this chapter:

> I think things through more than I used to. It's like before I used to just jump and do it, but it's like now I, I'll think it through. . . . In Listening Partners I've learned to speak out for what I believe without screaming.

Maureen reports:

> I think things through clearly. I try to. Before I would either not think about it because it was too hard to think about or I would just do the first thing that came along instead of trying to find the real, the best solution, for everybody involved. . . . Now I care about other people *and* myself, I have a new self-assuredness—that I can do it right *and* that I have rights.

Dawn explains:

> I guess I'm more outspoken now. But I think things through before I say things. I've learned that lesson. I get a lot of good ideas from the problem solving [strategies we learned in Listening Partners].

Each of these women comments not only about the merger of mind, thought, voice, and action but also on her new ability to think more about others and *simultaneously* stand up for herself—considerations all too often assumed to be at odds with each other. Ruth helps us understand this transition. She explains that at first she always did what everybody else wanted. Then she spent four years concerned with just herself. But now she does a lot more *real* thinking than she used to— she thinks of others and what they want *and* at the same time she sticks up for herself too. Ruth is describing for us the transition from silence to voice to more reasoned expression—moving from received to subjective and even to the beginning of procedural knowing. With increasing confidence in the strength and potential of her mind and voice, the perspectives of others become less threatening.

Rachel (whose story we heard in the introduction of this book) reveals a similar transition in broad dimensions of her life. Upon entering the program, Rachel described herself as able to acquire knowledge from the words spoken by others, but unable to learn from her own thinking. When asked how she thought of herself as a thinker, she said, "Well, I can understand things if somebody explains it to me." But she rejected the notion that a person can direct her own learning: "How can you learn on your own? You have to have somebody teaching you. . . . The teachers have, you know, been to school and stuff so they know how to teach it." She was confident in her ability to receive knowledge handed down by others, but she did not imagine ideas springing up from her own mind.

Within the year, things had changed considerably. In her second interview, nine months after the first, Rachel saw herself learning from her own experiences. When asked how people get knowledge and ideas, she said:

> From their past experiences, living life. [*laugh*] I get my ideas from looking over my life . . . I think with my head and my heart . . . I don't like to rush right into things. I like to think about them first and figure out if it's right for me.

As we have seen, images of agency appear throughout Rachel's second interview, a conversation that reveals her development of subjective knowing. With the ability to see the self as a source of knowledge, the whole way of conceptualizing the self expands rapidly (Piirak, Bond, and Belenky, 1995). In contrast to her previous passivity, Rachel speaks of her ambition, confidence, and ability to make decisions and say what she feels, thinks, needs, and expects from others.

By the third interview—the follow-up—more than a year and a half after the first one, Rachel was considering living again with her boyfriend. He had been sober for a year and was meeting other expectations that she held up for him. Rachel had also reevaluated her relationship with her daughter. When we first met Rachel, she had put talking *to* her daughter at the center of the educational process. Now she argues that it is also important to talk *with* her daughter. When asked how she was going to bring about her educational goals for her daughter, Rachel said:

> I will make sure that when she does things wrong that she's told that it is wrong and she's not supposed to do it. And I'll be there as a friend and talk and be able to talk about anything she wants to talk about, you know.
>
> UM HUM. HOW IS BEING THERE AS A FRIEND, TALKING ABOUT ANYTHING, AN IMPORTANT PART OF THIS?
>
> Because I think that if she felt she couldn't talk to anybody about things that she would feel alone and then she wouldn't be able to solve problems and wouldn't be able to know what's going on.

It may be that Rachel now seeks a relationship of greater reciprocity and mutuality with her daughter because she herself has felt the expansion of self that occurs when a community of peers think and talk together. And she relishes her newfound intellectual powers.

By the time of the follow-up interviews it was clear that many of the women had become more skilled in dialogue and more able to participate in mutually growth-enhancing relationships. The men in the lives of many of these women seemed to be less dictatorial and more dependable as well. Reflecting on her marriage, Dawn says:

> We talk things out a lot more. I think, rather than just, we used to just ignore each other, it's hard to explain. We used to go our own ways, more or less; I got stuck at home while he took off. Now he

stays home and, ah, we talk things out. We don't run away from problems or whatever. I can't say that he really heads right for them either, but if there's a problem, he'll help solve it. We've come a long ways, an awfully long way.

Maureen explains:

Before, we probably fought at least once a day, if not more. We were in a constant battle of wills . . . and he put me down for doing stuff. Now, he is really proud of me and brags [about my going to school]. He's changed a whole lot. He has accepted my feelings. Before we'd fight to the death. Now if we reach a subject that we don't agree on, we just either say we agree to disagree or we just, you know, say well, let's not talk about that. We just agree not to agree on that stuff, whereas before we'd try to make each other agree. . . . It's more fifty-fifty now than it used to be.

Pam is the most eloquent about such changes, perhaps because she—more than the other women—can articulate the procedures that shape the development of her ideas and discourse. Pam has gotten very comfortable stating her own desires, wishes, and opinions. She also has helped her husband put his ideas on the table. She says:

Now the lines of communication are wide open between us. When we first got married, my husband had the tendency to fly off the handle a lot. Because in his family, they didn't communicate well. I'm not trying to pat myself on the back—he would say the same thing—but I kind of taught him how to talk to me—you know, that I wasn't going to jump down his throat about things. He could talk to me about things, you know. If there was something he thought was going to upset me that he needed to tell me, that he could and I wouldn't just automatically go wild or something. I would listen to him. Do you know what I mean? I would understand or I would try to understand.

As the women reflected on the experiences that had led to their changes over the past year and a half, they so often pointed to the power of the friendships that they had developed, both within and beyond Listening Partners:

- "Learning to trust other people."
- "Having people really listen to you and care what you say."
- "I had to think about others and not just myself."
- "We were working it out together and not feeling so alone."

Tina explained that she did not have any friends while growing up, but now she does and that's what has been particularly important to her in her growth as a thinker.

> My friends were the important ones that helped me start thinking because I *had* to. Because I had to answer their questions to get somewhere. I couldn't depend on anyone else to answer those questions for me.

In contrast to her experiences in the past where people always provided her with the answers and didn't expect her to think for herself, Tina says:

> [The Listening Partners program] showed me that I did have ideas that I could maybe use later on. You guys listened to me.

Tina learned how to think for herself, express her own ideas, and speak her mind about others' perspectives; moreover, she learned how to make friends. She claims that all of this factored into her decision and ability to start college—venturing into a new context that could continue her intellectual and interpersonal development.

> Before if I wanted to go to college I would have to know some-one who was going so I wouldn't feel uncomfortable, but I don't know anyone in my classes and I just went in and made friends.

YOU COULD START FROM SCRATCH?

Yeah, before I couldn't.

Bonnie joined Listening Partners as a highly subjective knower who dwelled on her own needs and perspectives with limited interest in the experiences of others. By the end of the program, Bonnie had begun to move beyond her own world to cultivate an interest in what her peers had to offer at the same time she continued to value self-discovery. As she exclaimed at the end of the Listening Partners intervention:

[Listening Partners was] interesting, fun, exploreamentive. Kind of, something to explore because you get to explore other people, but yet you also explore yourselves.

Having never really gotten along with other women in the past, Bonnie says she grew more comfortable over time sharing her problems with others in the group and having them ask her questions.

It helped you to see more than what you had thought of yourself. . . . Because someone's not telling you what to do; they are helping you to see what you can do.

Listening Partners provided a context for discovering the multiple roles that friends can play and the notion that someone can have multiple types of good friends. Ruth explains:

Now, I mean, I can have a really good friend and she can be in the same situation I'm in. But yet I can have another really good friend that I can just go out and have a good time with—maybe sit down and have coffee. Before I always thought you only had one friend. Now it's like, through the group there's some of them I feel that I'm very close to. I could be a good friend to any of them.

Seeing friendships as more multidimensional, Ruth discovers that she is capable of playing multiple roles in the lives of others, as well—a discovery that brings her a sense of great satisfaction, accomplishment, and potential. For example:

I know that with myself I was able to help Patty [another Listening Partner] to speak out for herself and do things that she really wanted to do but she wouldn't do them.

Ruth is amazed at how much she enjoys supporting and helping others now that she has a stronger sense of herself as a capable individual.

It's weird. Like I like doing things for other people more than I used to. I'll go out and weed my parents' garden and stuff like that. Before you wouldn't of caught me doing that.

Whether in the context of friends, husbands, children, or other companions, Listening Partners were discovering not only mind, voice, and reason but the power of relationships for cultivating these capacities in themselves and others. Certain relationships were providing a safe forum for learning to take risks with others—learning to trust, to speak one's mind, to take a stand, to disagree; at the same time, they were learning to listen, to take another's perspective, to influence and be influenced, and to engage in a collaborative, respectful, and reciprocal manner to nurture an environment for mutual growth.

Many participants mentioned how important it was to hear the stories of other women—how it makes you "get beyond your own mess," "stop thinking just of yourself," "understand that you aren't the only one with these sorts of problems," and "be thoughtful and less impulsive." Ruth spoke of the equality, reciprocity, and mutual support that was the foundation of Listening Partners groups:

> I know I used to go to AA [Alcoholics Anonymous] with this guy sometimes [I wasn't a member; it was his group]. And it's like they were the only ones that had the problem. Nobody else had a problem, you know? They were the only ones; this is what they taught them. They come first and above anything else or anybody else. But like in Listening Partners it's like everybody is equal, you know. I'm not the only one that has a problem and it's not that yours ain't as bad as mine. It's like everybody was trying to help everybody out.

As confidence in intellectual and interpersonal skills grows, so too does willingness and ability to place ourselves in situations that will further our development. Tina, Bonnie, Maureen, Ruth, Pam, Dawn, Rachel, Lil, Sally, and Carol, among others, are coming to appreciate their capacity to learn and develop, to think things through carefully, and to use conversations with others to help them in that process. They seek out relationships where they feel safe and respected, where they can engage in high-quality dialogue with other women, where they can be listened to and be heard—relationships that have helped them gain a greater appreciation for themselves as knowers and as individuals who might raise up others. This change has empowered them to move further into the community, to build additional connections with others—

nurturing their developing minds and voices and those with whom they engage. Dawn, Lil, and Sally have jobs. Rachel, Lil, and Carol have completed their GEDs (high school graduation equivalency degrees). Tina, Maureen, Pam, and Carol have begun taking courses at a local community college. Rachel is taking courses offered to adults at the local high school. All are thinking about the careers they want to develop when their children are older. Moreover, we have learned that a number of the Listening Partners participants are now active members of volunteer community organizations, networks, or committees working, for example, with their children's schools, community education groups, and women's shelters.

In all, powerful images of agency flooded the final interviews of Listening Partners participants. We close with a few examples. First, Maureen:

> I think a lot more about things and whether or not they can be changed. If they can then, I try to think of [things] I can do to change them. If they can't be changed, then I try to think of ways of dealing with them, the things that can't be changed. I never used to think about anything like that before.

Lil said of herself:

> I'm spunky. I'm out to make my goals. Got my mind made up, I'm gonna do it. . . . I got a lot going for myself, you might say. I'm accomplishing my GED. This coming summer I'm gonna do my own business and get off welfare. . . . I'm not guaranteeing I'm gonna succeed, but I'm gonna give it my best shot.

Carol reflects:

> I think I've grown up. I'm just more serious about life. I can handle problems a lot better. Before, anytime problems came up I just couldn't take it. Now I think about things before I jump into them. Now I learn from my past. I just realized that I've got the power to change whatever I don't like. . . . Before my life ran me; now I'm running my life.

CHAPTER 5

MOTHERS AND CHILDREN

How's John gonna figure out what he's supposed to do if I don't tell him what to do? What are parents for, anyway?   ELAINE

Hey, that's why I got family—to steer me along. Sometimes I wish I could put a steering wheel on my back because I don't think I can stay on the road by myself, if you know what I mean. I need my mom as a full-time driver.   CARRIE

My mom always told me what to do; like she didn't think I could figure it out for myself. I hated that. It made me feel awful. How am I supposed to figure out how to take care of myself if no one gives me a chance to try to work stuff out myself?   TAMMY

At some point, you just gotta let go and let your kid experiment herself. I don't mean abandon them, but you know, you're not gonna always be there, so you gotta let them test the waters a little bit at a time when they're growing up. Otherwise, it's like suddenly taking off their life jacket and throwing them overboard when they've never practiced treading, let alone swimming on their own.   CHRISTINE

As Elaine asks, "What are parents for, anyway?" What is their role in sponsoring their children's development? What are their responsibilities and how are they to pursue them? The Listening Partners project sponsored women to gain the power of voice in private life with the expectation that this appreciation of mind and voice would be associated with more democratic and nurturing family and peer relationships—contexts that nurture development of others as well as self.

Throughout our work, we have had a special interest in the sponsorship of growth in the context of mothers and their children. Mother caring for children—cast as Other by Simone de Beauvoir; one traditional prototype for the immensely important role of sponsoring human development. Yet, while romanticized and sanctified on the one hand, mothering is not respected as an important endeavor. The matrophobia identified by Adrienne Rich (1976) pervades so much of our society, encouraging little regard for the painstaking work and thought involved in the nurturing of children.

As mothers' appreciation for their own abilities to think and act on behalf of themselves and their children is diminished by public images and systems that isolate mothers and limit their decision making, mothers' abilities to support their own growth and that of their children are diminished as well. In this chapter, we examine, in some detail, the documentation we were able to gather regarding the relationships between women's appreciation of their own minds and voices and their visions of and interactions with their children (see also Bond, Belenky, Weinstock, and Cook, 1996). These linkages provide the foundation for many of the "ripple effects" that we anticipate from the Listening Partners project as well as from the public homeplaces described in Part III of this book. The immense power of a generation to sponsor the development of another in both private and public life is a theme we encounter again and again among those who reflect on the sources of their own strength of vision, mind, and voice. Understanding the nature of these ripple effects permits us to build even further upon them.

There is a huge—almost overwhelming—literature, developed over many decades, that explores the relationship between various parenting practices and child and adolescent development outcomes (for reviews, see, for example, Baumrind, 1989, 1991; Eisenberg and Murphy, 1995; Maccoby and Martin, 1983; Sternberg and Williams, 1995). Like much of the research on human development, this work has been limited by an overreliance on studying white middle-class families. We are increasingly appreciating the complexities of parenting outcomes: parenting practices must be considered in sociocultural context (for example, Youniss, 1994), and parents' strategies are neither as stable across situations nor as global as was once assumed (for example Grusec and Goodnow, 1994; Smetana, 1994).

We have been especially interested in exploring those parenting practices that are associated with children's developing sense of mind and voice—the qualities upon which the Listening Partners project was centered. We had drawn from the parenting literature to design the Listening Partners intervention with the conviction that some of the same sorts of experiences that support children's growth of mind and voice similarly nurture adults. For example, as Nancy Eisenberg and Bridget Murphy (1995) summarize, highly moral children tend to have parents who "use inductive discipline, provide opportunities for children to learn about others' perspectives and feelings, and involve children in family decision making and in the process of thinking about moral decisions. . . . [These parents] model moral behaviors and thinking themselves, and provide opportunities for their children to do so," thereby fostering "the development of concern and caring about others" (p. 251). Robert Sternberg and Wendy Williams (1995) summarize the importance of parents providing "mediated learning experience" (a term introduced by Reuven Feuerstein with his colleagues, Rand, Hoffman, and Miller, 1980) as distinguished from direct learning experience, which "happens when a parent or teacher teaches us a fact" (p. 262). Parents and other mediators have been found to stimulate cognitive competence when they guide children in ways to think about what is happening so that they might learn from their own experiences. Sternberg and Williams conclude that helping children to *formulate* and *ask* meaningful questions is critical. Intellectual development is most enhanced when mediators encourage experimentation, question posing, alternative seeking, and evaluation.

What underlies or leads to parenting practices such as these that support children to develop and express the strength and potential of their minds, voices, and convictions? In Chapter 3 we presented a diagram of the Listening Partners project (Figure 3.1) and a table (Table 3.1) that illustrate our vision. Like many others who are currently writing about these issues, we believe that parents' child-rearing practices are shaped, in part, by parents' beliefs or "theories" about the nature and course of children's development (see, for instance, McGillicuddy-DeLisi and Sigel, 1995, for a concise review; Harkness and Super, 1996, who present an array of relevant cross-cultural research; and Pomerleau, Malcuit, and Sabatier, 1991, who describe their multidimensional study of mother–child interaction and child-rearing practices in three different cultural groups). Parents' understanding and beliefs regarding child development emerge from culture and experience and provide a framework for interpreting children's behaviors and setting goals for them (see, for example, Garcia, Meyer, and Brillon, 1995; Harkness, Super, and Keefer, 1992; LeVine, Miller, Richman, and LeVine, 1996; LeVine, Miller, and West, 1988).

We believe that parents' understanding and beliefs about child development, in turn, are tied to parents' broader assumptions about how people learn and grow and their conceptions of *themselves* as knowers (as we summarized in Table 3.1 in Chapter 3). These beliefs frame the context for defining and imagining healthy development including the experiences that are necessary, optional, or detrimental to assuring children's growth.

The relationship between mothers' own sense of mind and voice and their views of child development is not simple and, in fact, children's personalities, temperaments, and behaviors do much to inform their parents' evolving "theories" of child development. This situation becomes clear when we speak with women over time, as their children grow through various developmental phases, and it is equally clear as we follow a woman raising multiple children—her beliefs about child development are refined with the addition of each new family member. In addition, some people may make certain distinctions between the ways in which adults and children develop and learn. On the other hand, we find perspectives on ways of knowing to be deeply rooted and to serve as overarching frameworks or "philosophies," if you will, for *coding, translating,* and *interpreting* one's own as well as others' behaviors, feelings, and interactions. This structure for organizing information serves to minimize the changes or "reframing" that new experiences (including new individuals) introduce. The "new" experiences are coded and translated into old "systems" for interpreting and understanding the world, and so we find that different women interpret similar interactions with their children in quite divergent ways (see, for example, Dix, Ruble, and Zambarano, 1989).

For example, Elizabeth reported that her four-year-old son Charles is:

> mouthing off; just always mouthing off. Whenever I say anything to him, he asks me "Why?" Like I say we're going to the store and

he says "Why?" Or I tell him "Don't touch the bug 'cuz it's dead"
and he says "Why?" Like he's just trying to get me mad by never
listening to me. He never accepts what I say. He mouths off all the
time instead of believing me. It's like he just wants to tease me. You
know, he tests me.

In contrast, Joyce describes her four-year-old Peter:

Well, you know, he's got such an active mind, always going; like
he's never satisfied with just appearances—he's always trying to
figure out how things tick, why they do. So if I ask him to do
something or tell him to do something, he's always asking why. He
really wants to understand what's the goal—what's the purpose—
how come? He's really trying to piece the world all together . . .
and understand it all. It's wonderful. Or if I say, "We're going to the
store," he wants to know why. He's real interested in figuring out
how one thing leads to another. It's great, because sometimes he
helps me realize that I haven't really thought through why I'm saying what I am. And so we do think it through.

Of course, different interpretations of a child's behavior are likely
to lead to different reactions to that behavior. And so it is with Elizabeth and Joyce. Probing Joyce's last statement, we ask her "What do
you mean 'we do think it through'?" She responds:

I mean, he gets me to think it through—*with* him, you know. He
asks me why, and I realize we got to think it through together, because I don't really know why I told him to do what I did. I mean,
I have a feeling why, but I'm not really sure about it, so Peter and I
talk about some reasons why he should or shouldn't do what I
asked and we think through what really makes sense. It's really useful sometimes, you know?

Joyce's interpretation of Peter's behavior leads her to create a setting that encourages Peter to explore his mother's reasoning and learn
about the ways in which she selects goals, strategies, and actions. Joyce
also establishes a dialogue that permits her to learn more about Peter's
questions, skills, assumptions, and attempts to explore the world; that is,
she learns more about Peter's development and ways of thinking about

the world. With a growing awareness of the limitations of solitary decision making and an increasing appreciation of the power of dialogue,
Joyce sees her child providing her with an opportunity to develop her
own ideas more fully. Joyce draws Peter into the conversation as a truly
active participant, both communicating her belief that he can contribute to the interaction in a meaningful and thoughtful way and providing an occasion for him to observe himself doing so. All the while,
they both have the opportunity to experience their collaborative powers in thinking and reasoning together, providing both of them with a
context in which to witness and refine this potential in themselves and
one another for mutual support and problem solving.

Our probes with Elizabeth provide a striking contrast. When we
ask her what she does when her son Charles asks her "Why?" [or in her
words, "mouths off"], she explains:

> The best thing is to just stop talking to him. If I answer, he'll just
> keep going and then, you know, he knows he's got you. You're play-
> ing into it and he's jerking you around. I shouldn't have to prove
> myself, you know? If he doesn't trust me, if he doesn't think I know
> what I'm talking about that's not something I should have to prove,
> you know? So I just stop. Ignore him. I go and do something else.

Elizabeth's assumptions about Charles's motivation for asking
"Why" lead her to respond to him with silence—she ends their communication. She does not explain her position to Charles or her goals
and reasoning. She provides no framework for Charles to explore the
steps that she has used for posing, analyzing, and resolving problems.
Quite possibly, Elizabeth does not and perhaps cannot frame these issues and problem-solving steps even for herself. From this stance, she
interprets Charles's questions as revealing a lack of trust in her authority. Authorities' words should be accepted without question or doubt;
authorities should not have to explain themselves.

By ending the dialogue, Elizabeth not only restricts her son's opportunity to both explore the meaning of her words and engage in dialogue, in general; she also terminates her own opportunity to probe
Charles's thoughts, feelings, and strategies and to learn about the way
Charles tries to understand his world. Equally important, Elizabeth
does not establish a context in which she, herself, is likely to reexamine

her own logic and reasoning. She avoids the situation, evading a scenario that would invite her to reflect on and articulate her own perspectives—a situation that would encourage her to clarify her own mind and develop a more thoughtful voice.

What a different reaction we see in Joyce, who accepts and even welcomes her son's challenge to identify, clarify, and rethink her perspective. Joyce encourages these exchanges as opportunities to collaborate with her son as well as to articulate and refine her own thinking and reasoning. By working with Peter to reconsider her own views, Joyce is nurturing a setting in which she can grow; she nurtures an environment that supports not only Peter's sense of mind and voice but her own as well.

Women's Ways of Knowing and Their Parenting

Women like Elizabeth feel unable to use words to communicate and learn with others; they neither feel capable of nor value reflective dialogue. Because words come back to haunt, there is a fear of betrayal that encourages them to be wary, distant, and silent. Relationships are guarded; it is safer to share activities rather than feelings and ideas. Interpersonal differences are scary because they are seen as neither potentially understandable nor resolvable; often, therefore, there may be desperate attempts to avoid disagreements. In fact, the mere existence of questions, differences, or disagreements may suffice to define the relationship as critically flawed. In this environment of caution and restraint, it is difficult to discover or cultivate the powers of mind and voice—one's own or another's.

In contrast, a woman like Joyce, who sees herself as responsible for contributing to the creation of knowledge and as full of ideas that can be articulated, evaluated, and revised, is likely to search out the reflections of others, invite feedback, and look to others as important partners in the process of constructing, testing, and revising an understanding of the world. Articulation of differences and disagreements will be invited—it will be seen as providing rich opportunities for growth. Valuing others as a source of support and stimulation, these women will work to draw out the best of each other's thinking and thus promote their own and their partners' skills and confidence.

Similarly, as parents, women who rarely rely on words for problem solving and communication will be more likely to turn to power-oriented techniques for influencing their own children. Not feeling the power of their own minds and voices, these mothers will not imagine and draw out such capacities in their children. Not thinking and talking things through with their children, the mothers will be unlikely to explain what they themselves know. Nor will they ask their children questions that might help the children generate their own ideas, explanations, and choices. As we see in Elizabeth, a voiceless mother may well feel defensive and irritated when her children question and challenge her. Within the constraints of this context—where mind and voice are more likely to go unrecognized and unnurtured in both mother and children—the children may bring these thinking and parenting strategies to their own parenting when the time comes, in this way perpetuating these patterns and epistemologies through subsequent generations.

In contrast, a mother who sees knowledge as the dynamic product of an active, constructive process—a transactional process that involves the self and others—will be more likely to work *to draw out* her own and her children's thinking, to recognize and nurture their active involvement in discovering and, literally, constructing new truths. She will be more likely to engage in the sorts of interactions that will both cultivate the thinking and expression of her children and exercise her *own* powers of mind and voice.

EXAMINING MOTHERS' EPISTEMOLOGIES, PARENTING BELIEFS, AND PARENTING STRATEGIES

In order to examine these relationships in a more systematic way, we spoke with the women who participated in Listening Partners about the experiences they feel have been important in their own growth and development, and those they believe are important in their children's lives. In addition to discussing their views of mind and voice, we have explored their parenting beliefs and observed their interactions with their own children. These conversations, observations, and collaborations provide a variety of examples of the relationships we just described while they push us toward a more complex appreciation of the interplay between epistemologies and parenting.

To illustrate these relationships, we draw upon several aspects of our interviews. We turn to the Self-Description and Background Information (see Appendix A) to explore the women's thinking about themselves and their children. The Epistemological Development Interview: Ways of Knowing (see Appendix A) examines the women's thinking about truth, knowledge, authority, and themselves as thinkers: we asked the women to discuss how they go about learning new things, how that has changed over time, people and experiences that have been important in shaping their approach to learning and understanding, and their understanding and handling of disagreements.[1]

Parent–Child Communication   We also talked with mothers specifically about their goals in communicating with their children, especially in instances where they were trying to help their children learn or redirect their behavior and thinking. As we explored these issues with them, we worked to understand their assumptions about their children's learning and development—the women's reasoning behind their communication goals. What sorts of information or guidance do they imagine that their children need or will find useful? What sorts of interactions do they feel will be most productive and effective? What are the mothers' short- and long-term goals in such a scenario?

We structured these discussions around an interview developed by Ann McGillicuddy-DeLisi and her colleagues (McGillicuddy-DeLisi, Johnson, Sigel, and Epstein, 1980), called the Parent–Child Communication Strategy Interview. Using an abbreviated version of that interview (see Appendix A), we presented women with a series of four hypothetical situations that involve the interaction between a parent and four-year-old child. In one scenario, a child is playing with building blocks and begins to throw them around the living room when he has difficulty fitting them together; in the second, a child refuses to share her toys with a friend she has invited to her house for play; in the third, while the mother is bathing her child, the child questions whether the metal spoon he is playing with will float like his plastic bowl; and in the fourth, a child repeatedly asks her mother to play with her, although the mother has explained that she is very busy at the time.

For each scenario, we asked the women to describe the strategies they would use to respond to that situation and their rationales for their choices. After transcribing their interviews, we coded their responses into categories that reflected the degree to which their strategies invited active cognitive involvement on the part of the child (adapted from a coding technique developed by McGillicuddy-DeLisi, Johnson, Sigel, and Epstein, 1980).[2] The five most common categories of responses we found, and those most relevant to the focus of this chapter, were:

1. **Intellectual Facilitation**[3]   The mother used statements and questions that drew the child into the task as an active problem solver, to think through the problem at hand and focus beyond the concrete information presented, placing appropriately challenging intellectual demands upon the child.

2. **Rational Authoritative**   The mother provided the child with facts, rules, or information accompanied by a relevant explanation that appeals to reason or to social norms.

3. **Parent Activity**[4]   The mother demonstrated and/or performed experimentation for or with her child, with the mother serving as an active participant and/or a model.

4. **Direct Authoritative**   The mother made statements of fact or rule, without any further elaboration or explanation, that were directed toward affecting her child's behavior.

5. **Authoritarian**   The mother used power-oriented communications that rely on physical manipulation of her child and/or her child's surroundings or the use of verbal threat or abuse.

At one end of the continuum described here are intellectual facilitation strategies that explicitly demand the child's active mental involvement in the situation at hand; they call for children to go beyond the concrete information before them and actively manipulate and even create new ideas. At the other end of the continuum, authoritarian strategies impose pursuits that are parent directed and parent controlled rather than child directed and child controlled. The power and course of action are in the domain of the parent; rather than be generative or intellectually involved, the child is primarily to be reactive to the parent's exercise of raw power.

Observing Mother–Child Interaction   Not only were we curious about women's notions of effective ways to communicate with their children, but we were interested in understanding if and how these beliefs corresponded to the ways in which the mothers and their children actually interact with each other. What sorts of interaction strategies are used by mothers who emphasize the importance of engaging children in active problem solving? And what about those women who endorse more authoritarian techniques? Do their interactions with their children reflect such approaches?

We spent a morning or afternoon in each family's home so that we could observe the women and their children playing and learning together. Because the interview of parent–child communication strategies included four-year-olds in hypothetical situations, we concentrated our observations of mother–child interaction on a similar age group (four- to six-year-olds). In this way we could compare the women's reports of their preferred strategies with our observations of their actual interactions with their children. We analyzed observations and interviews of forty families who had a child in this particular age range.

As we visited each family's home, we recorded intervals of mother–child interaction using a small handheld videorecorder. This technology proved relatively comfortable to even the most isolated and impoverished families. Because many of the families had videotape players in their own homes that they used for viewing rented movies and recording television programs, we gave each family a copy of their videorecorded interactions once our work with them was complete. Many women expressed their appreciation for being filmed, pleased with both our interest in their family and their opportunity to receive a brief visual record of their lives at home.

We videotaped blocks of time in which each mother played informally with her child as well as other periods when we asked the mother to teach her child particular tasks. For example, we asked each mother to help her child learn to build a particular animal with Legos—small plastic interlocking blocks—and we asked her to help her child learn to assemble a particular puzzle we had brought along. The Lego blocks and puzzles for younger children were larger and less complex than those presented to the older children. The range enabled us to provide learning tasks that were appropriate to the children's various ages but offered sufficient challenge to place the mother and child in a situation in which they both had to stretch a bit. Finally, we ended the session by videorecording a cleanup period—each mother was asked to have her child help her put away the play toys.

We included these episodes of free-play, learning tasks, and cleanup because they represent, to varying degrees, situations that require interpersonal communication, cooperation, negotiation, and joint planning and problem solving between mother and child. Other researchers have found these settings particularly useful for identifying variations in patterns of family interaction.[5]

Translating meaning from hours of videotaped recordings can be extremely difficult. There are so many ways to consider the words and behaviors that transpire. We needed a framework for guiding the ways in which we observed the mother–child interaction and a structure for defining the important characteristics of the communication patterns. We adapted our coding scheme[6] from the Parent-Child Interaction (PCI) Observation Schedule originally developed by Jan Haugher and Irving Sigel (1980; see Appendix A). This approach analyzes the sorts of intellectual challenges that parents place on their children in the course of their interactions with them. The scheme records the degree to which a child is encouraged to become actively involved in mental interaction with the environment and the construction of knowledge.

For example, imagine three different mothers as each tries to help her child learn to build a house from blocks. There is a huge variety of strategies the mothers might adopt and each would engage a child in different ways. Think about Beth as she scoops the blocks into her own hands and says:

> Watch me; first put the large blue block here, then the orange blocks here, then these triangle blocks on top.

Picture Rhona, who places the blocks in front of the child and says:

> Why don't you put the biggest blocks on the bottom, the smaller ones next, and then see if you can find some blocks that are shaped like a roof for the top?

Or visualize Sara, who places a pile of blocks in front of her child and asks:

What kind of blocks would make the strongest basement for a
house? Why don't you start with those? How do you want to
build the side of the house? What goes on the top of the house?
What kinds of blocks would work best for the top? Why?

While these are only a few of the many strategies a mother might
adopt, it is clear that these approaches vary considerably in terms of the
intellectual involvement they encourage from the child. In the first
case, Beth calls for very little beyond rote memory or repetition. In the
second, through asking her child to analyze size and shape of blocks
and their relationship to parts of a house, Rhona demands more active
consideration of characteristics and relationships. Meanwhile, Sara, our
third example, engages her child even further, because she asks questions that encourage her child to speculate, analyze, compare, and evaluate. Therefore, Sara's questions put forth the greatest mental demands—drawing out her child's thinking and encouraging the
origination of ideas from the child. Moreover, if Sara is open to accepting her child's answers to her questions, the intellectual demands she
puts forth will be tailored to the child's level and should be stimulating
rather than a burden.

Of course, intellectual challenges, in and of themselves, are not always welcomed or useful, especially if they grossly and rigidly exceed
reasonable expectations for the individual. It is likely that if children are
repeatedly exposed to overly demanding activities, they will begin to
grow insecure and see themselves as incapable and inadequate. Meanwhile, situations that pose intellectual challenges on the leading edge of
the child's capability are beneficial in a host of ways. They provide opportunities for the child to "stretch," to experiment with emerging
abilities and exercise developing skills, to discover new possibilities and
affirm one's growth and potential for working and thinking through
new problems. Also, when these situations are presented in a supportive
context by family members and other acquaintances, they convey the
confidence that others have in the child's ability to extend and expand
to meet the new challenge. For these reasons, we were especially interested in looking for communication strategies that support high levels
of engagement by the child and nurture both growth and a sense of
potential.

Flaugher and Sigel (1980) have also made important distinctions among parents' "management" strategies with their children, that is, the ways in which parents direct their interactions with their children. Different management strategies engage the child in diverse ways and communicate distinct messages. For example, imagine a mother who wants her son to complete a puzzle. She might place her hand on his shoulder and say, "Stop talking and giggling now." With this child management strategy the mother tries to stop or change what she perceives to be "misbehavior" rather than an error in the task itself. Child management focuses on behaviors with little direct relation to the child's thinking or task. In contrast, task management strategies relate directly to accomplishing the task; for example, a parent might say, "Put the big piece here," "Look carefully at the differences between all the pieces before you select which one you want," or "What should the next step be?"

Child management strategies are more power oriented and less oriented toward strategy and problem solving—they are less clearly linked to the actual task at hand. They communicate that the child should obey the parent's directions because the parent is in control and has asserted her wishes; the parent holds power. Task management strategies convey a different message; they focus directly on the task. Although a child may not be pleased with being asked to change his or her behavior in either situation, task management strategies are more clearly oriented toward problem solving and achieving the task at hand rather than on disapproval of the child.

Confirming Our Hypotheses   As we have explained, we anticipated that mothers' epistemological perspectives would frame their beliefs about child development—their notions of how children learn and grow, the sorts of contacts and experiences that are important for this growth, and the role of adults, friends, and even the child in contributing to this development. We presumed that the women's personal theories of child development, in turn, shape their parenting behaviors, and their expectations, explanations, and interpretations of their children's behavior. Therefore, we expected to find strong relationships between mothers' epistemological perspectives and their beliefs about effective parent-child communications, as well as their actual interactions with their children during teaching and play.

Our research analyses confirmed our expectations. First, we discovered a strong relationship between mothers' epistemological perspectives and their beliefs about effective ways to communicate with children.[7] Silenced and received knowers, those with the least sense of power of their own minds and voices, were less likely than those with subjective outlooks to espouse strategies that encouraged children to think actively about the problem at hand and weigh alternatives for approaching the situation. Mothers with silenced and received perspectives were less likely to express the importance of providing children with information and explanations or to pose questions that draw the children into thinking through the problem.[8] In fact, not a single one of the women who expressed any silenced perspective endorsed primarily communications that draw out the thinking of the child and elaborate on reasoning and explanations. All but two of the fourteen silenced women exclusively endorsed highly authoritarian strategies as their dominant mode for communicating with children—placing little cognitive demand on the child and controlling through verbal threat or abuse, or physical manipulation of the child.[9]

Those mothers with a stronger sense of mind and voice placed more emphasis on providing children with explanations and alternative choices; they espoused strategies that draw children into a conversation about the situation and relevant options at hand so that the child will be an active intellectual participant in defining and constructing a response.

Our observations of mother-child teaching and play revealed similar findings. Mothers who expressed the least appreciation for their own minds and voices were the most likely to use child-management communication strategies that are power oriented and do not focus directly on the task at hand. In fact, mothers who expressed any silenced outlook used twice as many child management strategies as their peers; for example, they told their children, "Good kids don't fidget around," "Sit up straight," and they more often hit their children, physically restrained them as the children struggled to get away, or held their children's hands aside so that the mothers could manipulate the blocks.[10]

In the teaching tasks, we also found evidence that women with the least appreciation of their own minds and voices presented the fewest intellectual challenges to their children.[11] Silenced women were less likely to ask their children questions, talk through possible approaches and solutions, or raise alternatives for their children. We are reminded of Elizabeth, who went to the extreme of shutting off communication with her son altogether when she felt she was being challenged by him.

To summarize these quantitative analyses, mothers with a greater sense of their *own* powers of mind endorsed more cognitively demanding, nonauthoritarian, and nondirective parenting communication strategies—those that are more likely to draw children into active and reciprocal collaboration and problem solving. In addition, these mothers used more intellectually engaging statements and questions with their children, and focused less on controlling or restraining their children's behaviors in ways that were not clearly associated with the task.

MOTHERS' STORIES

To illustrate the relationships between women's beliefs about their own intellectual powers and their concepts of parenting and children, let us listen to a few of the women as they speak to us about themselves, their children, and their child-rearing strategies.

Susan: From Silenced   A woman we shall call Susan, like many others who are silenced, recalled a childhood with few friends or adult supporters, constant denigration, and little sense of ever having possessed, let alone spoken, her own mind. Barely clinging to the fringes of the social community, there is little opportunity to develop the skills or expectation to participate in dialogue. Susan described her childhood:

> I felt kind of dumb, very very. 'Cause for when I went to school, I was picked on for, [*sigh*] I don't know how long. Kids would say, "We don't want to play with you." You know, that kind of stuff. All the kids always picked on me . . . I felt dumb when I'd talk. You know, if I'd say something, it just didn't come out right. It just didn't sound right, and I felt like, oh, Susan, get out of here.

The lack of confidence in being able to pass meanings back and forth is profoundly isolating. The only kinds of learning projects that

Susan felt really competent to undertake involved knowing-in-action, unmediated by language. When asked how she would describe herself to herself as a learner or a thinker, Susan said:

> Well, I can cut hair but nobody's ever taught me. I can knit, I can make slippers, and I don't even know how to do it. I couldn't even tell somebody how to do it because I don't even know how to do it myself.

BUT YOU DO IT.

> Right. Well, um, I know how I do it but I couldn't tell you right now how to do it. You would have to watch me. Find out for yourself. Like cutting hair. People ask me, "How do you do it?" I say, "You have to watch me."

Susan describes her own son as having difficulties learning from others as well, and especially from their words:

> He's a very good kid but he has a problem on listening. He don't do nothing bad but I'm saying, say if I told him to stay on the side yard, like he'd adventure off a ways. I want to know where he is at all times. My older two, I know where they are; they have their boundaries too. They can't go out of the area [a small section of the whole yard]. . . . He knows what's gonna happen [if he disobeys], that he will be put in bed or be sit down. Well, if that don't work, then I have to spank him.

It appears that Susan does not ask or expect her son to learn or understand the reasoning behind the rules she imposes; she does not imagine that her five-year-old son can use relevant information to make appropriate judgments regarding reasonable behavior.

> I want to know where he is. There's a lot of things out here he could get hurt on that he's not aware of. A five-year-old, to me they're not aware of it. And I want to know where he is all the time until I feel he might be even older, until I feel he's capable of knowing right from wrong.

Asked about how she handles disagreements with her son, Susan states, "Um, if he's right, then he's right, but if he's wrong, then I have to take over, and I'll go, 'You did wrong,' 'You have to sit down,' or 'You have to give this back.'" Notably absent from Susan's descriptions of her child-rearing strategies are efforts to provide her son with explanations or rationales for the behaviors she expects, nor does she attempt to consider or explore her son's reasons for his behavior.

When we shared with Susan the story of a hypothetical four-year-old named Billy who was playing with blocks and began to throw them around the room when they wouldn't fit together,[12] Susan stated that the mother should direct the child to "pick them up . . . so that he'll realize he can't throw them around. . . . If he keeps throwing them, I just take them away." She tells us she would remove the toy, but she does not describe giving the child directions, explanations, or encouragement to work through his difficulties.

When Susan was videotaped teaching her five-year-old son to assemble an animal with interlocking Lego blocks, there was a striking absence of both verbal and physical interaction between mother and son. In fact, rather than enter into any apparent teaching relation with her son, Susan focused quite intently and exclusively on her *own* efforts to build with the blocks. Shortly after beginning the teaching session, Susan said to her son, "Let me try." She then took the blocks from him, yanked apart those he had struggled to clamp together, and resisted his attempts to manipulate the blocks with her, obstructing his view of her hands as she assembled the structure. Susan seemed relatively unaware of her child, except at several points when he approached her and reached for the blocks, only to have her push him away or twist in her seat so that he could not reach or even watch her maneuver the blocks. Throughout the entire period, Susan uttered literally only a few isolated, brief declarative statements (for example, "Hang on to it [a block]"; "Uh huh"). As it proceeds, the scenario becomes increasingly more painful to observe. Susan's son works to maneuver himself from behind to in front of his mother and to engage her in some sort of verbal or physical interaction. She responds to his efforts with silence and turning away. Eventually this five-year-old boy withdraws from his mother and retreats into silence himself.

Rachel: From Received Knowing   Rachel had a distinctly different perspective on herself. As we have seen from earlier discussions, Rachel originally described herself as able to gain knowledge from the words of others. When asked how she thought of herself as a thinker, Rachel said:

> Well, I can understand things if somebody explains it to me. . . . I know I can do good in school, but I got in the wrong crowd and started goofing off. I knew I could do good if I would have just stuck to it. The work and stuff I always understood. You know, I did good in my work and stuff.

But like other received knowers, Rachel saw herself acquiring knowledge from the words spoken by external authorities, not from the action of her own mind. In response to a question about the value of self-directed learning, Rachel replied:

> I don't think that's right. No. The teacher should be teaching you how to—what to learn and stuff. How can you learn on your own? You have to have somebody teaching you. The teachers have, you know, been to school and stuff so they know how to teach it.

This view that you have to learn from others, combined with a confidence in her own ability to learn from others, led Rachel to rely on explanations for educating children rather than punishment. Responding to the hypothetical scenario about the four-year-old who throws blocks when they won't fit together, Rachel responded:

> I'd explain to him that it wasn't right for him to throw it and tell him not to get so mad over it, to ask for help if he needs it, you know, and ask somebody to help him to do it instead of getting mad over it. I feel that you can teach a kid more by explaining to him why it's wrong than to hit him or something, than to holler at him.

Elsewhere in her first interview with us, Rachel described how she explains things to her own daughter; meanwhile, she did not present any images of drawing out her daughter's thoughts with good questions and mutual dialogue because she didn't imagine her daughter (or anyone else, including herself) as capable of active thinking and problem solving—of being a source of new ideas.

Rachel's first videotaped interaction with her five-year-old daughter fit within this received knowing framework. Unlike Susan, who assumed authoritarian physical control of the situation and the Lego blocks themselves, Rachel maintained control over the activity through verbal directions. Rachel drew her daughter into the building activity, but under the guidance of Rachel's very specific verbal instructions regarding which block to put where. The assumption seemed to be that her daughter could learn only from the transmission of specific, step-by-step instructions from her mother the expert. It is striking, however, that as the learning session neared completion, Rachel loosened her verbal grip on her daughter and began to include open-ended questions to guide the child's actions (for example, "Where does this go?" "Does that open?" "What goes in there?"). Perhaps Rachel felt her daughter had mastered certain block-building skills through her mother's instruction and was now ready to generalize these skills on her own.

Maureen: From Subjective Knowing   Over the course of our contact with Maureen, she had developed confidence and trust in her own inner voice. Like other subjective knowers, she had come to imagine and accept the existence of multiple and even contradictory truths—for Maureen, knowledge is lodged within the individual and arises from unique personal experience. Maureen had become accepting of the diversity of values, actions, and ideas she observes. She had come to value individuality of knowledge and truth. When there are disagreements, Maureen explained, "I just decide that everybody's different and I'm not gonna always agree." No longer preoccupied with conformity to rigid "rights" and "wrongs" or seeking approval from others, she also feels liberated from the judgment of others, and frequently refers to her pleasure and pride in being able to "stand up for myself" and "speak my mind" rather than depend on others' opinions. In fact, she is convinced that this stance earns her increased respect from others.

At the same time, like other subjective knowers, Maureen is not able to articulate procedures or strategies that she and others use to develop or test ideas—she does not consider knowledge to require or be available for testing. On the one hand, when asked to describe herself as a thinker, she said she is:

> Active. I think all the time. That's one of my favorite things to do at night, before I fall asleep, is to lay there and think or when I first wake up in the morning.

But she cannot describe what this thinking entails—the procedures she adopts, the processes to which she turns. Asked how she works through disagreements with others and, in particular, what goes on in her mind, Maureen explains that she simply turns to her "innate feelings" to figure out what's true.

Related themes emerged as we spoke with Maureen about the hypothetical situation in which Billy throws Lincoln Logs when he has difficulty piecing them together. Maureen emphasized how important it is for Billy to experience his thoughts and feelings in his own way; his mother should not guide his reflection. According to Maureen, Billy's mother should acknowledge and accept Billy's feelings as *he* sees them himself rather than try to describe or interpret them for him. Maureen cautioned:

> A lot of times you want to say, like, "I can see you're upset," but it doesn't work. You have to really try to see what the child is really feeling.

The regard for autonomy and individuality of experience is also striking when Maureen interacts with her own son Jacob. Asked to teach her son to build a figure with the Lego blocks, she placed the blocks squarely between Jacob and herself; unlike Susan's arrangement with her son, the blocks remained fully accessible to both Jacob and Maureen throughout the activity. Moreover, Maureen began the activity by inviting Jacob to suggest what to build, encouraging him to reflect and act on his own desires.

Soon we discover, however, that Maureen is not actually inviting Jacob to guide their *joint* interaction. Rather, she is encouraging him to chart his own course, independent of hers—to make decisions about what he will build from the Lego blocks, while she announces her plans to build a "man" from *her* blocks. Although Jacob makes several alternative suggestions for constructions—apparently trying to convince his mother to join him in a shared task—Maureen persists in announcing her plans to build a man, and then proceeds to work on her own. Finally, Jacob does likewise.

What follows is similar to the parallel play of young children—a laissez-faire approach in which both participants happily engage in their own activities, vaguely aware and supportive of the presence of the other, but uninvolved in the other's goals, procedures, or progress. Every once in a while, they chat with one another in a friendly way but without a common focus; both are idly speaking—essentially to themselves—about their own construction and progress. Actually, it is Jacob who intermittently watches his mother as she assembles her creation; Maureen does not reciprocate. Occasionally Maureen asks Jacob if she can have one of his blocks of a particular color, but she makes no attempt to engage him in her activity, or to monitor or encourage his construction.

When we inform Maureen that it is time to conclude the activity, she says, "Gee, do you mean I don't get to finish my man? [*laugh*] I've come all this ways [*laugh*]," and continues to assemble her blocks. What was introduced as a teaching task has been translated into an entirely individual and self-directed activity. Whereas Susan excludes her son from the building activity altogether and works alone in silence, Maureen welcomes her son as an active player but imagines parallel rather than mutually engaging activity; according to Maureen, creativity, knowledge, and potential are individual, subjective, and personal—not outcomes of interaction or collaboration.

Pam: From Procedural Knowing   Whereas subjective knowers attend to their own inner voices and imagine knowledge and ideas springing up from within, procedural knowers imagine themselves developing, analyzing, testing, and reconstructing opinions—discoverers rather than simply conduits of ideas who can also articulate some of the methods they use in the process of knowing. A woman we shall call Pam expressed some procedural perspective. For example, she explained:

> I think better when I talk, if that makes any sense. Just by talking
> about it. It's the feedback I get that brings up ideas in my head.

> Or it brings up certain feelings that tell me what I'm thinking about. . . . I can better come to a conclusion if I can talk to someone about it.

Not only does Pam imagine herself as an active participant in the thinking process, but she also regards the generation of ideas as a collaborative activity that benefits from dialogue. She points to the reciprocal ebb and flow of conversation to generate and clarify ideas.

When asked to comment on a statement made by another woman, "The student is giving her opinion. It might not be the right one. The teachers are always more or less right," Pam says:

> No, I disagree with that.

> BECAUSE?

> Because the teacher—a lot of times—makes up an opinion, states an opinion to get the students thinking—to get better feedback from the students.

Pam imagines the teacher manufacturing an argument to stimulate the student into active, independent thinking. She sees that conflict, disequilibrium, and good questions are powerful tools for drawing out embryonic thoughts.

When asked, "How do you go about understanding new things?" Pam replies, "I take on new ideas and things with a very open mind. You know, I try to see the good in it before I begin picking it apart for all the bad." Pam tries to embrace an idea before beginning its dissection, suggesting that she has begun developing some degree of both separate and connected procedural approaches. She also sees that both approaches can provide useful tools for sponsoring the development of ideas and the intellectual growth of others. While she recognizes the power of playing the devil's advocate for helping others clarify and develop their thoughts, she uses the connected approach when working with her four-year-old daughter, Alice; that is, she draws out her daughter's thinking, listens, and confirms rather than argues. Asked about the ways she and Alice handle disagreements, Pam says:

> We have to talk things out a little more than we used to. It used to be when we disagreed, Mommy was right and that was that. That

was the way it was, you know. Now, I have to let her voice her opinion. I have to listen to how she feels about things because she's thinking more on my level than on a four-year-old level, a lot of times. Not all the time, obviously, but a lot of times she sees it in a very logical way. A lot of times she can be right. She understands more than I think the average four-year-old kid understands.

Like Joyce, whom we heard from earlier in this chapter, Pam sees both herself and her child developing ideas through their conversations together. There is a sense of equality and reciprocity between this mother and child. Pam gets down to her daughter's level, and she sees her daughter rising up to hers. She listens to her child and appreciates the logic that she hears. When Pam describes her daughter, she sees the child's strengths, not the flaws:

Describe my daughter? Alice is a beautiful little girl; very bright. She enjoys spending time with people and talking with people. She loves books. She's got a load of energy that just doesn't seem to quit. Um, she's a mother hen. Things have got to be just so and she knows the right way for them to be. And if they're not the right way, she gets concerned about it. [laughs] She's a responsible child. A very responsible child. I'm starting to look at her more as a little kid than a baby. I realize that she's capable of doing things that, you know, that sometimes you don't become aware of and suddenly there it is. *You know, you realize that she's been doing it for two months. But you just haven't really noticed.* I'm letting her take on more little responsibilities and do the things that she wants to do. [emphasis added]

Pam reaches for a kind of double vision. She tries to bring her daughter's "growing edge" into focus, seeing Alice for what she is trying to become while also seeing her as she is at the moment. Pam realizes, as well, how difficult it can be to recognize something that is in the earliest stages of "becoming."

The videotaped interactions of Pam and her daughter are extraordinary. In contrast to Susan and Rachel, Pam is unconcerned with quickly and efficiently producing the animal we requested; her goal is to engage Alice in a shared, mutual activity. Pam begins by disassembling those Lego blocks that remain together from our previous session with another child, and she returns these blocks to the box so that Alice can take full control over selecting those she desires. Like Joyce, Pam's conversation is rich with questions followed by full pauses, a pattern that encourages her child to participate as a full partner: "Can we try to make him?" "Is that this part here?" "Can you get it?" Pam provides Alice with guidance, yet does so through questions that draw her daughter into the activity: "Now on the bottom of that we need what?" "Is that the one we need?" "And now what do we need to do on the top of his head?" Pam regularly refers to "we," suggesting that she truly sees the activity as coconstruction and shared problem solving with her daughter, a message that Joyce conveyed earlier.

In a step-by-step fashion, Pam orients her child through the task but slowly paces her guidance, allowing Alice to identify the next step and how to complete it. Daughter Alice performs all of the manipulation of the blocks; even when she runs into difficulty, Pam refrains from taking over physically or verbally, although she offers her assistance. At several points, we observe Pam begin to interject words or actions and then swallow her words or, in one instance, essentially sit on her hands, to refrain from taking over. Despite temptation to the contrary, Pam seems to value her daughter working through the problems herself as much as she is able. And as the session proceeds, Pam's communication becomes increasingly less directive, shifting even greater responsibility and credit for progress to Alice. At the conclusion, Pam invites Alice to compare her construction with the picture we had presented—Alice herself is called on to analyze their similarities and differences and, ultimately, to claim success for her accomplishment.

Summary

Our conversations, interviews, observations, and analyses have revealed an impressive relationship between, on the one hand, mothers' appreciation of their *own* powers of mind and voice and, on the other hand, their conceptions of child development and parent–child relations in both hypothetical and real interactions. A mother's understanding of her children, her expectations for her relationships with them, and her images of the role of these relationships in her children's development appear closely tied to the mother's broader understanding of human development including her own life course and the role of relationships therein.

We envision that bidirectional influences are important here, as portrayed in Figure 3.1 in Chapter 3. One's own sense of self, mind, and voice will frame one's understanding of both child development and the parent's role in supporting that development. These conceptions, in turn, will influence the parent–child transactions. On the other hand, a mother's beliefs and parent–child transactions contribute to establishing interactional contexts that reinforce and perpetuate the underlying assumptions. For example, not imagining the abilities of one's own mind and voice, a mother will be unlikely to draw on the minds and voices of others, including her children. This further limits opportunities for both her and her child to exercise, cultivate, and celebrate in the power of these personal and collective tools; it constrains possibilities for raising up one another, for supporting one another's growth of mind and voice. Conversely, a woman who perceives herself as a capable collaborator in the construction of knowledge will be more likely to engage her child in the active and collaborative creation of ideas; this, in turn, will contribute to a situation of reciprocity, collaboration, and support in which both mother and child are increasingly able to discover the powerful creations of which they are capable, and of which the *relationship* is capable.

PART 3

THE DEVELOPMENT OF VOICE IN PUBLIC LIFE

CHAPTER 6

PUBLIC HOMEPLACES

On the one hand, the quest has been deeply personal: that of a woman striving to affirm the feminine as wife, mother, and friend, while reaching, always reaching, beyond the limits imposed by the obligations of a woman's life. On the other hand, it has been in some sense deeply public as well: that of a person struggling to connect to the undertaking of education . . . to the making and remaking of a public space, a space of dialogue and possibility. . . . The aim is to find (or create) an authentic public space, that is, one in which diverse human beings can appear before one another as, to quote Hanna Arendt, "the best they know how to be." Such a space requires the provision of opportunities for the articulation of multiple perspectives in multiple idioms, out of which something common can be brought into being. It requires, as well, a consciousness of the normative as well as the possible: of what ought to be, from a moral and ethical point of view, and what is in the making, what might be in an always open world.

MAXINE GREENE (1988, P. XI)

Satisfied that the Listening Partners experience did enable a number of very isolated young mothers to gain a voice and claim the powers of mind, we wanted to continue exploring these issues. The next step, we thought, would be to look at well-established, successful, ongoing projects women have created for bringing an excluded group into voice and encouraging people to become fuller participants in community life. We thought that such a study would reveal important aspects of the work that could not be seen with a time-limited experiment like Listening Partners. We also believed that the study would reveal aspects of women's leadership that have gone unnoticed and unnamed.

Although the organizations selected for study were very dissimilar in many regards, they met the two criteria we required for participation:

155

(1) the organization was founded and is led by women who had reflected deeply on the experience of women and women's roles in society, and (2) the organization has as its primary mission the bringing of a marginalized group into voice. Personal testimony from scores of participants suggested that the organizations we selected were very successful in bringing an excluded group into voice. Indeed, these organizations nurtured the development of people and communities so well that we came to think of them as "public homeplaces."

THE ORGANIZATIONS

Four public homeplaces were selected for study. Two—the *Mothers' Center* movements in Germany and the United States—had nearly identical names and missions, although they were formed independently of one another. In both countries women decided to do something about the isolation and devaluation they were experiencing as mothers. Both movements developed a national network of Mothers' Centers where women could meet on a regular basis, supporting each other, and working together to make public spaces more responsive to the needs of women, children, and families. The endless array of local projects gives the women a good deal of hands-on experience; national networks encourage the women to view their work from a more global perspective. The combination has made a vivid impact on the lives of women in both countries.

A seed was planted for the third organization—the *National Congress of Neighborhood Women*—when an interracial, intercultural group of grassroots women created a neighborhood association to deal with some of the problems plaguing their divided and declining urban neighborhood in Brooklyn, New York, during the late 1960s. The women went on to build a wide variety of programs including one of the first shelters for battered women in the state of New York, a childcare program, and a center for the elderly. When the women realized that few of them had the credentials to fill the jobs they were developing, they created a college program located in the neighborhood and focused the curriculum on the rejuvenation of urban communities. Using their neighborhood association as a model for continued experimentation, the women teamed up with grassroots women from around the country who were engaged in similar efforts. This culturally and racially diverse group formed the National Congress of Neighborhood Women to support the leadership of grassroots women struggling to make their communities more responsive to the needs of women, families, and children. The Neighborhood Women are now extending this network to include women leaders from developing countries around the globe.

The fourth organization—the *Center for Cultural and Community Development*—grew out of the work of African American women from the Deep South who call themselves "cultural workers." They base themselves in a leadership tradition dedicated to drawing out and uplifting the community—a tradition that has been cultivated by black women since the middle passage and slavery times. The cultural workers foster all the arts and traditions of the African diaspora that strengthen and uplift. The cultural workers established the Center for Cultural and Community Development as a national network to support local leaders from different cultural groups who sponsor the development of people and communities denigrated and excluded by the larger society.

METHOD

Why have these public homeplaces been so enduring? Why have so many of their participants emerged powerfully voiced, speaking up for themselves and their communities? What has enabled these organizations to respond to diverse and changing needs while remaining quite cohesive and stable over long periods of time? How have they enabled their members to imagine that things could be different and then to develop the skills needed for realizing their dreams? Why have most been able to bridge vast differences of social class, ethnicity, age, and race so well? What accounts for the courage and strength of these women? In short, what enabled the founders of these organizations to establish such highly collaborative and creative learning environments? To answer these questions I, Mary Belenky, embarked on a new study. Although I took on the research and writing, I remained in close collaboration with Lynne, Jackie, and many others. First, I began spending time with each organization to see how their ideas were being played out in action. I took the subway to Brooklyn to visit the National Congress of Neighborhood Women. I interviewed the founder—Jan Peterson—and many other participants. I visited most of the community institutions and projects created by the neighborhood women. I traveled twice through the South with Jane Sapp, the founding director of the Center for Cultural and Community Development. Together we interviewed a number of African Americans who had been involved with cultural work over the years. I visited Mothers' Centers in the United States and interviewed two of the founders—Patsy Turrini and Lorri Slepian—and many other members, old and new. I traveled to Germany, where I interviewed the founders there—Monika Jaeckel and Hildegard Schoos—and visited centers in large cities as well as in smaller, more provincial towns.

The interviews with the founders helped me understand how each organization got started, how it evolved, and, most of all, the underlying philosophy that shaped its practices. I attended staff meetings, board meetings, workshops, institutes, and national conferences held by all of the organizations. I interviewed many groups of participants—the earliest as well as current members—to explore how they characterized these experiences and the impact of these events on the participants and their children, families, and communities.

Although some of the interviews were intimate, one-on-one conversations, most involved groups of people who had worked closely together. Experience with "focus group" interview techniques (Morgan, 1993) suggested that a collaborative, reflective process in small groups enables people to be unusually articulate about complex experiences they have shared. We found that to be our experience as well. During these discussions people probed the meaning of a transforming life experience in considerable depth. All of the interviews were transcribed so we could plumb the various meanings of these reflections and compare experiences across time and organizations for similarities and differences.

The interviews that were held with people who were involved with the organization in the early phases, decades ago, often turned out to be reunions—half interview and half celebration—because most had not met as a group for many years. Comparing their experiences with those of current participants, a remarkable continuity and stability of goals and practices in all of these organizations can be seen. Interestingly, many of the same goals and practices that have remained so important over time within each organization are similar to those that are shared across all of the organizations. As we will see in the concluding chapters of this book, these commonalities point to a philosophy and a set of key practices that sponsor the development of people who, in turn, go on to make their families and communities more nurturing places for others.

THE COMMONALITIES

All of these organizations began around the late 1960s and early 1970s with a very successful small local project that seemed worth developing as a model/laboratory. We link the two words *model* and *laboratory* because the model they started with always seemed open to experimentation and improvement. Each group continued to work year after year to elaborate and extend its model, gathering more people and more expertise as they went along. Each group became increasingly skilled at articulating the philosophy and practices of the kinds of leadership that have enabled them to create such nurturing environments. Each went on to build a national network that serves as a mutual support system for people all over the country who are trying to develop a version of the model in their local communities. Each has begun to travel the world, establishing international networks with people engaged in similar projects throughout Europe and a number of developing countries.

When measured by conventional standards, none of these organizations would be thought of as extraordinarily successful. They are relatively small, in terms of the numbers of people involved. With the exception of the German Mothers' Centers, all are chronically starved for funds. (European governments—unlike the United States—provide high levels of financial and programmatic support for families. In most European countries it is assumed that the development of children is as important to the nation as the development of industry, roads, and the military.)

These organizations are largely ignored or misunderstood by traditional leaders, the media, funding agencies, and the general public. There are many reasons for this invisibility. None have clearly and

narrowly defined objectives, target populations, and lines of authority—all of which are the mark of organizational success in the minds of
many. Organizations that are always evolving to meet the new needs of
people who are growing and changing can seem vague and uncertain
to anyone who does not appreciate a developmental perspective. Program officers from foundations and government agencies often tell the
African American cultural workers to narrow their focus and concentrate their efforts on well-defined "target populations." They do not understand that elevating the whole community is a goal of women's
leadership commonly found throughout the African diaspora.

Because the founders and leaders of these organizations adopt
maternal metaphors and language to describe themselves and their
work, they are often ignored. There seems to be a cultural blind spot
that leads people to dismiss outright anything associated with mothers
and mothering. It is the phenomenon that Barrie Thorne (1993) called
"girl stain" and Helen Haste (1994) called "metaphors of pollution."

Many simply assume that people who use maternal language are
members of the conservative right, trying to push all women back into
the most traditional of social roles. Mostly it seems that anything associated with mothering is ignored because mothering is seen as irrelevant
to public life. Modern technological societies are focused so intently on
generating commerce and profits that they have failed to evolve a common language for articulating civic enterprises that nurture human and
community development.

Outsiders also discount the women's claims that grassroots people
really do run the organization. There are several causes for this disbelief.
Hierarchical structures based on education and class are so common in
modern society that many find it difficult to imagine collaborative
processes that minimize these divisions. Socioeconomic status and intellectual performance are so strongly linked that many do not think it
is possible that people who function at a high level could have origi-
nated from the bottom rungs of society. Others assume that whatever a
person's roots are, once people do become educated and accomplished
they are a part of the middle class, even if they themselves maintain
their identity as members of the poor and working classes. Social mo-
bility is so highly valued in our society that many simply find it difficult
to imagine poor people voluntarily maintaining ties to their commu-

nity of origin once they have acquired the skills and resources that would enable them to move onward, upward, and out.

When funding agencies do see the importance of projects that sponsor human and community development, they are likely to provide resources for "a new and innovative project." Once the project is "tried and true," the funders move on. Once again the organizations must struggle with little or no institutional support. Needless to say, all of these organizations are likely to become increasingly stressed as the gap between "the haves" and "the have nots" continues to grow and the society withdraws more and more of the meager resources allocated in the past for supporting the growth and development of children, families, and communities.

LITERATURE THAT HELPED US FIND OUR WAY

While noneducational institutions dedicated to fostering the development of people silenced at the margins of society have no common name, we found a good deal of literature that helped us think about such organizations. Educational philosopher Maxine Greene (1988) calls such projects "authentic public spaces," while Sara Evans and Harry Boyte (1986), both political sociologists, use the label "free spaces" for organizations that enable people to learn a new self-respect, a deeper and more assertive group identity, public skills, and values of cooperation and civic virtue. Historian Aldon Morris (1984) says the civil rights movement grew out of these kinds of free spaces. He called them "movement half-way houses" because as organizations they had both public and private qualities. Emphasizing the importance of excluding controlling elites who might limit the group's ability to explore their situation, political sociologist William Gamson (1996) calls these forms "safe spaces."

In their study of people nominated as outstanding examples of moral leaders, developmental psychologists Ann Colby and William Damon (1992) seemed somewhat surprised to learn that the people they studied felt indebted for their own growth and development to organizations that intentionally sponsor the development of people and communities for their own growth and sustenance. Other developmental psychologists—Lawrence Parks Daloz, James Keen, Cheryl Keen, and Sharon Daloz Parks (1996)—were well aware of the importance of such communities before they embarked on a study of leaders highly committed to the common good. Indeed, a main goal of their study was to describe in detail the qualities of environments that nurtured the development of a sustained commitment to the common good. Selden Berman's (1997) extensive discussion of the role that educational environments can play in the development of social responsibility helps us understand why communities like these have had such a powerful impact on the development of their participants and on the society as a whole.

Gamson (1992, 1995, 1996) says these kinds of communities have been of utmost importance to people who have been cast as Other and excluded from society—sometimes through stereotyping that renders them invisible, sometimes through execution and genocide. Cultural critic bell hooks (1990) calls such communities "homeplaces" and explains why they have been so essential to the survival of African Americans:

> Black women resisted by making homes where all black people could strive to be subjects, not objects, where we could be affirmed in our minds and hearts despite poverty, hardship, and deprivation, where we could restore to ourselves the dignity denied us on the outside. . . . We could not learn to love or respect ourselves in the culture of white supremacy, on the outside; it was there on the inside, in that "homeplace," more often created and kept by black women, that we had the opportunity to grow and develop, to nurture our spirits. (p. 42)

This revisioning of both women's role and the ideal of "home" reveals the political commitment of black women to racial uplift, which was at the philosophical core of these resisters' dedication to community and home.

Ella Baker, a major figure in the civil rights movement and advisor to the Student Nonviolent Coordinating Committee (SNCC), also built organizations based on the ideals of a nurturing home (Baker, 1973; Cantarow, with O'Malley and Strom, 1980; Crawford, Rouse, and Woods, 1990; Grant, 1970, 1986; Omolade, 1994; Payne, 1989, 1995; Zinn, 1964). She thought of the movement as "the beloved community." Bernice

Reagon—one of the young students who worked with Ella Baker to create SNCC, SNCC's Freedom Singers, and some years later an all-women a cappella quintet, Sweet Honey in the Rock—describes how in the privacy of a nurturing "beloved community" people can free their imaginations and begin to see how the world *could* and *should* be organized. First and foremost, people must be free to have an extended dialogue among themselves without having to deal with the powerful "superordinates" who see them only as Others to be exploited and excluded.

> [T]hat space while it lasts should be a nurturing space where you sift out what people are saying about you and decide who you really are. And you take the time to try to construct within yourself and within your community who you would be if you were running society. In fact, in that little barred room where you check everybody at the door, you act out community. You pretend that your room is a world. It's almost like a play, and in some cases you actually grow food, you learn to have clean water, and all of that stuff, you just try to do it all. It's like, "If *I* was really running it, this is the way it would be." (Reagon, 1983, p. 358)

Pretending that the barred room is "the world" gives the excluded an opportunity to create a working model of a deeply moral society—a beloved community.

This kind of model building is of the greatest importance. Without a deeply experienced, well-articulated model of a beloved community, the best a subordinated people are likely to do is to impose a new pecking order on the old system. A subordinated people must have the experience of living in and creating a caring, generative community if they are to ever develop the vision and the skills necessary for transforming an unjust society. With solid experience of a beloved community behind them, people might be able to articulate the important ingredients of a more humane society well enough to build a version of it in a larger, more hostile environment. In this way, more and more people find themselves learning and teaching the form to others. When this happens the ripples radiate out through a society, just as a pebble tossed onto the water sets a pond in motion.

Evans and Boyte (1986) say that it is in the spaces between private and public life where people develop the freedom to gaze on old arrangements with a critical eye, dream of better ways, and actually build new models for living. Free spaces, they argue, are settings between private lives and large-scale institutions where ordinary citizens can act with dignity, independence, and vision.

To emphasize this bridge we decided to modify bell hooks's terminology and call groups of people organized to sponsor human development "public homeplaces." Without the word *public* we worried that those who draw a firm line between public and private life might think of homeplaces as serving only those with biological ties. This name seemed appropriate as the organizations we studied are public institutions dedicated to goals usually confined to women's work and private life—sponsoring the development of everyone, but most especially of the most vulnerable.

In the long list of names, "public homeplaces" keeps good company with Baker's "beloved community," Evans and Boyte's "free spaces," Gamson's "safe spaces," Greene's "authentic public spaces," hooks's "homeplaces," Mitchel's "half-way houses," and Reagon's "nurturing space." When a name is found that feels just right, more and more people will come to use it. Meanwhile, finding or inventing a common language that articulates an unnamed tradition seems to be a long and slow process. When a common language becomes available, it will help us get a better sense of how widespread this leadership tradition actually is—and has been.

METAPHORS AND CIVIC VIRTUES

In her book *Schoolhomes,* educational philosopher Jane Roland Martin (1992) envisioned educational communities where students are supported to develop self-respect, a deep sense of connection with others, the values of cooperation, and the other civic virtues embraced by the homeplace women. Believing also that these kinds of learning environments are built in the space between public and private life, Martin calls them "schoolhomes," joining "school" with the metaphor of "home." She says that schools, the child's first introduction to public life, should be organized around core values usually assigned to private life: care, concern, and connection. By bringing the values of home to the fore, Martin argues—as do we—that public institutions would be able to cultivate the civic virtues needed to sustain a more humane and democratic society. (See also Sharon Parks's [1989] discussion of "homeland pilgrimage," two other contrasting metaphors suggesting these ideas.)

Martin places her plea for schools as "a moral equivalent of home" alongside an appeal made by William James (1910/1970) in a celebrated essay titled, "The Moral Equivalent of War." Because modern warfare is so destructive, James argued, we need to construct other opportunities that are "the moral equivalent of war" if youth (that is, boys) are to continue developing the "martial virtues." His example: "All young men [would] be conscripted into an army and sent out as railroad men and miners, tunnel-makers and fishermen *to fight nature*" (Martin, 1992, p. 18. emphasis added). The "martial virtues" James wished to perpetuate include "intrepidity, contempt of softness, surrender of private interest obedience to command" (Martin, 1992, p. 17).

The psycholinguists George Lakoff and Mark Johnson (1980) say that the war metaphors like those venerated by James shape so much thinking in contemporary society that it is difficult to imagine a culture premised on a different notion:

> [It is difficult for us] to imagine a culture where arguments are not viewed in terms of war, where no one wins or loses, where there is no sense of attacking or defending, gaining or losing ground. Imagine a culture where an argument is viewed as a dance, the participants are seen as performers, and the goal is to perform in a balanced and aesthetically pleasing way. In such a culture, people would view arguments differently, experience them differently, carry them out differently, and talk about them differently. (pp. 4–5)

TWO OVERLAPPING CULTURES FOCUSED ON GROWTH AND DEVELOPMENT: WOMEN AND AFRICAN AMERICANS

Because of the almost universal division of labor based on gender (Bem, 1993), women everywhere create cultures intensely focused on promoting the development of people and communities—not warmaking. The themes that have emerged in the new findings in the psychology of women suggest this is the case: the ethic of care, as Carol Gilligan (1982/1993) would put it; self-in-relationships, as the Stone

Center group (Jordan, Kaplan, Miller, Stiver, and Surrey, 1991) describes; and the skills of connected knowing and midwife teaching, as delineated by the Ways of Knowing collaborative (Belenky, Clinchy, Goldberger, and Tarule, 1986/1997).

In her book, *Black Feminist Thought,* Patricia Hill Collins (1991a), professor of Afro-American studies, says similar themes reverberate throughout the African diaspora:

> Values and ideas Africanist scholars identify as characteristically "black" often bear remarkable resemblance to similar ideas claimed by [European American] feminist scholars as characteristically "female." (pp. 206–207)

Philosopher Sandra Harding (1986, p. 165) calls this similarity "a curious coincidence" and summarizes the overlap:

> Europeans and men are thought to conceptualize the self as autonomous, individualistic, self-interested, fundamentally isolated from other people and from nature, and threatened by these others unless the others are dominated by the self. . . . To Africans and women are attributed a concept of the self as dependent on others, as defined through relationships to others, as perceiving self-interest to lie in the welfare of the relational complex. Communities are . . . more fundamental than the persons that are individuated through their positions in the community. Nature and culture are inseparable, continuous. (p. 171)

Harding adds that contrasting ethics and epistemologies are said to follow:

> To Europeans and men are attributed ethics that emphasize rule-governed adjudication of competing rights between self-interested, autonomous others; and epistemologies that conceptualize the knower as fundamentally separated from the known, and the known as an autonomous "object" that can be controlled through dispassionate, impersonal, "hand and brain" manipulations and measures. To Africans and women are attributed ethics that emphasize responsibilities to increasing the welfare of social complexes through contextual, inductive, and tentative decision processes; and

epistemologies that conceptualize the knower as a part of the known, the known as affected by the process of coming to know, and that process as one which unites hand, brain, and heart. (p. 171)

Both cultures converge on the values and ways of thinking that would be central to any one focused quite specifically on sponsoring the development of people, families, and nurturing communities.

Many historical accounts show how black women's commitment to uplifting an entire people has permeated African American women's leadership for countless generations (for example, Brown, 1989, 1991; Collins, 1991a). Historian Gerda Lerner (1973) says the National Association of Colored Women's Clubs, an important organization that brought large numbers of women together at the turn of the century, reflected this understanding in their motto: "Lifting As You Climb." The historian Elsa Barkley Brown (1991) describes the tradition among a group of washerwomen early in the century:

[The washerwomen] took their laundry to the home of the woman with the largest kitchen. There they collectively scrubbed, rinsed, starched, ironed, and folded the pounds of laundry as they also talked. . . They created a community and a culture among themselves, turning what could have been a solitary act into a collective effort. . . . I came to understand the real connection between washerwomen and institutional development in the African American community. It was not merely the economic resources that the washerwomen wielded; I came to realize that those mornings spent scrubbing were also spent organizing. I discovered that a number of churches grew out of the discussions washerwomen had about the need for a place of worship in their own neighborhood; schools and recreational centers also had similar origins. When these women moved into developing mutual benefit societies and their affiliates, it was with clear planning and organizational skills that they had developed over the washtub—it was with a commitment to each other which had been born in mounds of suds. And so it was clear why and how it was washerwomen and washerwomen's daughters who organized . . . one of the most successful and prominent mutual benefit societies of the early twentieth century. They had the skills and they had long before dreamed the dreams and laid the plans together. And when they moved from there to organize a bank and a department store, and then to dream of beginning a factory, it was with the assurance and the skills that came from already having been entrepreneurs. (pp. 83–84)

Brown (1991) cites a study conducted by Carter Woodson (1930) in the 1920s that described in very similar terms the leadership that emerged from another community of black washerwomen. She says mainstream scholars dismissed Woodson's study as sentimental because they were unable to imagine black women capable of such feats.

To communicate black women's focus on the uplift of the community rather than the assertion of individual rights, Alice Walker (1983) replaces the word *feminist* with *womanist*. Although a womanist, she says, "appreciates and prefers women's culture, women's emotional flexibility . . . and women's strength, . . . [she is] committed to [the] survival and wholeness of [an] entire people, male *and* female" (p. xi).

Black studies scholar Patricia Hill Collins (1991a) says leaders committed to uplifting the most vulnerable members of the community have been crucial to the survival of African Americans. She calls women leaders of this sort "community othermothers." Her definition is as follows:

> Community othermothers work on behalf of the Black community by expressing ethics of caring and personal accountability which embrace conceptions of power and mutuality. . . . Such power is transformative in that Black women's relationship with children and other vulnerable community members is not intended to dominate or control. Rather, its purpose is to bring people along, to—in the words of late-nineteenth-century Black feminists—"uplift the race" so that vulnerable members of the community will be able to attain the self-reliance and independence essential for resistance. (pp. 131–132)

Collins says that the cultural traditions of community leaders who treat biologically unrelated people as if they were members of one's own family provide a foundation for black women's political activism that is little understood in the broader society.

In his definitive history of the struggle for civil rights in Mississippi, Charles Payne (1989, 1995) sees the kind of leadership described by Brown, hooks, Collins, and Walker as one of two distinct leadership traditions of black folk living in the rural South. It is, Payne says, a tradition that is seldom named and discussed by historians (or anyone else, we might add). The more commonly recognized leadership tradition, he says, is that of the articulate, charismatic leader who is likely to head the church and other important community institutions. Charismatic leaders, Payne says, are generally male, well educated, and ministerial; they lean toward the authoritarian. In this tradition the leader is a shepherd; the followers are gathered into the fold. He points to the Rev. Dr. Martin Luther King, Jr., as the outstanding example of a civil rights leader operating out of this tradition.

Leaders from the less understood developmental tradition, Payne (1995) says, are more often women with less education and little or no institutional support. They are not so interested in mobilizing followers as they are in supporting the oppressed to develop their own leadership capacities. (See also Moses, Kamii, Swap, and Howard, 1989; Payne, 1989; Reagon and Sweet Honey in the Rock, 1993; Seeger and Reiser, 1989.)

Payne (1995) believes that leaders like Ella Baker were successful in reaching people in the most oppressed areas of the segregated South because they created environments where people and their thinking could grow. They made personal connections, cutting through stereotypes and seeing people's human qualities and strengths. Rather than directing their "followers" as traditional leaders do, these leaders ask good questions and draw out a people's thinking so they can find their own direction. Leaders from the less understood tradition are not so interested in mobilizing followers as they are in supporting oppressed people to develop their own leadership capacities. They are, in Patricia Hill Collins's terms, community othermothers who uplift their neighbors by supporting their development as full human beings.

Payne (1995) says that charismatic leaders are likely to be well supported by the social institutions they head whereas developmentally oriented leaders seldom have institutional backing. More often than not, they work on a voluntary basis without titles and salaries. They are likely to be working class, rural, and female. They draw their strength from their folk culture, re-creating the spirit of the nurturing, self-sufficient, egalitarian families and communities in which they grew up.

> [They bring] back to the rural Black South a refined, codified version of something that had begun there, an expression of the historical vision of ex-slaves, men and women who understood that, for them, maintaining a deep sense of community was itself an act of resistance. (p. 405)

Payne says that most historical accounts of the civil rights era see charismatic leaders like the Rev. Dr. Martin Luther King, Jr., as the movers of the movement; the developmental leaders have been largely lost to history. Payne suggests their invisibility stems from the fact that most of these leaders were women, and that their goals were too long term and not well understood. Historians were more drawn to record the dramatic and dangerous events that coalesced around the charismatic men who more easily fit Western definitions of leadership.

Payne argues that it was actually the developmental leaders, not the charismatic leaders, who developed the infrastructure that upheld the movement when it finally came through the Black Belt into Mississippi. Without the support from leaders who focused on development, Payne questions how it would have been "possible, within a few years, to move large numbers of dependent and, to all appearances, apolitical people—none of them having any semblance of legal rights at the local level, all of them vulnerable to violence—. . . to a position of actively working to change the conditions of their own lives" (1995, p. 2).

We detail the work of both Ella Baker and Septima Clark, two of the exemplars among developmentally oriented civil rights leaders to whom Payne calls attention. We choose Baker and Clark because their stories helped us see the shape of this leadership paradigm with unusual clarity (Baker, 1973; Cantarow, with O'Malley and Strom, 1980; Clark, 1990; Crawford, Rouse, and Woods, 1990; Forman, 1972; Grant, 1970, 1986; McFadden, 1993; Morris, 1984; Omolade, 1994; Payne, 1989, 1995; Ransby, 1993; Zinn, 1964).

In the early 1950s Ella Baker cofounded an organization called "In Friendship," setting a pattern for all of her subsequent work. In Friendship identified and supported people who were risking their lives to uplift black communities in the Deep South. At that time such people were faced with intense and violent opposition from white Southerners while people throughout the nation averted their eyes. In Friendship supplied these local activists with a whole range of financial and moral support that enabled them to continue developing their leadership in their own community. The organization also linked people working on a local level with others around the country, enabling them to gain a larger perspective on the work they were doing. Without this organization, Payne says, most of these early activists would not have survived to lay the foundations for the movement in the 1960s.

Ella Baker was later appointed as the first executive director of the Southern Christian Leadership Conference (SCLC), an organization firmly rooted in the charismatic tradition exemplified by its founder—the Rev. Dr. Martin Luther King, Jr. Baker struggled to get the SCLC to make a bigger investment in developing the leadership of youth and the poorest people living in the Deep South. The organization ignored her pleas and continued to focus on developing the leadership of the clergy and its charismatic leader, the Rev. Dr. Martin Luther King, Jr. Miss Baker felt her views were discounted for two reasons: she was a woman and she thought it was important to draw out the leadership of people at the bottom of the social-political hierarchy. That approach simply did not register with the clergy focused on cultivating a devoted following.

Later Ella Baker would play a key role in the development of the Student Nonviolent Coordinating Committee (SNCC)—an organization devoted to the goals that the ministers in SCLC did not seem to understand: developing the leadership of youth living in the poorest and most oppressed regions in the South as well as more privileged young people from across the nation. It was SNCC—not SCLC—that finally galvanized the movement in areas of the Black Belt that the older, more established civil rights organizations saw as too resistant and too dangerous to organize.

Following the example set by In Friendship, the young people in SNCC identified potential leaders in local communities and supported them to take the lead in their community's quest for social justice. SNCC also brought these people into a national network with others who shared their overriding goals. As SNCC provided these supports, the people's vision of what was possible grew and the movement took off. Generations of pent-up aspirations came spilling out. Even though white resistance stiffened as never before, the civil rights movement was able to transform the social order.

Septima Clark founded Citizenship Schools throughout the South to support blacks who wished to register to vote. In the process she enrolled a large percentage of rural blacks in the civil rights movement. At that time, getting on the voters' list was a difficult and humiliating process for all blacks, but particularly for those with limited literacy skills. In some communities it was extraordinarily dangerous to even try to register. In Clark's mind the overriding goal of the Citizenship Schools was not so much to attain literacy and voter registration but to discover and develop local leadership. She would engage the most respected informal leaders in an area to run the schools, supporting them to become teachers/coaches who, in turn, would draw out the leadership potential of their neighbors. Clark's intention was the same as Ella Baker's: to broaden the scope of democracy to include everybody and to deepen the concept by including every type of relationship. Looking back on this effort some twenty years later, Clark writes,

> Even with [intense] harassment, the Citizenship Schools really got into full force. . . . In 1964 there were 195 going at one time. They were in people's kitchens, in beauty parlors, and under trees in the summertime. . . . The Citizen School classes formed the grassroot basis of new statewide political organizations in South Carolina, Georgia, and Mississippi. From one end of the South to the other, if you look at the black elected officials and the political leaders, you find people who had their first involvement in the training program of the Citizenship School. (1990, pp. 69–70)

Septima Clark founded the citizenship schools while she was on the staff of the Highlander Folk School (now called the Highlander Center for Research and Education), but moved her base of operations to Southern Christian Leadership Conference (SCLC) headquarters when it became clear that the local authorities would soon close down Highlander and jail its leaders or run them out of town (Clark, 1990; Payne, 1995).

Like Baker, Clark felt that her philosophy was neither well understood nor shared by the staff at SCLC. Clark says,

> I sent a letter to Dr King asking him not to lead all the marches him-
> self, but instead to develop leaders who could lead their own
> marches. Dr. King read that letter before the staff. It just tickled them;
> they just laughed. . . . I thought that you develop leaders as you go
> along, and as you develop these people let them show forth their
> development by leading. That was my feeling, but that was too much
> for them. They didn't feel as if that should be. (1990, pp. 77–78)

Although she wasn't so conscious of gender at the time, Clark
now realizes that SCLC had as little interest in developing women's
leadership as they had in developing the leadership of the poor:

> I think that there is something among the Kings that makes them
> feel that they are the kings, and so you don't have a right to speak.
> You can work behind the scenes all you want. That's all right. But
> don't come forth and try to lead. That's not the kind of thing they
> want. (1990, p. 73)

Payne (1995) summarizes the characteristics of the civil rights
leaders who worked out of the developmental tradition:

> [They were] insistent on the right of people to have a voice in the
> decisions affecting their lives, confident in the potential of ordi-
> nary men and women to develop the capacity to do that effec-
> tively, skeptical of top-down organizations, the people who led
> them, and the egotism that [form of] leadership frequently engen-
> dered. Therefore, they were committed to participatory political
> forms because people develop by participating, not by being lec-
> tured to or told what to do. They all thought that if one worked
> on "local" problems with an open mind, one was likely to learn
> that the roots of those problems lay elsewhere. They all liked to
> think of themselves as non-dogmatic, able to hold strong beliefs
> while open to learning from new experiences. (p. 101)

While these leaders were passionately centered in strong moral
beliefs, they were always questioning and open to new learning. They
encouraged people to look on their projects as experiments that could
be studied and improved upon. This "let's try it and see" attitude helped
people feel freer to make mistakes and try again. (A mother from the

Listening Partners project called this kind of approach "exploreamentive.") The people kept trying until they found themselves overcoming obstacles that many assumed were insurmountable. Payne thought it was the exploratory and participatory process of thinking everything through for themselves that enabled people to withstand the violence of the opposition they faced. Recently the educator Mike Rose (1995) traveled through Mississippi studying schools that educate poor black children to become powerful, articulate thinkers. He heard kids belting out a rap song about Septima Clark: "a mother to my nation/she taught my ancestors so they could control their destination" (p. 308).

Payne's description of developmental leaders fits both the African American and the European American homeplace founders we studied remarkably well. It is of great interest to us that many other studies of outstanding leaders committed to the common good also exhibit these same paradoxical qualities: a steadfast commitment to deeply held principles while continually reexamining old ideas and experimenting with new ones in the most collaborative fashion. (See, for instance, Berman, 1997; Colby and Damon, 1992; Daloz, Keen, Keen, and Parks, 1996; Oliner and Oliner, 1988.)

INVENTING AND REINVENTING THE TRADITION

Payne (1995) argues that leadership oriented to development is characteristic of folk cultures in general. Payne supports his assertion by pointing to the developmental leader Myles Horton, the founder of the Highlander Folk School. Horton is the only leader from the white community who worked in the civil rights movement that Payne holds up as an exemplar of the developmental tradition of leadership. Horton grew up in great poverty among white folk in one of the tiny hill communities of the Appalachian Mountains. During the Great Depression he established Highlander as a school dedicated to the empowerment of grassroots peoples. Like Ella Baker and Septima Clark, Horton rejected the notion of elites coming into poor communities and leading the way. Instead, Highlander brought grassroots people together and supported them to develop their own leadership. Before the civil rights movement brought down the practice of segregation, Highlander was one of the very few public spaces in the South where people from different races could meet as equals. (See Adams, with Horton, 1975; Horton, 1990.)

While Payne sees Horton's development as an educator/leader as an outgrowth of his folk heritage, Horton (1990) himself credits opportunities to study with some of the most innovative thinkers of his time. As a young man he had scholarships to study at several of the nation's great universities. He obtained a grant and traveled to Denmark to study the folk school movement. Many believed it was the folk schools that had enabled the Danes to move so quickly from a feudal order to a well-functioning democracy. (For a history of the folk school movement and its effects, see Borish, 1991.)

Horton also spent a good deal of time in Chicago with Jane Addams and others who were applying similar ideas being developed by John Dewey and George Herbert Mead to the education of adults living on the edges of society. Addams thought that dramatic alterations in an unjust society could be accomplished by providing a nurturing meeting place where two very different groups—educated women and impoverished immigrants—could grapple together with the problems facing the city of Chicago at the beginning of the twentieth century. Both groups were extremely marginal to the political process at that time. Women were denied the right to vote and speak in public forums; immigrants were facing the devastating effects of industrialization and urbanization in a strange and unwelcoming society (Addams, 1965; see also Deegan, 1988; Hayden, 1984; Lagemann, 1985; Leibowitz, 1989; Muncy, 1991; Seigfried, 1996).

Addams, like Dewey, was confident in the ability of ordinary men and women to participate in a democratic process; they would develop a far more humane city than the current leaders who had little regard for most of the city's residents. Addams picked the most stressed area of Chicago and built a place she called Hull House. A large group of educated women moved in They opened the doors of their home to the immigrants living in the neighborhood as well as to visitors like Myles Horton, interested in the development of a more just society. Both groups worked together studying the problems facing their community, making art that reflected on and communicated the condition of their lives, and carrying out one action project after another to address the problems they had identified. Addams, like Dewey, saw education based on this kind of community involvement as a form of liberation. When people take responsibility for governing their communities, they learn to understand complex issues, to articulate their dreams, and to back up their positions well; the society becomes a more democratic and life-enhancing place for everyone.

Hull House began what came to be known as the settlement house movement in the United States. The movement established public homeplaces in cities across the nation, supporting immigrants from all corners of the globe to work together on the issues they were facing as Others—blamed for many of the nation's ills.

Whereas the generation of African American women that participated in the public homeplace study also had opportunities to travel and study, their mentors seldom had had such options. The oldest of the lot, women born into slavery, would have broken the law by learning to read and write. No one gave poor rural Southern black women of Horton's generation generous scholarships to attend the nation's great universities. Indeed, they would have been barred from most, even if they themselves could pay the full tuition. Even so, African American women have been evolving since slavery times a tradition of developmental leadership that has many similarities to the approach to education and to participatory action-oriented research that Myles Horton learned from the Danish folk schools, Jane Addams, and the Hull House women early in the century.

Ella's Daughters

Barbara Omolade (1994), the educator and activist leader who called black women's leadership oriented to development "a tradition that has no name," says that she has been well trained in the tradition. This training began in earnest when she left college to join the civil rights movement, enlisted in SNCC, and apprenticed herself to Ella Baker. She said SNCC and Ella Baker provided a laboratory where she and many others could learn to address social problems within a democratic organization of rich and poor:

> Bringing white and Black college students into SNCC enabled
> Ella Baker to influence and train leaders who became part of

national movements promoting changes [in and beyond the
Black community]. . . . The white men she mothered brought
the New Left Movement into being. The white women she
mothered in the movement inspired others, creating second-wave
feminism. . . . Her Black daughters combined and took from feminism, nationalism and the New Left, adding their own unique
notions, to birth womanism. (p. 165)

Bernice Reagon (Reagon and Sweet Honey in the Rock, 1993),
one of the many whom Ella Baker mothered, described the nature of
Baker's leadership and teaching:

Ella Baker believed in young people. . . . As a leader [Miss Baker]
was strong, powerful. She would speak out; she would lead and be
in front. But she also led by the way she listened and questioned.
In her presence you got the feeling that what you felt inside made
sense and could be offered up to the group for discussion as policy
or strategy. Miss Baker put nothing in front of teaching others to
organize for themselves. She urged us as organizers to understand
how to create structures that allowed others in our group to also
be leaders as well as followers. (pp. 21–22)

Summing up Baker's life, Barbara Ransby (1993) writes:

Ella Baker was, above all, a bridge connecting young people to
their elders, northerners to southerners, Black people to white
people, and intellectuals to common folk in a web of organizational and personal relationships. Moreover, she was a historical
bridge connecting the social movements of the 1950s and 1960s
to the legacy of Black resistance and social protest in the decades
that followed. (p. 74)

Reiterating the same idea, Barbara Omolade (1994) says that the
social movements that blossomed during the 1960s and 1970s were
rooted in the apprenticeships with Ella Baker that she and many others
held during the civil rights movement. It was here that so many new
leaders learned how to create structures that allowed others to be leaders as well as followers. They are all, she says, Ella's children. (For a detailed history of these links, see Evans, 1979, 1989.)

As we will see, the founders of the public homeplaces we studied were also among Ella's many daughters. Each had participated in civil rights groups and/or women's organizations that sponsored action projects on the local level. The women portray these projects as highly collaborative endeavors that grew out of the group's sustained analysis of the situation. Each learned from their movement experience the importance of creating a "beloved community," like the model that Ella Baker and her many colleagues nurtured throughout the civil rights movement.

Public leadership devoted to promoting the development of the most vulnerable members of society arises in many cultures and eras. Even so, its appearance is so intermittent it is a tradition that needs to be reinvented time and time again. As we have seen, African American women have carried on the tradition since slavery times. Jane Addams, the Hull House women, and their allies in the neighborhood cultivated the form at the turn of the century. The Mothers of the Plaza de Mayo reinvented the form more recently in Argentina. With the "disappearance" (a euphemism for execution) of their politically active children, the Mothers turned their private despair into a public force. They created a free space that enabled poor and working-class women to resist, openly and successfully, one of the more brutal dictatorships to occur in our hemisphere in modern times. In an extensive study of the Mothers' philosophy and practices, the poet Marguerite Guzman Bouvard (1994) says these women were able to mount such a powerful, persistent, and effective force against this brutal dictatorship precisely because they infused their politics with maternal values. Their practice of nurturing development, pacifism, cooperation, and mutual love revealed the military values of hierarchy, obedience, and the unchecked use of physical force so clearly that the Argentinean people could no longer stand back in silence.

The developmental approach to leadership evolves in urban neighborhoods, in religious communities, and in great universities as well as in rural folk cultures. The only requirement is that people think carefully about the processes involved in homemaking and the raising up of young people and those silenced as Other to become fuller participants in a more deeply democratic and caring society.

Women's ability to raise up people (whether in private or public homeplaces) is not inherited. It is cultivated through continuous reflection on highly valued work in a subculture where the ideas can be discussed, tested, consolidated, and taught to the next generation.

The study of the philosophy and practices common to this diverse group of homeplace women reveals an approach to public leadership that is rooted in maternal practice and maternal thought. Because this way of thinking, as Sara Ruddick (1994) suggested, is so far beyond "normal ways of thinking," this tradition of leadership has gone unnamed; its philosophy and practices are seldom acknowledged and articulated. Because the approach is seldom taught in a systematic way, it is a tradition that has to be continually invented and reinvented.

The homeplace women have worked hard to cultivate the developmental approach, to articulate its philosophy and practices, and to school others in its methods because they also feel a great urgency to transform the more "normal ways of thinking." The following chapters lay out the history, goals, and structure of the four public homeplaces we studied, describing the common visions and root metaphors that have shaped these organizations. Mostly we concentrate on the genesis stories, as the same processes that gave birth to these organizations have nurtured their development from beginning to end. We conclude our story with a discussion of the philosophy and practices of the kind of leadership that has made public homeplaces such powerful sources of personal and civic renewal.

◈ CHAPTER 7 ◈

THE MOTHERS' CENTER MOVEMENTS

We wanted to create a public space where women would be able to reflect on what it means to be a mother. There is no space in society for this.

HILDEGARD SCHOOS
FOUNDER, THE MOTHERS' CENTER, GERMANY

Mothers need a place where they can give voice to what they need and have that voice validated.

PATSY TURRINI
FOUNDER, THE MOTHERS' CENTER, UNITED STATES

In technologically advanced societies mothers who work full-time in the home have become increasingly isolated and excluded. More than ever, women raising children are likely to feel like an Other—left out and deficient. While some sense of exclusion is felt by most mothers, the experience has been particularly intense for the many women who try to raise children outside of any real community: affluent mothers living in suburban areas whose most intimate community facility might be the shopping mall, urban mothers bringing up children in anonymous buildings often set in violent and deteriorating neighborhoods, mothers living in rural areas depopulated and demoralized by the waning of an agrarian way of life. Now that so many women are in the professions, any woman who leaves to raise children is likely to feel her status in society slipping away. When she meets former colleagues, she often finds eyes glazing over and the conversations stilted. In the United States, government programs and policies can be destructive to poor families. Under some circumstances a father must abandon the family before the government will provide economic assistance for his children. The women are then stigmatized as single mothers and by their dependency on public welfare.

180

Many modern nations have witnessed the proliferation of centers designed to serve mothers and families coping with these strains. For the most part, these centers have been developed by women to meet the needs of women and their families. Most often they are called family centers, parent centers, or parent–child centers hoping to support fathers as family caregivers as well as mothers. Some centers provide a range of traditional social services for families under stress. Others are most concerned with ameliorating the social isolation, self-devaluation, and sense of powerlessness experienced by mothers so they might become a united force for social change. Some, like the Lamoille Family Center in Vermont that hosted the Listening Partners project, provide both kinds of programs. A recent study by Ann Rath (1995) traces the impact that family centers in Ireland are having on the lives of poor Irish women. Not only are the women supported to improve their personal and family situations, but a remarkable number have gone on to become leaders in their communities. This is the first widespread effort in that country to bring the voice of grassroots women into the public arena.

We selected for study two groups that are a part of this broader trend—the Mothers' Center movements in the United States and Germany. Of all the groups we studied, the Mothers' Center movements have been the most flamboyant in embracing motherist values and rhetoric. Mothers' Centers were launched in both countries by women who wanted to do something about the social isolation and devaluation of mothers ghettoized in the private world of the family. They would bring the voice of mothers into the larger arena by creating supportive public spaces that honor the values, knowledge, and art that women have always cultivated in the private world of home.

In the United States, Mothers' Centers are mostly located in middle-class suburbs and serve a fairly homogeneous population. The lack of funding available for such projects in the United States has made it difficult for this movement to have a broad reach. Because there are few suburbs in Europe, German Mothers' Centers are set in towns and cities where they are geographically accessible to families from all socioeconomic classes. The generous funding in Germany for families themselves and for programs that support families has enabled the German movement to develop programs that support women from all walks of life. Mothers' Centers have spread throughout Germany including through the newly annexed states in the East. There they help mothers adapt to the rapidly changing social conditions brought about by the dissolution of the German Democratic Republic and the Soviet Union.

Although there are important differences between the German and U.S. versions of the Mothers' Center movement, there have been many similarities from the beginning. Both decided to call their projects Mothers' Centers rather than taking a more inclusive name like family centers or parent centers. That brought widespread disapproval in their respective countries. Some criticized them for focusing on the needs of mothers rather than on those of children or the whole family. Some feminists charged that the name reinforces traditional values and harms the cause of women.

The decision to retain the language of mothering has been a very costly decision for the Mothers' Center movement, especially in the United States. American funders from both the public and private sectors have made it clear that monies will not be forthcoming unless the women adopt more gender neutral language like family centers or parent centers. The Mothers' Center women refuse, noting that projects for men raising children are readily funded even though terms such as *parent* are seldom used as a substitute for *father*. The women also note that the available literature on adults raising children is almost always based on women's experiences. In these writings maternal language referring to women's child-rearing activities is often avoided in favor of gender-neutral terms like *parent*. On the rare occasions when authors write about men similarly engaged, they almost always present the men as *fathers,* not as *parents.*

Mothers' Center women on both sides of the Atlantic remain steadfastly committed to the use of maternal language and metaphors. Because many of the women feel they have been excluded and discriminated against precisely because they are mothers, they reject the constant exhortations to use gender-neutral terms like *parenting.* They say the avoidance of maternal language is a good example of "girl stain." As Hildegard Schoos, one of the founders of the German movement, said,

"Mother" is a devalued word in most modern societies. It also has fascist connotations in Germany. Here it is a taboo word. In the Nazi time mothers were only good for giving birth to soldiers. Women supported men so they would be more capable killing machines. Women had no value in their own right, only their products were valued. In themselves, women were nothing. Many accuse the Mothers' Center movement of perpetuating this view. No. We want to bring the values of mothers into the middle of public life. We are not interested in producing soldiers, but in promoting the development of full peoples. Not killing machines.

Following a pattern common to other groups who have decided to resist stigmatization and marginalization, the women from the Mothers' Center movement place symbols naming their Otherness at the center of their identity. As women invested in the demeaned activities of raising children, they insist on being known as "mother," just as some people abhorred for the color of their skin proudly name themselves "black," and some gay men and lesbians authorize themselves as "queers." A group of menopausal women call their basketball team the "Hot Flashes." A community of Canadian women, long active in the peace movement, realized that the older they got the less they were being heard. They adopted "Raging Grannies" as a name, donned nineteenth-century dress, and took to the streets. Their songs and speeches now get excellent press (McLaren and Brown, 1993).

The Mothers' Center women say that when they are deeply engaged in the work of raising children they feel like mothers; the language of parenting just does not name their experience well. The women find that the analysis of their work as mothers is greatly inhibited by the use of gender-neutral language. They say that when they try to avoid the language of mothering they simply cannot reflect on themselves and the conditions of their lives as well as they might. Sara Ruddick (1994) makes a similar point in her book *Maternal Thinking*.

The women on both shores reject the notion that the Mothers' Centers reinforce traditional roles that have kept women subordinated. Instead, they argue that the opportunity to participate in a warm, caring, democratic space in the public domain enables women to develop exactly the kinds of skills needed for democratizing their homes. Women from both movements go further and argue that a more democratic society will be achieved when and only when that spirit radiates throughout most of the homes in a nation. A more deeply democratic society is the ultimate goal for many women involved in the Mothers' Center movement here and abroad.

The U.S. Movement

The U.S. Mothers' Centers began on Long Island, New York, when social worker Patsy Turrini and several associates decided to do something about the isolation of mothers in their community. Speaking from her own experience, Patsy described the problem:

> I experienced terrible feelings of inadequacy when I could not understand or act with certainty with my new infant. My fully-prepared-for-motherhood mental image of myself (I was a social worker, I'd read, I'd taken all of the courses) was in complete contradiction to the uncertainty. And then there was my isolation: no job, no neighbors, no mother nearby, and no place to find out what this new mother experience was about. With the awareness of these feelings I began to hear clients and friends speaking about the stresses of mothering in a new way. (Zimmerman, 1980, p. 1)

Patsy and her colleagues believed if more were known about mothers, they would be better supported by the community and its various institutions. In 1972, Patsy and her colleagues designed an interview study of mothers. They received support for the research from a local Mental Health Center where Patsy worked as a clinical social worker. The research goal was to lessen the isolation of mothers and help the women and the community think more carefully about the needs of mothers in contemporary society.

They would invite new mothers to share their knowledge about early mothering in a series of group discussions that would take place over a six-week period. The children would participate in a well-run play group while the mothers talked. To guide these discussions the women created a postnatal questionnaire with carefully developed questions on all aspects of pregnancy, childbirth, and the care of infants.

The questions would encourage the women to explore their individual and collective experiences in considerable depth. Although a similar format was used by many women's consciousness-raising groups of the sixties and early seventies, it was rare at that time for researchers to take such an approach. More recently, the mode has become quite common. It goes under the rubric of focus group interviews (Morgan, 1993).

After extensive piloting of their questionnaire, Pasty and her friends placed an ad in a local newspaper announcing the study and asking for volunteers. They were completely unprepared for the overwhelming response. To help deal with the large numbers of women who wanted to participate in the research, they called on several women in the community to help lead the extra discussion groups. Lorri Slepian and other women with a good deal of experience with the women's consciousness-raising (C-R) groups that were burgeoning at that time volunteered to help cope with the torrent of applications. They could see that Patsy and her friends were creating a C-R experience much more intensely focused on women's mothering than most. While Lorri disagreed with many critics who accused the women's movement of being "against motherhood," she believed it was a topic poorly explored in most C-R groups. She thought Patsy's approach had the potential of broadening the movement to include many women who were still standing on the sidelines. Lorri volunteered to lead one of the initial discussion groups. She and many others stayed on to help Patsy turn the research project into an ongoing national organization.

One of the women who answered the original newspaper ad looks back on the experience some twenty years later:

> I was a mother That's all I was. I had nothing else. I was isolated. No car. Husband going to school, husband going to work. When I read the ad, "young mothers to assist in a research project on women's needs during pregnancy, childbirth, and first experiences with an infant," I thought, "*I* was needed for a research project! Someone wanted to know about *my* experience." When the person who answered the phone said, "Someone will get back to you," I said to myself, "No, they won't." Patsy Turrini called back and said, "Oh, we would be so delighted to have you." I said, "Nobody is delighted to have me on any level." That was how I was

feeling but I went anyway. They really *did* want to hear something from me! It was wonderful. I intended to do it for six weeks. I lasted seven years.

For six weeks the women met in small groups while their children played together in a nearby room. The researchers recorded what the women had to say with care, taking notes, tape recording, and using videotapes—technology that was rather new at the time.

When the six weeks were over a number of the women decided to continue meeting on a regular basis. They thought of the group as a continuing experiment with an evolving model. They would try to articulate the underlying principles, structures, and practices that had enabled them to hold such a collaborative dialogue and create a highly democratic community group. If they could articulate the principles and train new facilitators, the model could be replicated in many other communities. As Lorri Slepian said,

> We saw it as an experiment in doing. We were making things happen in a different way—a female way, "the Mothers' Center way." This way was synergistic, inclusive, and consensual. We thought that women who participated in the experiment would be more able to bring the Mothers' Center way into their homes and communities.

As the conversations continued, it became increasingly clear to the women that many of the problems they discussed were rooted in social arrangements that could be ameliorated if they worked together. For instance, the women could see that many of the difficulties they had experienced around childbirth and early mothering were a function of hospital policies and practices. Twenty years later Patsy Turrini describes the feelings she had had listening to the tape recordings of these discussions:

> I was surprised at the depth of suffering. I am still traumatized when I think of myself sitting alone listening to those tapes and hearing of the assaults on women in the delivery room. . . . I had to pace myself as I listened to the material; I had to keep calming myself down. It was chilling to hear of the sadistic words that were said to the women. It was chilling that others could not understand how traumatic these assaults were for women.

The women decided to do something about the problem. First, they conducted an extensive study of the treatment women were experiencing around these issues. They polled women throughout the community and documented wide discontent with the maternity services local hospitals were providing. They also conducted an extensive study of the policies and practices of the hospitals. Once they had collected enough data, the women approached the hospitals with requests for reform. As was their practice, they videotaped the interviews.

Watching the videotapes they had made, the women were amazed by the quality of the data they had collected and their presentations. They were also startled to discover how contemptuous the doctors and administrators were of them and their arguments. As the women began to edit their films and present their case to other community groups, the hospital personnel began to see themselves through the eyes of the women they were supposed to be serving. It was not long before all the local hospitals had completely redesigned their maternity services.

The hospital project was so successful that the women decided to focus on other discriminatory practices that mothers were encountering in the community. Local libraries and businesses that had ruled out strollers and carriages were persuaded to reverse their policies. The libraries also began providing changing tables and a place for the toddlers to play so women with small children could easily use the facilities. These experiences encouraged the women to make research and social action projects a key component of Mothers' Centers. They called it the research–service–advocacy model.

These ongoing discussion groups and action projects claimed the attention of women from surrounding communities who wanted to start their own groups. A group called the replication team was formed. It was their job to figure out how other communities could be supported to develop their own Mothers' Centers. First, they articulated the model. Each new Mothers' Center would provide research-service-advocacy groups for mothers and developmental child care for children. Information about child development, mothering, and psychoanalytic theory would be made available. Referral services would be established for women needing and wanting other forms of professional treatment.

The replication team designed and ran workshops for training women as group facilitators. By showing the women how to design their own questionnaires whenever they had a new topic to explore, they taught the kind of question posing that generates a highly reflective and collaborative dialogue. By teaching the skills of empathetic listening, they helped women create a safe space where people could speak openly and honestly about themselves and their lives. They codified a nonhierarchical governance process that local groups could adopt that would help maintain the collaborative problem-solving approach the women found so valuable. Each center would be guided by a steering committee to plan the organization's overall direction. Each would also have a social action committee that would plan community projects whenever the conversations revealed a need. Leadership roles would be shared as much as possible. Everyone would be encouraged to take turns guiding the organization. A manual (Zimmerman, 1980) was published outlining all of the principles and practices that had been so useful. Essentially the women had articulated the philosophy and practice of connected knowing so well that they could teach the discipline, routinely bringing others to a very high level of competence in a very short time.

Once the Mothers' Center way was well articulated the women set out to disseminate their model more widely. The Mothers' Center Development Project (MCDP) was established with a toll-free phone number. Requests for help in building centers came in from far and wide. Well over a hundred different communities were helped to establish their own centers. A journal was published and a conference was held once a year. The movement spread across the country.

The National Association of Mothers' Centers was established in 1991 with an independent board. It was thought that the more complex national structure would better meet the needs of communities across the country, involve more women in shaping the organization, and secure better financial support for the movement. The women have worked hard to construct a national organization that can operate in the Mothers' Center way—egalitarian, nurturing, and as concerned with the development of each individual person as with the organization as a whole.

The national board and annual conferences have brought women together from all corners of the United States to develop a mutual support system. Mothers who had opportunities to develop a public voice in their own communities are now developing a national perspective. Some have begun traveling to meet their counterparts in other countries. A group of women from U.S. Mothers' Centers visited German Centers and attended their conferences. A large group of women from the German Mothers' Centers came to the United States, fanned out, and visited centers in many different communities across the country.

Because the women have been so successful in articulating and teaching the Mothers' Center way, most new groups are able to create a space where mothers can carry on an expansive and generative discussion. The conversations lead to an endless array of personal and collective projects. Mothers, who had all too often felt quite "brain dead," find themselves operating "on all cylinders," developing a fuller range of their capacities. Communities that had ignored the needs of mothers, families, and children are becoming better places for human beings.

THE GERMAN MOVEMENT

The Mothers' Center movement in Germany also started with a research project. Sociologist and feminist Monika Jaeckel and a small group of other feminists—all highly educated politically active professionals, most childless, some lesbian—had begun to notice how alienated mothers were from feminist politics. Something seemed wrong. Not only did the women question a feminist stance that excluded mothers, but they also realized that they themselves knew next to nothing about women living traditional lives as homemakers. As Monika says,

> The housewives couldn't count on being able to talk with us; we couldn't count on talking with them. Our worlds were so different and there were no bridges between them. We were not listening and taking up the issues that were important in the daily lives of most women. When I became aware of that, it made me very uncomfortable. I knew that if so many women were alienated from our politics we would not have much of an influence. I wanted to change things. We were not going to make any kind of influence

on the male world, if all categories of women were not in it together. I just felt that the women's movement was going to be
weak if it continued to be limited to the kind of women that were
in it then. That was very clear to me.

To remedy the situation, Monika and a colleague, Greta Tüllmann, obtained a research grant to study homemakers. The granting
agency wanted to know why homemakers did not use the standard educational programs available in their communities. To answer the question, Monika and Greta interviewed a large number of young mothers.
The homemakers found the educational programs uninteresting mostly
because women were treated like children. The role of student was
continuous with childhood status at a time when the women were
struggling to define themselves as adults. This problem was further ex-
acerbated by the fact that many teachers seemed to look down on the
homemakers and their lives. In "serving" the women, educators had
taught the women what they thought mothers needed to know. They
never asked the mothers what they wanted to know. The young homemakers also criticized programs and people who tried to "serve" them
or "cure" them as patients or clients. They did not want "service" and
they did not want "treatment." They were looking for more. They
wanted to be respected as competent adults who could contribute to
society. They wanted to develop their competencies through participation in the activities of the community.

In extended conversations the researchers and the homemakers
began to envision the kinds of programs that would make a difference
to mothers. One theme appeared again and again: There should be a
meeting place where women could drop in with their children to carry
on the same kind of highly reflective, "hard-nosed conversations" they
had been holding with Monika and her colleagues. The place would be
called a *Mothers' Center,* because it would put mothers in the center—
something few other public institutions do. It would be like a public
living room where children could play and make friends while the
mothers talked around a coffee table. Everyone would share responsibility for the organization, which would be run in a collaborative, democratic fashion. While the women dreamed of many other possible

facets a center might have, the coffee table was always the focal point. The women were funded to test out their plan by building centers in three different communities.

While these discussions were progressing, Monika and Greta, the urban feminists, teamed up with Hildegard Schoos, a housewife, and a group of provincial homemakers who were searching for a way women could enter into public life as mothers focused on children and families. These homemakers had been active in the Haus Frau Bund, an organization of highly educated women who had tried to professionalize homemaking by making it a serious subject of study. The group's collaborative way of working had two consequences that Hildegard and the other women had not anticipated: (1) having learned to work democratically in their organization, many of the women went on to democratize their own families, giving women and children a greater voice in family decisions, and (2) having become articulate about homemaking, many developed a public voice as politicians and professionals. But when they entered into public life these women lost much of their identity as homemakers in their own eyes and in the eyes of their professional colleagues.

Hildegard wanted to go into public life with her identity as mother fully intact. Her own mother was a highly successful businesswoman who delegated much of the care of her eight daughters and five sons to others. Whereas Hildegard's seven sisters followed their mother's example and devoted themselves to a career, Hildegard chose a different route. She would build an organization for homemakers that would hold a series of goals not fully embraced by the Haus Frau Bund. The new organization would include the empowerment of women and the democratization of the family as explicit and publicly stated goals. It would encourage the participation of women from all social classes. It would support women to enter into public life without abandoning their perspectives as mothers. Hildegard also wanted a group less interested in attending lectures given by outside experts and more interested in developing action projects where these particular values could be brought into play and new ideas could be tested.

When Hildegard and the urban feminists first met, it was—everyone agrees—like hot fusion. As Monika said,

We fell in love. We were fascinated with each other. Hildegard was the sort of woman we wanted to meet all along. We were the sort of women that she wanted to meet. It was instant recognition.

They were like emissaries from two cultures meeting. Monika recalls the early conversations:

We talked for hours—in the car, on the phone. For hours, just telling each other about our lives. "How did you think about this?" "What about that?" "Did you ever hear about the feminist movement? What did it look like to you?" "What kind of images of feminists did you have?" Those were my questions for her and she gave me her questions.

Sometimes the differences were so great they were like travelers in a strange and distant land.

Hildegard was saying to me, "What? You don't have children? You don't want children? I can't imagine that!" And I said to Hildegard, "How can you enjoy being confined to that kind of marriage?" We were very curious to understand what the other was doing. Being in a friendship mode allowed us to take in more of the other's whole culture, to be more open and curious. We enjoyed our differences! We could see that our differences complemented each other. We could join the differences and use them as strengths. It was extraordinary.

Hildegard and several colleagues from the Haus Frau Bund joined Monika's group and helped them build the three centers the granting agency had agreed to support. By all accounts, the three were a great success.

Although the grant stipulated that Monika and Greta would publish a report on the effort, they realized that the mothers themselves should be the ones to author such a book. Monika said,

We spent a whole year getting this book together. We would have seminars and talk about the issues. The women would tell their stories. It was a back-and-forth process. We would type the stories up, edit them, and send them back. They would create their article from there. Then we would edit the work again. This process re-

sulted in a book (Jaeckel and Tüllman, 1988) that was so alive that
the book itself created the Mothers' Center movement. Everywhere women read the book they said, "We can do it too. What
those women did, we can do in our town."

When local women requested a Mothers' Center in their community, ample funding was usually available from municipal and federal
governments. Given a level of financial support that women from the
U.S. movement find astonishing, the German women have been able to
develop Mothers' Centers all over their country. The last count to reach
our ears was over four hundred. Most towns now have a public space
designed by mothers for mothers; many of the larger cities have several
centers. After the fall of the Berlin Wall the Mothers' Center women
helped women in the East establish centers throughout the area. These
have played a crucial role for women struggling to find a way during
very turbulent times. The movement has opened up the main avenue
for dialogue and collaboration for grassroots women from the two
halves of this radically divided society.

The Mothers' Center that Hildegard Schoos and her peers
founded in Saltzgitter has been able to realize the fullest version of the
movement's vision in Germany as it commanded substantial grants for
purchasing and renovating a large building as well as for innovative pro-
gramming. This center will be described in detail because it has become a model studied by women from all over the world interested in
developing similar programs.

Hildegard and the women in Saltzgitter designed a building that is
so homelike it is difficult to imagine that it is actually a large public institution with a staff of seventy-seven that facilitates programs for over
eight hundred people. When you step into the building you find yourself in the middle of the so-called "public living room." The room is an
inviting sun-filled space with nine or ten dining tables as well as comfortable sofas and overstuffed chairs. The room opens to a professional
but homey kitchen, so women are not cut off from others as they prepare the meals. Throughout the large building are facilities for a variety
of other services the mothers provide for each other. There is a well-
appointed playroom with an outdoor play yard for the children; a laundry that serves the center as well as mothers who do not have their

own equipment at home; a hair salon where children and adults can get their hair cut and styled. The basement houses a secondhand store for recycling children's furnishings and a pottery shop and carpentry shop where women can learn these crafts and supply other women with goods made to order. The second floor is quieter. Besides offices for administrative tasks, there is an attractively furnished apartment that is used for a wide range of functions. Elderly persons might elect to stay there while the people they live with are sick or away on vacation. They might share the apartment during the day and early evening with napping children or small groups needing a quiet meeting space. The attic houses several large thickly carpeted rooms. When the tables and chairs are up, these rooms can accommodate large conferences, seminars, and sewing circles. The ironing boards and furniture can be moved away for dancing, exercising, singing, and games.

On any given day two hundred people might come through the door; breakfast and lunch will be served to more than a hundred people. Like a large family, the Saltzgitter Mothers' Center brings together people of all ages. Besides children and young mothers, there are middle-aged women who continued to work on one or another of the center's many projects long after their own children were grown. There are childless adults who volunteer their time so they can have children in their lives. There are elderly men and women who come for a whole range of services and programs provided by younger women at the center.

Because women in the German Mothers' Center movement criticize social arrangements that allow everyone but mothers to be compensated for the work they do, they do not ask mothers to volunteer their time. All of the services are provided by mothers who are paid for their work. The pay scale is pegged at a level that is comparable to twice the minimum wage in the United States. It is similar to the wages check-out clerks receive in German supermarkets. Women are charged modest fees for the services they use at the center. Between the salaries women earn at the center and the ample child support allowances paid to mothers by the German government, the Mothers' Centers are accessible to women of all income levels. Low-income women, traditionally nonjoiners, are likely to participate because of the economic incentives. The income makes their participation more understandable and acceptable to spouses, who might otherwise recoil at the idea of a group dedicated to the empowerment of women. More privileged women are probably not greatly influenced to join the organization because of the financial incentives, but the income helps validate their worth, as it does with low-income women. This is no small matter, given how devalued educated women in modern societies feel when they do not develop a professional career.

The German Mothers' Center movement has been able to do something that is exceedingly rare in any society. It has created public spaces in towns and cities all over Germany where women from all walks of life can gather for a common conversation. It is difficult to imagine this situation occurring in the United States on such a regular and widespread basis. Suburbanization has profoundly isolated the middle classes from the rest of society. Yet, the gap between the poor and the middle class is not just one of geography. Even though the United States is one of the richest nations in the history of the world, the level of maternal and child poverty is among the highest of any industrialized nation; the level of social supports for families and children is among the very lowest. When the German women were able to show how well the Mothers' Centers were meeting the needs of families, local and national governments as well as private foundations usually made funding available to the communities where women wanted such a program. Because this kind of funding has not been available in the United States, Mothers' Centers here are primarily funded by the women themselves who volunteer their time and pay most of the organizational expenses out of their own pockets. Poor communities are unlikely to have the necessary resources. Suburban middle-class mothers are so removed from the poor both geographically and psychologically that they find it hard to imagine how they might begin bridging the gap.

The ability of the German Mothers' Center movement to have mothers run their own organizations and be paid for their services affects the social relations within the organization in many ways. Whereas a more conventional social service agency will ask a prospective client, "What is the problem that we can help you with?" someone from the Mothers' Center asks a prospective member, "What kind of contribution would you like to make *to* this community?" Hildegard paraphrases a typical encounter:

What talent do you want to contribute to the Center? We want you to bring these talents into public life. Now it is just your family that is profiting from your talents. We want you to bring these talents into a larger environment. We want to create a space here for you to come in and do whatever it is that you are good at.

The point of the Mothers' Center is to draw out talents from women who may not even be aware that they have them. At first they might focus on what the women are already good at and comfortable doing. Later they might encourage the women to develop new interests and skills. Thus a woman who likes to bake might begin by working in the coffee shop, another might choose to work in the children's playroom, and another who likes to iron might work in the laundry. An artist when it comes to haircutting might open a beauty shop, another skilled in handling governmental red tape might become an in-house lawyer and help other women obtain their benefits and rights. Others might run the second-hand store for recycling children's clothes and equipment. Still others might maintain all the houseplants growing at the center and keep the coffee tables supplied with flowers from their own gardens. Others might help develop an after-school program for children of working mothers. One group of women put together a traveling art exhibit that depicted the negative stereotypes of mothers that the women had garnered from the public media. The central image of the show is an enormous gilded cage. The women felt they had made a powerful statement summing up experiences they could hardly have named when they began the work.

When a woman wanted to develop a theater group, the Mothers' Center found her a coach. Hildegard says,

> If someone needs more skills to do what they dream of doing, we try to find them a coach. Coaching is another one of the jobs at the Mothers' Center, training and talking to the women. Coaching is a long process, building up the consciousness and self-confidence. The woman who created the theater for the movement was living on welfare. She was very much on the margins when she first came. She had a great gift for acting and we found someone who could coach her to start a theater group.

This theater group now travels around the country performing plays developed from the consciousness of mothers. German homemakers are startled to see an art form that mirrors their lives well. It is, after all, rare to have women's experiences with mothering articulated in a public forum. For the first time many women are feeling that they might have a significant voice in the larger conversation.

MOTHERS' CENTERS ON BOTH SHORES

One difference distinguishes the movements in the two countries that seems important to note. The German Mothers' Centers made a decision not to codify and articulate the processes that might support the development of highly collaborative and creative learning environments; the U.S. movement set out the procedures in bold, clear terms. The German women argued that all that was needed was the provision of a public living room; the development of the caring community would evolve in the wake of the ensuing conversation. Clearly, they were right in the case of Mothers' Centers like the one in Saltzgitter. The Saltzgitter Center is so complex they are able to retain many open-minded, older, former members who trained themselves through years of involvement in building the movement. In the public living rooms of these centers, the older women model the skills of connected knowing and teach by example—all day, every day. Smaller centers in more remote, provincial towns neither achieve this level of complexity nor do they have the daily input of so many experienced older women.

Young women who are trying to build centers in small places say it is hard to break through the narrow-minded conventions that govern their communities. They say that the women are apt to be so judgmental of deviance they find it hard to listen to each other with the kind of open-mindedness that has been so essential to the movement's success. When the German women from some of these out-of-the-way places visited Mothers' Centers in similar communities in the United States, they were astonished at the quality of the dialogue small-town women in the United States were able to achieve. They thought the difference could easily be attributed to the way the U.S. women articulated, codified, and taught the processes that support the development of a highly reflective, free-ranging, dialogue.

Even with such differences, the two movements have a remarkable number of similarities in their approaches and in their achievements. The development of a highly reflective public conversation is seen as *the* core activity of Mothers' Centers in both Germany and the United States. Women from both countries place the matter of voice at the forefront; they have many stories about their own coming into voice. They also describe how they have taken the skills they acquired in the Mothers' Centers out into the larger community. Mostly, they talk about how they now bring others into voice. The following comments by a founder of the U.S. Mothers' Center movement is typical of things women in both countries said:

> As a mother I had lots of feelings but I did not have any words for them. As I listened to other women speak, I realized that they were putting words to my experience. That was so empowering. There were words for what I was feeling! The women also listened to what I had to say in a very active way. That gave me the freedom to begin speaking. Now I go out to other places and listen in this active way. I convey to others that I want to know them, I want to know their feelings, I want to know their ideas. I think these kinds of conversations make a ripple in this world.

When the women talk about how their Mothers' Center experiences have changed the way they relate to their families, women in both countries give very similar descriptions. They say they have democratized their families by teaching to other family members the skills of dialogue and collaborative problem solving they learned at the Mothers' Centers. At first many of their spouses fought the changes, but now most appreciate being in a more equal relationship with a strong, resourceful, and engaged woman.

Women from both Germany and the United States say their children benefitted greatly from the Mothers' Center experience. As evidence they quote teachers who say they easily spot the Mothers' Center children at the beginning of every school year. Mothers' Center children, the teachers say, are unusually engaged, inquisitive, and self-directed. Most of all, they say these children have a lovely way of relating to younger children and making the school a more hospitable place for everyone. The older founding members marvel at how outspoken their children are as young adults. Even though it has caused some of their children difficulty with people who like to avoid controversy, the women believe they sponsored the development of a generation unusually well prepared for adulthood. They say their grown children have established egalitarian marriages with spouses interested in building democratic families. Their daughters are equal partners with the men they marry; their sons are deeply involved in the daily nurturance of their children.

The Mothers' Center movements in both countries have been especially important to women who have felt particularly unprepared for family life and parenthood, a problem widely shared by many women with highly evolved careers in traditionally male-dominated professions. Many of these women found that the distancing, argumentative discourse of the public culture they had cultivated through years of schooling and professional practice were detrimental to the task of creating a caring, connected family. Untrained to speak in a connected mode suitable for bringing young children into voice, many of these women found they could hardly speak at all when they began raising a family. A German woman gives a moving account of the problem:

> As soon as I became a mother I lost my voice. I literally could not speak—I stuttered, I could not find words. Up to then I had been highly involved in speaking and writing as a professional. But it was a male-dominated profession and I had been doing the kind of thinking and talking men do. I looked down on women's talk and the kind of speech that you need to use with children. I thought I had regressed because I was no longer able to talk and think like a man. Of course, when I was at home no one spoke with me at all. Then when I began coming to the Mothers' Center I found myself speaking with women without feeling a sense of shame. Here everyone listens; we pool information. We see the problems we are faced with as common problems, not a function of our personal inadequacies. Here we keep our minds open and are always learning from each other. We find everyone has so much to contribute. Everyone becomes so much more active as learners.

Everyone is sharing knowledge; everyone gets the satisfaction of being a contributor, a helper. Everyone is always learning; everyone is always teaching. It wasn't long before I got so confident in what I was saying that I could enroll in the university and begin developing a more balanced professional career.

A number of highly professionalized U.S. mothers have said similar things in almost identical words. Interestingly, many professional women in both countries found that the collaborative form of problem solving they learned in the Mothers' Centers greatly enhanced their careers when they returned to work. Many of the women also believed that the careers of their spouses were greatly facilitated by the more collaborative, democratic practices they learned at the Mothers' Centers and taught to other family members. The women say the impact is easiest to see in the careers of spouses involved in advanced, rapidly evolving technologies that require high levels of collaboration and creativity.

Women from both shores have also found the Mothers' Centers an important source of support in building a public life. While many women go on to develop professional careers that are not directly related to children and homemaking, many others create professional lives that clearly focus on promoting the development of people and communities.

Whatever their professional commitments may be, most Mothers' Center women remain actively involved in their local communities without losing their perspective as mothers. Not only do these women continue working to get the needs of mothers and families met; they are a part of a large network of women skilled at collaborating and speaking out. Hildegard put it this way:

A center like this brings together women who have a tremendous amount of competence caring for people of all ages. Nowhere have I met any kind of institution that values and supports all of this kind of expertise. It brings the expertise that mothers have into public life. To be at the Mothers' Center is a political act in itself. Once a woman gets involved she changes in a way that is visible everywhere she goes. She gets used to dealing in ways that are different from the public culture. She creates an aura around herself that is different. She expects public life to be different. She communicates differently in the supermarket. Mothers expect people to slow down for the children, to accommodate them. If things are not right, they say so. They are no longer so intimidated. They have created a different kind of public space here. Everywhere they go they take this experience with them. The women used to adapt themselves to the public institutions, saying, "This is the way it is." Now they ask, "Why is it this way and not another way?" They challenge politicians who speak to housewives in a condescending manner: "Why are you talking to me that way?" They teach people to be more responsive to the needs of children. It is very subtle, but it is constant. The world is not created like the Mothers' Centers, but the women from the centers have decided that this is going to be the world.

CHAPTER 8

THE NATIONAL CONGRESS
OF NEIGHBORHOOD WOMEN

It's not that neighborhood women don't dream. Their dreams aren't voiced because they don't think anyone is listening.

None of us had any idea what we were doing, we had to figure it out as we went, right?

JAN PETERSON
FOUNDER, NATIONAL CONGRESS
OF NEIGHBORHOOD WOMEN

The National Congress of Neighborhood Women (NW) grew out of a dream Jan Peterson began cultivating in the 1960s. She would help to create an interracial, intercultural force for community development in a poor and working-class neighborhood in Brooklyn, New York. The travels that brought Jan to Brooklyn began in 1968—the year Martin Luther King, Jr., and Robert Kennedy were assassinated. That fall Jan set off from her small Wisconsin hometown for New York City on a Greyhound bus. With college behind her, she wanted to take a "year out" before she married the boy next door to live in a place where ideas flowed more freely.

> I figured I'm like the Australian, New Zealander, women. There you are supposed to get a year off before you get married. They go off to Europe for a whole year and they could do whatever they wanted. For a whole year they could do wild things. Then they'd come back and never leave New Zealand or Australia again. That's what I felt I was doing. I was going off for my year. I went by Greyhound bus to New York.

Jan soon found herself a job with the Department of Social Welfare in the South Bronx. This spritely petite blond woman collected her

202

worldly belongings and moved uptown, miniskirts and all. To Jan, the South Bronx was bursting with vitality. Recalling the pleasure she gained from her job as a social worker, she says,

> I thought, "This *is* great!" I loved it. I loved talking and listening to people. I was constantly running up and down all these steps in urine-infested stairwells. Everybody always lived on the fifth floor and the elevators were always broken. Of course, I found that 90 percent of the people were extremely hardworking and decent. Their homes were peaceful islands in all of this disorder. They were doing their best under incredible circumstances.

Jan also signed up to work with CORE (Congress of Racial Equality) in Harlem. CORE was a national organization of local groups that worked for social justice in their own communities. Committed to direct-action projects, nonviolence, and civil disobedience, CORE played a central role in the development of the civil rights movement, especially in the northern states. As a white CORE member Jan said she was "like a member of the ladies' auxiliary. I was just happy to go in there, type do the filing, and clean the toilets." She threw herself into the work. She thought she had found her community in the civil rights movement.

Jan's quest for family, community, and social justice had been set in motion by a series of childhood events. When Jan was ten years old, her father, a lineman for the power company, was electrocuted. Within the year her mother remarried. Jan's father and stepfather were a study in contrasts. The father, a Dutch American working-class man, was a progressive. He was very political and extremely outspoken. He loved debate and discussion. As young as Jan was, he expected her to enter into the fray along with everyone else. A devil's advocate par excellence, he mostly advocated for the underdog. Jan's stepfather was a first generation German émigré. He was a strict conservative who advocated for the authorities. He ruled out discussion, questioning, and debate. Children were to be seen but not heard.

Jan's reconstituted family moved from Port Washington, Wisconsin, where poor and working-class people—many new to the United States—took care of each other like "one large extended family." They resettled in Cedarburg, where her new neighbors, like her new father, were much more conservative. She was, she said, the only Democrat in a sea of Republicans.

After a year or so of incredible sadness, Jan began to throw herself into her new community. She explains that

> Mostly, I ran with the boys because they had very little for the girls that had any action in it. I ran with the pack, played basketball, and all that. I remember all of a sudden the boys weren't supposed to play tackle football with me. That was very upsetting.

Jan also found the way Cedarburg teachers and students picked on the farm kids very upsetting. She worked hard to become friends with everyone, the farm kids as well as the children of the community's leaders. In the process she became, she said, "a bridge person," a label claimed by most of the founders of the public homeplaces we studied.

A few years later, Jan again threw herself into a community of people who were quite different from herself. The work in the South Bronx and Harlem CORE provided her with two very different kinds of apprenticeships working with one of the most marginalized groups in the society. CORE's commitment to and skill at empowering people at the margins to tackle the problems facing them and their communities was just the kind of ability Jan wanted to develop in herself. Essentially, Jan wanted to devote her life to supporting grassroots people who long for the kind of nurturing communities she enjoyed as a child in Wisconsin.

As Jan's involvement in the black community deepened, the evolving "black power" movement made the role of whites working in the ghetto increasingly problematic. When it became clear she should leave, Jan was devastated. Once again she had lost her community. Marshall England, one of Harlem's political and moral leaders whom Jan most admired, talked with her at length about how she should work in her "own" community. Jan realized that "her" community was really the working-class émigrés who were being blamed for much of the racism in the United States. Jan decided to follow her friend's advice. She would move to a poor and working-class neighborhood teeming with immigrants. There she would create an interracial, intercultural force for social justice. From her childhood years, Jan knew poor and working-class people to be fully capable of creating communities where diverse peoples live together in harmony.

Jan moved to Brooklyn, New York, where she found a job directing an antipoverty program (CETA) in the Williamsburg and Greenpoint neighborhoods. A short subway ride from Manhattan, the area housed many small industries along with many new arrivals from all corners of the earth. Modest single-family homes, often meticulously maintained, were interspersed with triple-decker houses, shops, factories, public housing projects, and small apartment buildings. Many of these structures were deteriorating; others were boarded up and abandoned. The triple-deckers often housed two or three generations of an extended Italian family still living a way of life traditional in "the old country." Although the immediate neighborhood was predominately Italian, there were Hispanics, Polish Americans, African Americans, and many others living in the area. The people, some of who were already among the poorest in New York City, were facing a steady decline in the manufacturing industry—the economic underpinning of the whole community.

Just as in Cedarburg and the South Bronx, Jan got to know everyone. She says, "You know, I feel really happy when I'm walking around the neighborhood talking to people." As she visited, talked, and worked on one community project after another, Jan came to see the community through the eyes of her new neighbors. Where many outsiders would see only alienation, fragmentation, and blight, Jan saw people working together, caring for their families, and doing what they could to keep the whole community together. As in the South Bronx, she found most people were coping amazingly well with incredible hardships. She also saw that the white working class was feeling quite ignored by the government as much of the new antipoverty legislation being generated by the war on poverty sidestepped them and their concerns. This feeling would turn to anger during the following decades as the globalization of the economy continued to undermine the way of life of many working people.

Drawing on her undergraduate training as a historian, Jan also studied the governance structure and the lines of authority—formal and informal—that ran through the community. She observed what she called a "plantation mentality," a way of thinking that develops when

the "overseers" who run the schools, services, and industries live elsewhere and do not allow local residents to have a say in the affairs of
their own community. She also observed the fracturing of community
that occurs when the children of poor and working-class people move
up and out—Horatio Alger style. Seeing her interest, the women in the
neighborhood took it upon themselves to educate Jan, sharing their extensive knowledge of the people, the politics, and the history of the
neighborhood.

As in Cedarburg, Jan was always on the lookout for people who
were being left out. When she realized that the traditional leaders were
not listening to her or any of the other women, she began to think systematically about gender for the first time. She joined a consciousness-
raising group in Manhattan that would play a key role in developing
the women's movement. She also became intensely involved with the
burgeoning antipoverty movement. Maintaining her contact with the
civil rights movement, Jan would go on to build a bridge linking all of
these movements.

Jan began this bridge building by observing the role of women in
her Brooklyn community more carefully. She could see that the "overseers" and many local leaders were in agreement on one thing: a
woman's place was in the home. Even so, many ordinary "housewives"
were actually working very hard to sustain and enhance the life of the
community through PTAs, block associations, tenants' groups in the
projects, political clubs, and churches. Hull House's founder, Jane Addams (1965), would have called these women "municipal housekeepers." Municipal housekeepers, by Addams's definition, are those who do
the things that must be done if a community is to be worthy of the
name "home": they get streets and alleys cleared of garbage, find places
for children to play, advocate for a stop sign here and a stoplight there,
protest overcrowded and underfunded schools, get the branch library
reopened, and so on.

Jan saw many outstanding, broad-minded women leading these
efforts, most of whom had little formal education. Some were lavish
with the care they bestowed on the community, even though they
themselves had very limited access to material resources. A few were
even traversing ethnic and racial lines to create cross-cultural alliances
to work on common problems. Jan was particularly drawn to the fight-

ers, women who could bring zest and courage to the political battles that racked the borough. She found women in the Italian and African American communities who were undaunted by conflict, having grown up in cultures that often support women to be more forthright about feelings and demands.

Most of the women leaders with whom Jan identified worked in isolation on one discreet project or another. They had little support for the work they were doing from others in the community. There was no structure that would bring them together, enabling them to support each other and develop a comprehensive long-term plan for developing and directing their leadership.

Although Jan thought of these women as leaders, their leadership was invisible to almost everyone else—including the women themselves. Not thinking of themselves as leaders, the women would stand back and let the men step in and take over whenever they got something together that might lead to budgets, salaries, and buildings. As housewives fighting for the interests of mothers, the women did not think of themselves as political; no one else took the political work of the mothers seriously. These women had no official standing, no institutional support, and no public recognition for their efforts. Like women's work in the home, their "municipal housekeeping" was uncounted, unpaid, and unnamed.

It galled Jan that these women and the needs of their families received so little recognition from the formal institutions that controlled the community's resources. Realizing that these "municipal housekeepers" could be a powerful force for change in the neighborhood, Jan set out to organize them. She put it this way:

> You know I have a very good ability at seeing the strengths of everybody. I connect people. I get people involved with each other. I bring people and ideas together to make things happen. And once we got things happening the "overseers" had to listen to us.

As a director of the local CETA program, Jan was able to hire a number of these municipal housekeepers and see that they got some institutional backing for the work they were doing. With this unprecedented source of support, Jan and the Brooklyn women began to dream of a rash of new projects to improve the community.

The women began to see that, because they were wives and mothers, their leadership and contributions to public life were being rejected by traditional leaders. The women also realized that there were numbers of women in all of the different ethnic communities who wanted to make things better. It was clear they would make much greater headway if they began working together. They would create a challenging and supportive place where they could develop their leadership. With that support they would be able to make the larger community a more nurturing place for others. Elizabeth Speranza, one of the members of the original group, gives some sense of the impact Jan and the group had on her:

> We would have never went up to City Hall alone to fight but Jan kept saying, "You have to go up there and voice your opinion. You have to say what you want. You are the same as everyone else. You are equal, you know." The things that we have accomplished would have never been accomplished without the help of Jan, 'cause she knew where to open the doors. Even though we had our ideas about what we wanted, we didn't know how to go about it.

When the women tried to characterize their organization they reached for images and metaphors of home and family: "I really felt at home here." "We were like a family." "People were here for me yesterday, they will be here for me tomorrow, next year, ten years from now, whatever—just like a family." "Because we were going to be together over the long haul, we could take on very long-term challenges." It pleased Jan that her own mother would have been happy to join the kind of organization they were putting together.

Like a family, their organization tied several generations together. Many of the women Jan brought into the network were literally "old enough to be her mother." She was always casting other women in the roles of mother or teacher and herself as a daughter or learner. As a newcomer to the neighborhood and urban life, Jan had much to learn.

The mother-daughter theme was further elaborated in an unusual way. Many of the original members of the group were Italian as this was the predominate group in the neighborhood. In Italian culture the family is central and family members are apt to be very close. Three generations often live within easy walking distance from each other. Many take apartments in the same triple-decker house. While tradition demands that women remain in the family, women are allowed to be out and about as long as they remain in the company of a family member. Tillie Tarantino, a founding member along with her mother, Molly, and her sister Millie, explains:

> At that time, if you are the woman, you are in the house; you stay in the background. You just bring up the children. You do whatever you have to in the home and that's it. That was our culture. But if someone from your own family would go about with you, you didn't have to stay at home. It was our culture.

Needless to say, under these conditions the bond between mothers and daughters who wanted to venture out in the world could become very tight. Tillie describes how essential the support of such a closely knit group was to her progress:

> I don't think anyone of us could have done it on our own; we needed the support of the group. If we had to go somewhere it had to be as a group. I know that I didn't have the push at that time to do it on my own. I would say I was a little backwards then. I was always wanting to know, "Am I doing the right thing?" "Am I doing the wrong thing?" Now it's a whole different ball game, but at that time I didn't have that confidence. I did need the Elizabeth Speranzas. I did need my mother, my sister, and the Jan Petersons. I did need the Marian Variales and the Angie Giglios. We had to work together.

Jan recalls her astonishment and irritation at the closeness of the mother-daughter teams that joined them in those early days:

> The women came in family blocks. I never even thought about block voting until I met Molly, Tillie, and Millie. You'd be trying to get something happening and they would vote as a block, whether they agreed or not. They would drive me absolutely nuts.

While this depth of connectedness and the tendency for relatives to enter into public life as a family unit is characteristic of many ethnic groups, it is at odds with more mainstream U.S. culture. As Jan points out, the more general assumption is that everyone will operate more or less independently as a separate, autonomous individual. This supposition is reinforced in the public sector by antinepotism laws that make close working relationships among family members illegal.

The umbrella agency administering Jan's program and other antipoverty projects was rattled by all of the women's many plans and activities. Accustomed to providing "services" and "charity" to those in need, they were unnerved by "clients" and "beneficiaries" initiating their own goals and claims. As Jan said, "Nothing had been done from the bottom up before. When we tried to tell them they needed to share power, bring everybody in, and build the leadership of the community, they just couldn't understand it."

In 1969, when the director of the agency could no longer tolerate the women's assertiveness, he tried to fire Jan and shut down her program. The women were determined to continue their work. They would free themselves from this administrator and the constraints he tried to impose on them. The women gathered up all of the records and combined forces with the Conselyea Street Block Association—a neighborhood association begun by some of the women who had been working in Jan's CETA program. They set up an office in a shoe repair shop donated by a neighborhood man who was retiring.

The director never dreamed the women would fight back. The director's own negligence as an administrator gave them the ammunition they needed to win the ensuing battle. The agency was required by law to have a majority of low-income people from the community on the governing board. Not only were all the agency's decision makers high-income professionals, but most lived outside of the community. As an agency mandated to empower the community, the poverty program had failed to fulfill one of its most important obligations. The director had to face Jan, the group, the law, and a powerful moral argument. Seeing no other choice, he released the women and their funds to establish an independent operation. This was the women's first major battle and their first victory. As Jan said,

> The Italian political leaders, the men, and other people in the
> community were very threatened by this because they were used

to controlling the neighborhood. All of a sudden there was this whole new group moving into public space. It was a mixed group of women—black, Hispanic, and Italian, but mostly Italian. That was a big thing. Nobody had ever seen anything like that happen before in the whole history of the neighborhood.

The second major battle ensued when the women began acquiring funds for a building to house programs for children and the elderly, two kinds of programs desperately needed by families in the neighborhood. Local politicians and community leaders told them in no uncertain terms, "Go home and do your dishes." The women were clearly violating many community norms. They were working across ethnic and racial lines; they were raising funds to build a public building to their own specifications; they planned to retain ownership of the building and control over the programs; their programs would be open to everyone; they would govern the programs in a highly participatory and democratic manner. Up to that point all the public buildings in the community had been erected and controlled by men who championed very hierarchical governance structures. All too often the programs they created kept the various groups in the community separated and divided, with many being excluded altogether.

An open war was declared on the women. They would come out of meetings to find their car tires slashed. Their phones would ring in the middle of the night. The ensuing silences were unsettling; the threats of violence against their children were terrifying. Some of the children were sent to live with relatives elsewhere; others were given police protection. Jan describes the battle:

> The politicians and whole groups of Italian men and women tried to use race to control us. They said that the day-care center is not going to be for Italian children; it's going to be for black children. The whole community was up in arms. The Italians organized petitions and a candlelight vigil against the day-care center. We kept organizing to push it through. Of course, we had some Italian women on our side who were able to withstand the onslaught. In the long run we prevailed because our position was morally stronger. How can you say, "There shouldn't be a center for children"? Really! It was a ferocious battle.

Tillie Tarantino looks back on all of the strife and describes the ways ethnic stereotypes were exploited to keep the people divided against each other. She says,

> People who are still leaders working with us now on everything all over town looked down on us then. They looked on us like a piece of nothing. We were like the lowest of the lowest because we were working with the black community and others who were trying to get something in our community that we felt was needed: the senior citizens' center, the day-care center. "Oh, no—you're bringing that in? That's terrible. You are going to bust the block and blacks will ruin the neighborhood." I mean they wanted to kill Jan Peterson.

When Elizabeth Speranza's daughter accepted a staff position with Jan's CETA program, Elizabeth was told, "Your daughter is going to be a communist." Relatives called her husband to say, "Your wife is disgracing the family." Another husband was taunted for having a lesbian for a wife. The women were demonized as "dykes," "reds," and "nigger lovers." While some of the women dropped out, most refused to be manipulated by such tactics and the group persevered.

When the traditional community leaders saw they could not stop the project, they tried to take it over. Late one evening, Elizabeth and her husband were startled by knocking on their door. Two large men stood in the doorway. With hats pulled down and cigars dangling, they looked every bit like gangsters from a Hollywood film. The men said that Elizabeth had to come with them if she and her friends had any hopes of building their community center. They would take her to "the club" where the borough president was waiting to see her. As was his habit, Elizabeth's husband encouraged her, asking only that she take a friend along, which she did. The two women were driven to the smoke-filled club in a long black limousine. The president and his men interrupted their card game to lay down the law. They informed her that "her women" could have their building if they agreed to put "their men" on the board. "That's okay," Elizabeth recollects saying, "but remember, the women run the place. The women are the ones that are going to be doing everything." The men could sit on the center's board, but they would be there only as tokens. The struggle was suddenly over.

The threatening calls stopped, police protection was discontinued, and the children who had been sent out of town returned home. The women were successful in building their center and maintaining control of its programs, just as Elizabeth said they would be.

Building and housing an institution of their own was an incredible challenge for the women. The clear victory gave them a sure footing in the neighborhood. Because the new building housed programs that met a variety of needs articulated by people from all segments of the community, it became a meeting place for young and old, men and women, as well as Italians, African Americans, and Hispanics. Even the local politicians were quick to see that this was the place to be and began hanging out at the new center. Many people familiar with the area believe that this inner-city neighborhood is much less stressed by the intense racial and ethnic divisions that have buffeted similar communities throughout Brooklyn and other urban areas. They attribute the relative harmony to the fact that Jan and the neighborhood women have created a number of meeting places like their storefront office and the senior center, where diverse people can meet and find common ground. The fight for a physical place to house their projects was so intense, and having space they could control for an office was so rewarding that Jan and the women felt they had learned an important lesson: Groups that want to empower themselves must claim physical space to house the structures they are trying to create. The theme of claiming space would continue to be elaborated by the women over the years to come. Clearly, claiming space is a primary step in the empowerment process—an insight reminiscent of Virginia Woolf's argument in *A Room of One's Own* (1929/1957).

Jan's dream of a more inclusive, democratic society led her to reach out to women leaders from grassroots communities all over the nation. In 1974 she collaborated with Barbara Mikulski, now a senator from Maryland, and Nancy Seifer, the author of *Nobody Speaks for Me* (1976), to give a conference in Washington, D.C., for women leaders of grassroots communities across the country as well as women politicians, academics, and policymakers. It would be the first of many small, working conferences, workshops, and forums to support the work of neighborhood women leaders and community organizers from poor and working-class communities. It was here that neighborhood women began to develop partnerships with professional women.

The Brooklyn women, many of whom had never been out of their neighborhood before, began to travel. The conferences brought them together with women leaders from many different kinds of grassroots communities around the country. These conferences were eye-opening for everyone. The women began to look at their local communities and themselves from a new perspective. Placing their local problems in a larger context, they could visualize more of the broad social forces that were affecting them and their communities as well as others around the world. They pooled their resources and learned from each other. They helped each other see the significance of their leadership. With such a broad base of support, local leaders began to dream of goals and projects that would have been beyond the wildest imagination of women working in isolation.

In 1975, a federal grant from the Carter administration enabled the women to convene a second conference of women leaders from grassroots communities. Before the conference was over, the participants decided to form a national organization. Their ways of working together were so rewarding and there was so much knowledge to be shared they would continue the process. An ongoing national organization would enable women leaders from grassroots communities all across the country to provide each other with this kind of mutual support year in and year out. They called the new organization the National Congress of Neighborhood Women (NW).

The National Congress of Neighborhood Women's primary goal was to build women's consciousness of their power to define and solve the problems facing them and their communities. The organization would do this by recognizing the women's strengths, by offering education and skill-building in a manner that does not alienate the women from themselves and their roots, and by developing a strong national network so women from all corners of the nation could pool their insights and resources. The governing board of the new organization brought together a wide variety of grassroots leaders and professional allies. Over time the board itself would become an outstanding working model of the kind of support system the women were trying to create nationwide.

NW wanted to establish the national office in a poor and working-class neighborhood. Jan and her colleagues agreed to set up an

office for the new organization in Brooklyn. The national organization
would also continue the work of the Conselyea Street Block Association as a working model. Furthermore, they would look to the other
organizations in the network for models and insights.

As the women built the national organization, they continued to
create new programs in Brooklyn—the first being a college program.
As soon as the women got the senior center and the children's day-care
program in place, they realized they would have to hire outside professionals to run these programs. Even though there were many gifted
women in the neighborhood, none of them had the training and the
credentials that staff members of these kinds of organizations are required to have. Needless to say, that was a great disappointment to the
women. Their whole thrust had been to empower neighborhood
women to envision build, and run the kind of community they wanted
for themselves and their families. All this was to be done in the most
democratic fashion. In their experience, these were not goals and
processes shared by most professionals who came into the community
to staff and administer social programs.

The women saw no other option but to found a college program.
Their college would serve mature women who were trying to improve
their neighborhoods. They would recruit women from the different
ethnic and racial groups, building bridges between all of the groups that
live in the area. Many of the women they recruited had not finished
high school. Most would not have felt welcomed in the established institutions scattered throughout Manhattan, even if they had resources
for fees and transportation costs. Furthermore, established programs
were not well designed for people who wanted to uplift declining
inner-city neighborhoods. Indeed, going to college seemed to discourage such activities. The women regularly observed their neighbors who
were able to get a college education subsequently pulling up stakes and
moving away. The graduates seldom looked for ways to use their education to the benefit of the community.

With funding from the Rockefeller Brothers Foundation and the
cooperation of Laguardia Community College and, later, other accred-
ited institutions, the women designed and opened a college program in
1977 (see Haywood, 1983; National Congress of Neighborhood
Women, 1993). They worked with local women to select a teaching staff

and develop a curriculum focused on improving urban communities. Courses in group dynamics, community organizing, public speaking, political science, and the sociology of the family were standard offerings. They also instituted a peer-counseling program and a student government. They quickly established an ethos that made it clear to all that this college would be a supportive place where everyone would work together. It would be a place where every voice is heard and considered. The two-year program awarded an AA degree, giving the women the training and the credentials they needed to run most of the programs they had in place or were thinking of creating. If the women attended their own college they could hire themselves instead of outsiders.

Almost all of the women who completed the college program continued to live and work in the neighborhood. Plowing their new confidence and capacities back into the community, the women have taken on a vast array of jobs and responsibilities in the many institutions that NW has spawned and in the neighborhood as a whole. Most have been able to lift themselves and their families out of poverty in the process. Tillie Tarantino gives us a sense of the impact the college program has had on her and her life:

> I used to think I was a nobody. Now people look upon me with respect because I am not afraid to pursue something, to argue with something. Jan kept saying, "You can do it, you can do it, you can do it." "Go to school!" "You have to go to college, you have to get a degree." "Let's get a college program in this neighborhood." She was the driving force.

With her degree, Tillie was hired as the founding director of the Swinging Sixties—the new senior citizen's center the women worked so hard to create. While running this highly successful community program for more than two decades, Tillie has had a voice in New York State, effecting programs for the elderly at all levels of municipal and state government.

The design of the college program rested on two basic assumptions: It should be neither intimidating nor culturally alienating; the students' development should be intertwined with the development of the community. All of the women involved in the organization were encouraged to further their education for the benefit of NW, the community, and themselves. The program's broad interdisciplinary curriculum centered on solving problems that were of significance to the women, their neighborhood, and the broader society. The curriculum provided both specific skills and a broad liberal arts perspective, helping the women place their situation in a wider context. Course work was augmented with apprenticeships in various community agencies, such as the shelter for battered women NW helped create, and the city's legal-aid program. The women also participated in a research project investigating some aspect of the community. Working in small collaborative groups, they would study a problem, design an action project, or make recommendations to government and civic organizations for future action.

The college program also emphasized the kind of peer "family-like" support of women helping women that was NW's usual practice. They took special care to involve the women's husbands so the men would have a greater understanding of and engagement with their wives' studies. In these and many other ways the college program replicated many of the processes that had permeated the Conselyea Street Block Association and the National Congress of Neighborhood Women: It provided a caring, supportive environment where women could nurture each other's development. It maintained a dual focus on each person's individual growth *and* on the development of the larger community. It sponsored collaborative projects demanding active participation, intensive experimentation, and problem solving. And it encouraged groups of women to reflect on their situations, articulate their visions, lay out detailed action plans for meeting their goals, and evaluate their efforts carefully whenever a project was completed.

From the beginning, the student retention rate at the college was far higher than the rate obtained by the standard on-campus programs in the greater metropolitan area. Community groups from all over the world sent delegates to Brooklyn to study NW's college program. Although the college program was later disbanded due to cutbacks in the financing of educational programs for the poor, the model has been used in six other communities across the country.

As NW was developing the college program for local Brooklyn women, it obtained a federal grant that helped them think about grassroots women's leadership in broad terms. The women conducted a wider and more systematic study of the nature of women's participation in the development of communities across the nation. They documented and publicized community programs across the country that were supportive of women as models to be examined and built upon. They also arranged a series of conferences so women leaders could continue to meet on a regular basis and develop a more elaborate system of mutual support. The range of grassroots women who attended one or more of these meetings included Karen Means from South Dakota, a leader of Women of All Red Nations; Helen Powell, the leader depicted in the film *Harlan County*, who organized thousands of Appalachian mining families against black lung disease; Maria Garcia and Ester Cota, who led a Chicano community to secede from a town where they felt voiceless and establish the town of Guadelupe, Arizona, as a place where the people would be heard and their values respected; and Bertha Gilkey, a leader who had organized the residents to take over and run a notorious project housing many of St. Louis's poorest blacks. When the tenants redesigned, remodeled, and ran the projects themselves, they were able to virtually eliminate drugs, crime, and vandalism—making their project a relatively safe and homey place for people to live and raise a family. There was a range of professional women as well, many of whom joined the NW's board, dedicating themselves to the organization for decades. Ronnie Feit, a corporate lawyer well connected in Washington and founder of the National Women's Political Caucus, has helped NW establish working relationships with policy makers and deal with a variety of legal issues. Marie Cirillo, founder of the Woodland Community Land Trust in Clairfield, Tennessee, and Sandy Schilen, a political scientist, have helped NW develop a very sophisticated understanding of the social, economic, and political forces that affect grassroots communities.

This extraordinary mix of women leaders sparked many new ventures. For instance, Ethel Velez, a young woman from the James Weldon Johnson Houses, a housing project in East Harlem, decided to follow Gilkey's example. She would organize her neighbors and they would transform their dysfunctional housing project in East Harlem just as Gilkey had done in St. Louis. With the National Congress of Neighborhood Women to back her up, Ethel created a tenants' organization that succeeded in taking over the management of the place. The tenants' association mobilized the residents and the city to completely overhaul the project. They refurbished the buildings, redesigned the grounds, and designed a governance system run by and for the tenants. Good lighting, well-placed trees, strategically located paths, and comfortable park benches created a variety of safe and pleasant outdoor spaces. Community space was created indoors as well. For the first time in the history of the project, people had common spaces where they could gather, socialize, and look out for one another. The tenants' association also built playgrounds that were well designed to meet the needs of children at various ages. All of the public spaces are maintained with the greatest of care. One never sees a single piece of trash littering the lawns or walks. When graffiti appears on a wall the tenants see that the damage is repaired immediately. Because young people are given special responsibility for maintaining the facilities they too take pride in the place. The tenants' association has also developed a democratic workplace, giving young people a range of opportunities to develop work skills and their capacities for community leadership. Today, Ethel's tenant-governed project is viewed as an outstanding example of a public housing project that is well designed, beautifully maintained, and democratically run.

NW found that their goal of getting diverse groups of women working together to solve common problems and realize shared dreams was extremely difficult, particularly when the women came from vastly different cultures and social classes. All too often the women would not take time to understand each other. Misunderstandings and conflicts could flare up at any moment. To be successful creators of the kinds of learning-working environments NW had in mind, the women would have to figure out all the steps involved in creating these kinds of social forms. Then they would have to create structures that would encourage participants to take these steps on a regular basis.

Seeing the importance of this task, Lisel Burns, a longtime NW member, took on the responsibility of articulating the philosophy and practices that would support these goals. Lisel made an extensive study of mutual-aid groups that have been successful in empowering diverse groups of people to work collaboratively on common problems and concerns. NW experimented with different practices in the college program and their national conferences. The women formally adopted the practices that seemed to be the most effective. They called these practices the Leadership Support Process (LSP).

NW encourages women to work in small Leadership Support Groups that meet on a regular basis. These groups are safe spaces where women can think out loud about themselves, the society they live in, and possibilities for a better way. Examining one's situation in terms of gender, ethnicity, race, and social class can be painful and frightening. Imagining new possibilities requires a sense of freedom, openness to the unknown, risk taking, and courage to explore the forbidden. Such qualities only flourish in dialogues between people who value each other's ideas, listen to each other with care, and build on each other's contributions.

The following were among the practices the women found helpful in cultivating this kind of dialogue: learning how to ask the kinds of questions that draw out people's best thinking; becoming adept at stepping into other people's shoes and seeing the world through their eyes; becoming skilled at seeing dreams unfold and affirming each other's most embryonic attempts to move forward; becoming proficient at discerning shared themes among diverse dreams so that common ground can be found, enabling them to move forward together.

Jan, herself, is a gifted question-poser, in part because she is so interested in people. She wants to know everything about them. She is always asking the kinds of questions that invite people to reflect on their experiences and articulate their thoughts, feelings, and visions for the future. Jan also works hard to put herself in each of the women's shoes, to see the world from their eyes. She says this is extremely difficult for her. Having modeled herself after her beloved, outspoken father, Jan says it is almost impossible for her to imagine the voiceless constricted lives that many women lead. The women appreciate Jan's struggle to understand them, even though they say "she often gets it wrong." Needless to say, they too find the task of understanding people with very different perspectives extremely difficult. People who haven't developed these skills make the assumption that empathic role taking or connected knowing is effortless. That Jan is so open about her difficulties undoubtedly alerts everyone to the fact that the process takes a good deal of effort and skill building. Lisel got everyone in the organization trying, in a systematic way, to figure what those efforts might look like.

Jan has another practice that has become part of NW's culture. She is always looking for the strengths of individuals and cultures. She is always trying to find ways these might contribute to the movement. She is especially interested in drawing on any cultural traditions that enhance family and community life, traditions that are still practiced and highly valued in many poor and working-class communities. Diverse people who pool their individual and cultural strengths greatly enlarge their vision of what is possible. For instance, the powerfully voiced Italian and African American women who take bold, direct stands in the face of conflict are important models for those who come from cultures that advocate silence for women and/or the avoidance of conflict. Black women who are raised with the expectation that they will become powerful community leaders are very helpful to women who come from cultures that are more likely to confine women to the home and subordinate roles.

Jan is always looking for ways to document and mirror the women's strengths. The organization institutionalized giving "appreciations" as part of the Leadership Support Process. Most of NW's meetings end with people sharing their observations about each other's strong points and advances. The women also bring these kinds of observations to the attention of the wider public. For example, they have collected and published oral histories documenting each other's strengths and the strengths of their cultures. A film on Neighborhood Women has been made and distributed to a wide variety of interested groups. The group also has a practice of sponsoring ceremonies and awards to make women's leadership more visible to the larger community.

Like a midwife, the National Congress of Neighborhood Women is always helping to give birth to new projects. The range has included the first shelter for battered women in New York, an experimental high school for students disaffected from the local public school, and many other job training and cultural programs. They nurse the "fledglings" along, and when it is time, they send the "child" out into the world with separate staffs, boards, and budgets. NW always remains interested and supportive even after their progeny are fully independent and self-supporting. As soon as one project is strong and standing on its own feet, the women begin again asking each other what they call "vision questions": "What is it that this community needs?" "If we had the support we needed to achieve our goals, what is it that we would be reaching for this time?" Once a common vision gains some clarity, they begin asking each other, "And how on earth would you do that?"

The women even got involved in developing new housing in the neighborhood—a formidable undertaking for any citizens' group. When the women heard that an abandoned hospital in the neighborhood was going to be demolished, Neighborhood Women became committed to saving it. The women could see that the brick and stone buildings—four in all—would provide a wonderful setting for the many families in the area who were in desperate need of decent housing. The buildings were surrounded by a high stone wall that muffled the sounds of the city. The enclosed grounds, comprising several acres of land, were dotted with ancient chestnut trees, a thing so rare in this neighborhood that a famous novel was titled *A Tree Grows in Brooklyn*. This peaceful place would be well suited for housing designed to bring out the best in families coping with the stresses of urban life.

Neighborhood Women and five other community groups (mostly led by women who graduated from the college program) formed a coalition to block the demolition of the hospital. Because of dramatic and persistent efforts, they succeeded. It was finally decreed that the building would stand and that it would be renovated for housing. The coalition decided it would develop the project itself. They would create model housing expressly designed to fulfill the needs of urban women and their families. The proposed housing would bring all segments of the neighborhood—old and young, poor and not so poor, white and black—together as a caring, supportive community. And, of course, the complex would be managed democratically by the tenants themselves.

Needless to say, when NW became a developer, the women had to acquire a huge range of new knowledge and skills. Indeed, their wish that the development process be guided by a feminist perspective and the values of the community required that they invent much of it as they went along. Feminist thinking has simply had less of an influence on architects and city planning than on most other human endeavors in this century (Hayden, 1995). The women began learning the ropes. Some of the local groups they were working with had considerable expertise in housing. They also sought out urban planners, social scientists, politicians, and others interested in bringing the perspective of community women into the planning process. They got Katrin Adams, a feminist architect, so interested in the project that she ended up donating years of her time to the effort.

Although the women anticipated that the undertaking would be complex and difficult, they never imagined the magnitude of the difficulties they were to face. It took ten years of intense effort, but they finally got housing built in the two buildings the community consortium allotted to them for development.

While NW's success in developing the project was a remarkable achievement, the women were unable to realize many of the innovations that they had proposed in order to make the housing more supportive of modern urban families. The maze of rules, the layers of bureaucracy, and stubbornly conventional analysis of cost effectiveness were overwhelming. These left no room for the women's more innovative design concepts and new ways of thinking about housing for modern families. No doubt one day we will read about a ground-breaking housing project planned by neighborhood women specially designed to enhance their lives in urban neighborhoods.

Under the auspices of NW, the Brooklyn women have engaged the traditional leaders of their city in one battle after another, year after year. Indeed, a central commitment of their organization has been to fight back whenever the established leaders do not listen to them and take their point of view seriously. They challenged the patriarchal control of the community by staging public demonstrations and strikes. They went to jail for civil disobedience. The organization encouraged women to run for local offices; they worked to get women appointed to the planning board and other important civic functions. They did everything they could think of to support the women to develop the quality of their leadership, once in these leadership roles.

The Brooklyn women have been able to command an increasingly large say in the affairs of the community because they absolutely refuse to be ignored, and their positions are well thought out and boldly articulated. They also prevail because they try to stand on a high moral ground. Because the women work with so many diverse groups and struggle so hard to bring in voices that are seldom heard, their positions are likely to envisage the common good more fully than are the positions of those who only consider the interests of a narrow segment of the population.

By the mid-1980s, the National Congress of Neighborhood Women felt it was focusing too much attention on projects in Brooklyn. The organization wanted to expand the national network and spend more time supporting women leaders in other communities. To prepare for the shift, NW spent three years working with community women in Brooklyn to create an independent but affiliated organization that would carry on the local work. They called the new organization the Neighborhood Women of Williamsburg/Greenpoint.

The National Congress of Neighborhood Women board was able to secure grants from the Ford Foundation and others to fund an enhanced outreach effort. They wrote an extensive manual (National Congress of Neighborhood Women, 1993) giving a highly detailed account of the processes involved in the leadership support process and their approach to organizing for promoting the development of women leaders and grassroots communities. NW also developed a series of workshops to teach these skills.

NW began reaching out to grassroots women all across the country in a more systematic way. By the late 1980s, the members had co-hosted many community forums with local grassroots women leaders and their allies; in 1990, they held five regional forums. All in all, they told over a thousand women about NW, demonstrated their leadership support process, and listened to what other women had to say. They found that the experiences and needs of grassroots communities across the country were very similar, with minor regional variations. Everyone was concerned about poverty and welfare reform. Everyone was having difficulty confronting or working with the existing power structures. Everyone was struggling with lack of funding, internal conflict, and burnout. Everyone wanted training in leadership development, help with strategic planning, policy information, sharing of program ideas that worked, and support for their efforts. Since then, NW has sponsored an annual weeklong Community Development Institute for sixty or so very diverse leaders from around the nation. By the end of these long, intensive sessions, the women shared a great deal of each information, honed their skills, and developed strong working relationships with community leaders from all corners of the nation. Women leaders emerge from these sessions with a greatly broadened view of the problems they face. of possible solutions, and of themselves as leaders. Each year the network seems to grow larger, more complex, and more effective in meeting the needs of the grassroots leaders.

It is not by chance that the Neighborhood Women's network has begun to circle around the globe. Highly democratic structures that are effective, inclusive, open, and committed to development are likely to radiate outward—encompassing ever larger numbers of people, a greater range of ideas, and more of the earth's territory. When Jan Peterson and other NW members attended the United Nations' Third World Conference on Women held in Kenya in 1985, they were disturbed to see so few grassroots women had been included. Professional women spoke eloquently of the problems and concerns of poor and working-class women, but poor and working-class women did not speak for themselves.

NW made a commitment to change all of that. Members teamed up with Caroline Pezzullo, a consultant on women and development to the United Nations, and grassroots organizations from six developing countries. Together they created an international network supporting grassroots women leaders all over the world to gain a voice in international forums. They called the new group GROOTS (Grassroots Organizations Operating Together in Sisterhood) International and obtained a substantial grant from the United Nations Development Fund for Women (UNIFEM) to financially support the effort.

GROOTS mounted a major campaign to bring the voices of grassroots women from developed and developing countries to the United Nations' Fourth World Conference on Women held in China in 1995. They held a number of forums in the United States and abroad to hear what grassroots women had to say and to gather women for the journey to China. They led workshops in community development for delegates from NGOs (Non-Government Organizations) at the European and North American regional preparatory meetings for China held in Vienna, Austria. Among the 30,000 women who attended the China conference, many were grassroots women GROOTS and NW helped to bring from Africa, Asia, Canada, Europe, India, Latin America, and the United States. They raised money to help cover the women's travel expenses. They kept the women informed of developments through meetings and publications. But most of all, they stressed the importance of having their voices heard. The thirty-member U.S. delegation named itself "the 50/50 delegation," because half of them were grassroots women and half were professional partners.

NW and GROOTS knew how important it would be for grassroots women to have a meeting place at the conference if they were to find their way at the largest gathering of women in the history of the world. They successfully lobbied the NGO Forum organizers to provide a tent on the conference grounds. They called it the Grassroots Tent. Grassroots women who might have felt quite lost in such a sea of humanity found a homeplace where they could gather themselves and move forward together. The tent was open all day long with a daily program. Delegates from different regions of the world took turns planning the events so each nationality could see that their stories were told, their songs sung, and their dances danced. A daily meeting was held in the tent at which the women would sum up their thinking, review the progress of the conference, and plan their strategies. Translators were arranged whenever possible. Everyone was encouraged to use LSP methods so a dialogue might flourish even though the women came from such different cultures and spoke so many languages. People could learn about aspects of Africa one day and South America the next. Soon themes began to emerge that linked the women to each other in powerful ways. Women from fishing villages around the world described the impact the death of the seas was having on their communities; others talked about the death of rain forests; still others spoke of the death of great cities. The women shared strategies, methodologies, and insights. Lyn Pyle's (1996) video, *We Are the Leaders: A Look at the World Through Grassroots Women's Eyes,* gives a good sense of the connections that were made in the Grassroots Tent.

It was not long before the word was out that one of the most vibrant conversations at the conference was going on in the Grassroots Tent. Officials from the United Nations and other organizations began sitting in and listening to the women. They realized, many for the first time, how rare it was to hear the voices of grassroots women at an international conference. They could see how important it was that these voices be included.

Before the China conference came to an end, a series of events was set in motion to assure fuller participation of grassroots women in future meetings. GROOTS, NW, and other network members would play a lead role in the Habitat II, the United Nations' conference on Human Settlements in Istanbul, Turkey, in 1996. The women agitated until the Istanbul Conference allocated them a tent and child care, and recognized them as a caucus. Again, they created a space—a public homeplace—where women from around the world could gather, figure out what needs to be said, and find a way to be heard. The perspectives of grassroots women were given an unusually full hearing at Habitat II. As of this writing, GROOTS and the National Congress of Neighborhood Women are gearing up to open an office at the United Nations. No doubt it too will become a public homeplace.

Looking back on the distance Neighborhood Women has traveled over the past decades, Sandy Schilen, a key player for many years in NW, gives this summary:

> Jan could see that gender was left out of the civil rights movement, that women were left out of the neighborhood movement, and that grassroots women and the neighborhood were both left out of the women's movement. The women in Williamsburg/Greenpoint ignored the women's movement because they believed it ignored the concerns of poor and working-class women like themselves. All that changed as they saw Jan redefining the women's movement from the perspective of neighborhood women. They essentially said, "Oh! You believe in the importance of families!" "You see how important it is that we care for our families!" "You believe in the importance of communities!" "You see that women are the ones that are holding up this neighborhood with or without resources." "Oh, you see we are pitted against each other around issues of race and that is why the neighborhood suffers." "You have a vision of women cooperating rather than competing with each other." "You see that women have the capacity to tackle and solve the problems that plague this neighborhood."

Women have always worked to make their communities more nurturing places for themselves and their neighbors, but women have not always named this tradition. Neighborhood Women is making this kind of leadership visible. By fighting for the right to have public homeplaces wherever they go, whether in concrete buildings or canvas tents, Neighborhood Women has shown how important it is that all excluded people have a place where they can feel at home. By working to have the voice of "municipal housekeepers" heard, NW gives us a clearer picture of how we might make our society a more hospitable place for everyone.

CHAPTER 9

THE CENTER FOR CULTURAL AND COMMUNITY DEVELOPMENT

People of color, all of us—women, poor men out on the street, all of us—live as an act of resistance, like the keepers of a flame. We are in active resistance to those who can only see themselves and think that their image should be the image in which everybody else is cast. As a resister I am always looking for people whose voices have been histori- cally shut out in this country, people whose voices seem to be silent, people that other folks see as invisible.

JANE SAPP
FOUNDING DIRECTOR, CENTER FOR CULTURAL
AND COMMUNITY DEVELOPMENT

Do you know the gospel singer Jane Sapp and her work with CCCD—the Center for Cultural and Community Develop- ment?" This question kept coming up in conversations with people around the country about ways of sponsoring grassroots women to gain a voice and claim the powers of mind. Invariably our matchmakers would add, "If not you should." "Jane," one informant said, "works with African Americans and other disenfranchised groups all over the coun- try to develop the philosophy and practice of something she and her colleagues call 'cultural work.'" He went on to explain that they call themselves "cultural workers" because they draw on the arts and tradi- tions of the African diaspora that enable them to create nurturing homeplaces where the silenced find themselves coming into voice. Jane Sapp and most of the other women who have helped develop the idea of cultural work grew up in the Black Belt, a fertile strip of dark rich soil that cuts across the Deep South, spanning Georgia, Alabama, and running into Mississippi. Because cotton blossomed easily on this land, the Black Belt housed an enormous African American workforce during slavery times and afterward. While some refer to the area as the Cotton Belt, those who cherish African American culture always seem to call it the Black Belt. In giving it this name they allude at once to the fertility of the bounteous soil and to the richness of the African cultures preserved by the area's dense and highly segregated black population.

After locating the cultural workers' origins, our informant went on:

> I believe you would call Jane Sapp a constructivist in that she is always getting communities of people actively engaged in rethinking everything. What she calls cultural work is an interesting elaboration on what you are calling "connected" or "midwife" teaching, because cultural workers get to know people extremely well and are very gifted in drawing out people's very best thinking. Jane is a powerful, gifted musician. She could have had a major career on the concert stage. She has chosen, instead, to use her art to elevate her people. Actually, elevating the country is probably more like what she really has in mind.

When we decided to include CCCD in the study, Jane took the risk and agreed. She arranged for the Belenky and Sapp families to travel together through the rural South talking with people who had been involved with cultural work over the years. We would interview Rose Sanders—the activist, lawyer, educator, organizer from Selma, Alabama—who has played an important role in developing the idea of cultural work. We would also interview a number of people who had participated in one or another of Jane's projects as adolescents or young adults.

Jane had also been interviewed extensively by Dean Elias (1993), an educator interested in social transformation, and Gwendolyn Kaltoft (1988/1990), a musicologist interested in the transformative power of music. Both made their interviews available. Kaltoft and Elias's interviews and their subsequent analyses opened up issues we might not have explored. We are grateful for their generosity.

The ease with which I, Mary Belenky, fell into the data collection phase of the project with Jane and the Center for Cultural and Community Development was to me surprising. I could not have anticipated the openness and the seriousness with which Jane approached the project. I was also overwhelmed by the generosity, warmth, and hospitality extended to us by Jane's friends and colleagues in the Southern black communities that we visited. Without exception, everyone we talked with took great pains to help us understand what cultural work was about and how it had affected them and their communities.

Because the gathering of information had gone so smoothly, I was unprepared for the difficulties I faced when it came time to analyze the data and articulate what I had learned. My goal of viewing the cultural workers in their own terms was, I found, surprisingly difficult. I had analyzed the interviews from the other homeplace women with methods my colleagues and I had developed during previous studies. Although all of that went well, I kept putting off the task of reading the cultural workers' interviews. When I finally started the process I began to doubt the methodology we had used with Listening Partners and other projects. It took me the longest time before I got comfortable with the process. I will describe the struggle in some detail because it ultimately illuminated the power of our approach and may help others embarking on cross-cultural research for the first time.

I believe that my anxieties about working across this cultural and racial divide had caused me to frame the task in a way that was immobilizing. When faced with this set of interviews I conceptualized the task of stepping out of my own framework much more literally than I ever had in the past when trying to understand the perspective of others. In previous studies I simply worked without being so self-conscious until I could get a good grasp of the person's point of view. This time I felt an awesome responsibility to transcend my own biases and yet I could not just set aside the lens—or the interpretive framework—that we had developed over the years. To do so would be to abandon the only tool I had for bringing the cultural workers' world into focus.

As I struggled with the problem my sense of the task began to change. When I became more comfortable I no longer saw myself trying to exchange one set of lenses for another. It seemed rather that I had simply expanded an old conversation about women's lives by adding to the dialogue two groups of African American women who had thought deeply about their cultural experience. One group was the African American cultural workers (mostly women) I had interviewed in person. The other was the black women writers I was reading.

As I read and reread the interviews, following our standard

procedures for analyzing interviews, I began to feel that we were all simply participants in an ongoing conversation. Because the interviews had been carefully transcribed, I could pore over them along with the annotations and excerpts from the books I had read. I would underline the text whenever someone addressed an idea that seemed important. The emphasized text would be given one or more labels, naming the topic(s) being addressed. Next to each quotation I would sum up what I thought the person was saying in my own words. I also tried to indicate why I thought the idea was important. Once I had decided that my own framework was a given to be expanded rather than denied, I no longer tried to deny my perspective. Indeed, the practice of putting my words side-by-side with those of the authors I had read and the women I had interviewed helped me articulate and expand my perspective. I allowed myself to explore any issue that seemed particularly promising, problematic, or puzzling. I did not try to assess the significance of the themes by counting their frequencies. Instead I tried to construct a narrative that captured the underlying structure of the women's thought.

After all of the materials had been read and reread many times, I began grouping the women's words in a myriad of different ways. Mostly I used the labels I had attached to the quotes to establish the categories for organizing the clusters. Thus Jane Sapp's thoughts on a particular subject might be placed alongside of Zora Neale Hurston's, Toni Morrison's, and Alice Walker's. Soon it almost seemed as if these women were talking with each other. When I could read similar ideas held by many of the African American women one after another, the notions became more elaborated and differentiated in my own mind. Things that had puzzled me became more understandable. I could almost hear the women saying to me, "Yes, but you should also look at it this way," "Did you notice this?," and "Look at that!" As I worked I began to hear nuances in what the women were saying that I had missed in earlier readings.

Because I disciplined myself to spell out my own thoughts next to each of the quotes I had excerpted, it felt as if I was being included in the conversation as well. Mostly I found myself saying, "Oh, I see! Now I understand. You and so-and-so were really trying to say such-and-such." As time went on I realized I had many things that I wanted to add to the ongoing dialogue. I also realized that I was carrying in my head the voices and viewpoints of the women from my own culture whom I had been interviewing and reading for decades. When I stopped denying these voices for fear of drowning out the black women's, they too seemed like important contributors to the discussion. Clearly many voices and angles of vision are useful whenever you are trying to grasp the shape of something new.

One more step extended this dialogue in very important ways. Jane Sapp read draft after draft of these chapters as they were being written. After each careful reading we would set aside time for another long reflective conversation. Jane would correct me patiently whenever I made an inference that seemed wrong to her. When I hadn't understood something well enough she would push me to delve deeper. She had a lovely way of showing her excitement whenever I achieved an insight that she particularly liked. Sometimes when I was trying to develop a hunch on the basis of very little data she would provide me with many new examples and stories to back up the case I was trying to make.

The lenses that I brought to this task were so much a part of who I am that I was hardly aware of their existence. Only as I began to see that the cultural workers were systematically approaching the world from a different cultural perspective could I better appreciate the organizing power of my framework forged in the experience of my culture. The dialogue helped me expand (not abandon) my point of view, enabling my vision to include more of the cultural workers' perspectives. Or, switching from a visual to a voice metaphor, as my own internal dialogue was enriched by the cultural workers' voices, I was able to hear more clearly what they were trying to say to me. Of course, what I came to see and hear was always my interpretation of the cultural workers' visions and voices. Although they worked hard to help me "get it right," I am certain that none of them would have put their own work forth in exactly the terms I have chosen to use. Thus the observations I have made about African American and European American women are offered here as simply one report on a careful and thoughtful dialogue between groups of women who are just learning how to talk with each other.

THE ROOTS OF CULTURAL WORK

Cultural work is rooted in the memories of Black Belt communities like "the Bottom" in Augusta, Georgia, where Jane grew up. Of "the Bottom," the name given to her neighborhood as well as to many other black communities throughout the South, Jane says,

> People looked down on people from the Bottom. They thought that is where you were. You were on the bottom of life. It was a low life. It was nowhere. You had "low potential." Your potential for getting out of the Bottom wasn't too great either. You were just nothing.

Jane's own experience of the Bottom was the total opposite:

> A great protective net was thrown over us there. It was a place full of incredible people—people with talent, people with wit, humor, and insight, people with creativity—not low ability as some would have it. It was a place you could feel at home. It was a place where you could sing. It was a place where you could love, where you could trust.

Cultural work is also rooted in memories of many community othermothers—that is, women leaders who work out of the developmental tradition to uplift the people and the community. These are the mothers and grandmothers, the woman next door, the choir leaders who built and maintained homeplaces as sites of resistance in communities all across the Black Belt. The cultural workers not only had direct access to a wide array of these community othermothers as teachers, models, and mentors, they had a wealth of cultural heroes like Harriet Tubman to ponder as well. (For further discsussion of women's role models, see Chapter 1.)

Music and Development   Cultural work is also rooted in the memories of the music that reverberated throughout the Bottom, as Jane testifies:

> Growing up as I did, you learn early on—somewhere in your soul—that music has power. When you grow up seeing people break up a church with their singing, you just know that music has power. Watching everyone becoming overcome with a kind of

spirit was a powerful experience. It was an overwhelming force that ignited everybody with a fierce energy. Everybody moved to that energy in their own way. Some people may cry, some people may run, some people may throw things. Some people may be standing up and shouting. Some people may be moaning to them-selves. Some would be patting their feet, others clapping their hands. Everyone was vibrating and sending their energy all through the church. (Kalcoft, 1988)

The power of black song for developing the spiritual and emo-tional lives of people and knitting them into a cohesive community has been long observed and much discussed (see, for example, Levine, 1978). Less noted is the power inherent in this music that can be har-nessed for the construction of knowledge. The philosophy and practices that Jane and the other cultural workers have evolved show how this traditional musical dialogue can be developed to draw out the minds of children and adults as well as their hearts. But first, let us look at why Jane believes that music plays such a powerful role in the development of mind and voice, and how she uses music to develop and test her own thinking:

There is something about singing. It's not that singing washes away thoughts but it opens up the mind to let something new come in. Like sleep and dreams, music relaxes the barriers of the mind. Music is a way to unlock what is waiting to come out. Mu-sic shakes up all of your preconceived notions. We have those tapes of set ideas that we play in our heads. Music shuts out those tapes and allows you to hear new ideas. When I play the piano I see things I didn't see before. I understand things I didn't understand before.

Music allows you to take risks, to explore the most difficult issues, to see beyond what others see, to go beyond the given.

Music and that dash of passion allows you to take risks. Wherever that place is that art takes you to, it is a place that enables you to take risks that you would not take ordinarily. I know that place be-cause I am an artist. It is that place in which intellect and feeling or passion have come together in a way to forage something new, something bold. From my personal experience I know I am more willing to take risks when I am at the piano. Understanding where I am when I can take those risks, I try to get to that place when I am not near the piano. It's like in a jazz combo when people begin to improvise. When you begin to improvise, at first you are taking a risk. You're just out there trying to figure out something new. You're not worried about who is going to laugh.

Jane uses the power of music to help her think through everything:

Music allows me to think. When I feel confused, or when I feel I can't think straight, or I feel I can't stand on solid ground, I have to play the piano. Somehow the music helps me to get clearer about what I think, where I am, and what I want to do. . . . In many ways the piano and music became that place for me where I found my voice. So for me to think of not singing or not having the music is like condemning me to silence or something. [She laughs.] But that's where my voice is: it's in the music. It's where my strength is; that's where my life is. It flows in my blood.

She describes the process of developing her thoughts through music:

The different notes don't mean anything until you are able to interpret the many different sounds you put together so that the interpretation and the synthesizing of it begins to *mean* something. Then taking that meaning and acting on it.

When you do all this, she says the music unleashes the whole person:

When people really understand that they have a voice and experience the freedom of their voice, it's like unlocking what's already been wanting to come out. Music does that so easily.

But Jane says that freeing an insight, inspiration, or intuition is not enough. Too often people do not understand that ideas must be explored, developed, and tested.

There is the spontaneous risk that you take, but then you don't just leave it there. It becomes scaffolding to build on. It's never just left there. It gets kneaded again and again. That's the thing that people don't understand: the feeling, the inspiration is just a beginning. It took me here, but how do I work it now? What is that saying—"creativity is 1 percent inspiration, 99 percent perspiration"?

Knitting, crocheting, weaving, and kneading are some of the metaphors Jane uses to describe how she develops and refines an idea:

> You keep kneading it and kneading it, until you really understand it, until it becomes a part of you. To me kneading is always the most important part of the whole process.

She says that an idea and a person become joined when the person comes to a full understanding of the thing being pondered, when all aspects of the thing have been taken into consideration.

> You keep kneading an idea until it feels a part of you, not separate from you. When it feels joined with you, it's right. When it is fully absorbed you no longer have to go and reach for it. When you have a full understanding, you have created a whole. Everything comes together. You have pulled in all the threads; all the stitches have been worked together. Kneading is working it so it starts feeling like a whole.

Others who listen to the music will also experience the wholeness that the artist has created.

> When I work on a song, what I work for is for that song to feel like one note just naturally follows another, like there are no disconnected threads. So when others hear it everything will sort of weave together for them too.

Jane says that in the kneading process she tests out the ideas she is developing against her own experiences:

> When I sing a song I want every word to be true to the experience that I sing about. It would be very difficult for me to sing about something that I haven't experienced and kneaded. To me

there wouldn't be truth in the song. I would just be singing out of emotions that I hadn't experienced. I wouldn't sing a single word from any song that I can't conjure up from my experience.

Jane also uses her audiences to help test out the "truth in the song." Does the idea she has been reaching for ring true in the audience's experience? Does it help the audience to bring together the loose ends with which they are concerned? To weave a new whole?

Singing gives me the opportunity to test the words with audiences. Points would be clarified in the singing. I had an opportunity not only to test the saying of it, but to test the thinking of it. Singing about something helps me see if the thinking stands on a solid moral and logical ground. I can speak with a certain kind of assurance, clarity, and commitment when things have been tested in the music.

Jane says that once the truthfulness of an idea has been tested through music it becomes the basis for commitment:

I'll keep working that song and working that song until it feels like it is wedded to you. So there is no separation between the words, the emotions, and you. You want to be committed to every word you sing. Saying things through music gives me the courage to say them without the music.

Commitment leads to action:

You look at the specific information and try to figure out what it's trying to say to you, if it makes sense to you; if it speaks to something inside of you and the outside of you in terms of what you're doing, then you do something with that. You take what you've been able to pull together and you go out, you share it with others, and you act on it.

Jane is interested in moving the whole community to act:

Mainly the acting on it is the sharing. You want other people to be *moved* by what you do. When a group of people are moved, they will begin to act in harmony with one another. That is where the real force in the music comes pouring out.

Jane sums up the role of music in her life:

> Music flows in my blood. I carry it in me, so if I speak, it's a song.
> I hear it being composed and coming out of my mouth like a
> song. I want to shape everything as if I were singing it. I know that
> it sounds strange, but that's how it feels to me. It feels like life flows
> like a song. Life flows with the rhythm and beat of a song. A lot of
> times I hear the song developing. I'll be looking at something, and
> in my mind I'll be trying to shape it into a lyric. Then I say to my-
> self, "No, Jane, that's not a lyric, that's just a theoretical reflection
> on the world. That is all it is. You are not going to be able to shape
> it all into a song." But I think I'm always going for the song. But I
> don't always need to be singing, per se, because the song—it's here.
> I mean it's happening now. Life is the song.

THE FOUNDING OF THE CENTER FOR CULTURAL
AND COMMUNITY DEVELOPMENT

The concept of cultural work with all of its philosophical underpin-
nings began to take shape in the minds of Jane Sapp and her allies during the civil rights movement of the 1970s. When Jane and her husband, Hubert Sapp, finished college, they returned to the Black Belt,
where they were at the center of the movement. They joined the faculty of Miles College, a black institution in Birmingham, Alabama. It
was not long before they had turned their house into a homeplace for
students and community people active in the movement. They created
a powerful collaborative learning community around their kitchen
table. Everything was discussed there—the protests, the civil disobedience, the philosophy of nonviolence, the killings, the police violence,
the nation's history, the world's history, the centuries of black struggle,
the movement's politics and strategies, along with each individual's personal stories and choices. All of the intellectual disciplines were related
to this historic struggle and the students' academic work took on new
meaning. The students emerged from the process as highly articulate
adults with strong leadership skills and a deep commitment to building
a new society.

The conversations around the Sapps' kitchen table always ended in song. Because most everyone was from the Black Belt, the power of song for drawing a community into conversation was understood from long experience. Soon Jane and a group of women students formed themselves into a singing group they called the African Ensemble—Jane's first large-scale project as a cultural worker.

The spirit and purpose of the African Ensemble was very much like the Freedom Singers that Bernice Reagon and a group of civil rights workers from the Student Nonviolent Coordinating Committee had developed earlier in nearby Albany, Georgia. Bernice Reagon would also found Sweet Honey in the Rock, the all-women a cappella quintet that has elevated the country with black song for the past twenty-five years (see Reagon and Sweet Honey in the Rock, 1993). In her music making and in her work as a scholar, Bernice Reagon has helped develop the idea of cultural work by harnessing the power inherent in the music for promoting the development of a people and their quest for social justice.

Like the Freedom Singers, the African Ensemble traveled up and down the road to support the civil rights groups that were bursting into action throughout the Black Belt. The Ensemble bolstered the people's spirits with singing, it communicated the spirit of the movement to the broader world, and it helped raise funds to sustain the effort.

Jane and I interviewed women from the ensemble still living in the Birmingham area. Because this was their first meeting in many years, it was also a reunion. Needless to say, there was a good deal of singing at this gathering.

In the interview the women spoke again and again about how Jane had insisted that the members of the Ensemble use the music to make a statement about themselves and the era in which they were living. Listening to them tell about singing their way through those heated times, it is clear that the women's musical statements became richer and bolder over time, as did they themselves.

Reflecting on the effect that the Ensemble has had on their lives, the members realized that almost all of them have continued the work of the Ensemble in one way or another. Valencia Power Bell, an educator with the Birmingham Community College's satellite program in a local prison, gives but one example:

Each of us has a story like this to tell. Mine is about the work I do with prisoners. They are all male. Ninety percent of them are black males. Most are very intelligent and *very* good-looking. [Everyone laughs.] If somebody would allow them to speak, there's no way that they would be incarcerated. They should be allowed to offer what they have to offer to the world. I am there as a mother figure, as an educator: I am constantly reminding them that they're intelligent human beings and what they have to offer is wonderful. This is so even though the world won't let them express themselves.

Valencia collects the prisoners' stories, like an oral historian. In the process she encourages them to reflect on where they have been and where they want to go. She says,

I am always saying, "You should look at yourselves as black men who have had a struggle. That struggle is supposed to make a statement. What you do, what is happening to you now, who you are— all of this—should be used by you to make your statement to the world." All these men have a story to tell and that story is valuable. I encourage them to speak it and to write it. All of them have value. It's such a waste. The beautiful gifts they have are just wasted.

Valencia says if these black men can find the freedom of their minds they will shape a better life:

Education can give these men an avenue. It frees the imagination. In the freedom of their imagination they can decide who they are and how they want to live. They can choose how they will manifest their lives. That education can do this is shown in studies. Prisoners who get an education have lower recidivism rates because they have found the freedom of their minds.

The Sapps went on in 1973 to Eutaw, Alabama, where they helped Miles College establish a satellite campus. Eutaw is in an area with an extremely high concentration of African Americans, poverty, and rural isolation even for the Black Belt. Some (Chestnut and Cass, 1990) have called the area "a citadel of racism," so fierce was the resistance there to any aspirations arising from the black community. Educational opportunities for black children in the area had always been extremely sparse and higher education was entirely absent. Resistance to blacks who would aspire to anything but the most menial of work was intense. Many of the area's whites wanted to see themselves as superior to blacks and they themselves had low levels of education. It also served their purposes well to have a very large workforce that was docile and poorly paid.

Because of their numbers, African Americans would outvote whites and rise to leadership roles now that they had finally achieved the right to vote and were exercising that right. A high-quality educational program was clearly of the utmost importance to the future of the whole area and beyond.

The Sapps planned to bring the students together in Eutaw as a family, just as they had done in Birmingham. They would create a homeplace where they and the students would study contemporary problems in light of the history and the culture of their own African American community. The study of the local culture could be conducted with unusual thoroughness because Jane was awarded a substantial grant to conduct the first extensive oral history project in the region. Not only did Jane get this unprecedented support, but she joined a new community of black scholars who were embarking on similar efforts.

> With the black power movement there was this energy within the black community to understand our history and our culture as thoroughly as we could. Before the sixties you primarily had white folklorists and anthropologists going into the black community and doing research. They were scholars who had little interest in promoting the development of the community they studied. Indeed, some even wanted the development of blacks blocked, so their folk culture would remain in stasis. Now for the first time, blacks were finding support to do this kind of research in their own community. The African Diaspora project Bernice Reagon started at the Smithsonian Institute gave us a space—an institutional base—from which we could reach out to each other, come together, and make a major presentation of African and African

American history, culture, and traditions. If it had not been for the space Bernice was able to create for this group of black scholars through the African Diaspora project, their voices, thoughts, and work would not have had a place to develop. While most of the scholars she brought together continued to take the disinterested stance of a traditional academic, a small number of us were interested in seeing how the study of black culture could contribute to the ongoing growth and development of the community.

The model Jane worked out in Eutaw, linking the study of culture with the development of people and communities, provided a template for her subsequent projects as a cultural worker. She describes the spirit that pervaded the project:

> The students who enrolled at Miles College in Eutaw could not really read or write. They were so silent. I had to find the imagery and the spirit that would communicate with them. We had to leave the classroom to get to this deeper level of understanding. We left the classroom and started driving all over the county. I'd get out and say to folks, "I just want to know who you are and what you do. I teach at this new college in Eutaw. I think who you are and what you do ought to be a part of what we teach." There wasn't anybody I wouldn't talk to. We talked with people who made all kinds of things—from the blacksmith to the jug blower. We interviewed one family who still lived basically as people lived in the thirties or forties. They were still sharecropping, although now they call it renting. The guy still had the wagon pulled by the horse. She still cooked out of the fireplace. We interviewed everybody. We collected their stories. We got hundreds of wonderful photographs. Then we would put all of this together in various ways. It would all be available for our students as well as for students at the local high school. In this way the community gets its knowledge back. The community can see that it has a knowledge base to build on.

Asking people what they thought and carefully returning their words had a transformative effect on everyone. Jane says,

> You have to remember that this area of Alabama was one of the poorest areas in the country. It was probably the first time someone

was asking the people there, "What do *you* think?" You could just feel this burst of energy coming from the people.

Thus two unprecedented events occurred simultaneously. A black educator was given substantial support to collect materials that would help the faculty and the students better understand and value a way of life that had been written off as "just nothing." And students who never even dreamed of college found themselves in a learning community where they felt welcomed, understood, and valued. With this kind of support, the students were able to make better use of the whole curriculum the college was providing.

Elzora Fluker, one of the first students to enroll in the new program, explains why she had never dreamed of getting an education:

> I came from a large family. My mother was a single parent. It was a struggle for her just to keep everything going from day to day. Even though we lived only 27 miles away, coming to Eutaw was like going to Las Vegas. It was a long distance. There were no phones. We had never even talked to people that lived far away. Going to town was a rare thing. Hardly anyone had a car. Very few people from my community ever even thought of going to college. It was something rare.

Elzora also helps us understand how the oral history project helped the students see their community as valuable and worthy of their commitment. She says,

> Before I started going to school at Miles I'd see my mother quilting and other people doing other things. Those things would happen, but we didn't look at them as being important. We figured it was just the thing they were doing. Jane taught us to be appreciative of these things, the art of them doing it, the beauty in it. Before that the only thing that we really wanted to do was leave; we didn't know there was anything here that was important. . . . Thanks to Miles College, I didn't leave. I work as a deputy here at the county, and I serve on the Board of Education—thanks to Miles College. We have so many that went to Miles College who are still here in the community doing all sorts of things.

Mollie Gaines, another student who also stayed after graduation to become a community leader, spoke of the transformation that occurred for her while she was at Miles. She says,

> Now I am a thinker but I didn't start thinking 'til Miles College and Jane Sapp came to Eutaw. In those days your parents thought for you: "You do this, Mollie. You do that." We were farmers—essentially sharecroppers. My father had died. We had to work very hard. You would get up every day, you dressed, you went to school, you came home, you went to the field, you picked cotton, you came home. Your mom told you what chores you had to do and that's what you did. You didn't really have to think. You didn't have choices. Jane gave me the courage to think for myself. Jane made me feel that I could think and make good decisions for myself. That I did have choices. That I could decide what's best for me in my life.

Mollie links her ability to think for herself with a new view of her culture:

> Just by knowing Mrs. Sapp, the way she carried herself and her dress, made me know that I was an African American, and that as a black person I could be proud of what I was, that I could be something, that I could stand for something. That's the image Jane pictured for me: a black African woman who was about doing things, who was moving forward. That's what I wanted to do—move forward.

As Jane accumulated oral histories of people in the area, she discovered people who were using the traditional arts in ways that were transforming the lives of the people in their local communities. A blues singer from nearby Pickens County, Alabama, by the name of Willie King was among their number. Pickens County was an unusually poor county, even in the Black Belt. Willie had gathered together some of the poorest and most marginalized young men of the area and was busy teaching them the blues. When they formed a group and began to sing and speak in communities all over the countryside, these young men began to blossom.

Jane explains why being reconnected to their culture was so

liberating for the students at Miles-Eutaw and for Willie's musicians in
Pickens County:

> In every community people have a culture, a set of "how-to's":
> how to build institutions, how to build relationships, how to make
> themselves feel good. Culture also provides the strategies, the
> "how-to's," for social change. All of this knowledge is a part of cul-
> ture. It is the knowledge that people have created together. The
> "how-to's" link us historically; they give us the basis from which
> we create. Without the "how-to's," people just float aimlessly with-
> out even thinking that somehow it could be a different world.
> Culture is the knowledge that has helped us to understand how to
> struggle, how to live *through* struggle, and how to live *with* struggle.
> It cannot be overlooked. It's what's gotten us through thus far.

Jane describes how cultural work supports people to engage in
struggle:

> To me cultural work is about how you nurture people, how you
> affirm people, how you help people to know what they know,
> how you help people to know that they have a culture and a
> knowledge base to build on, how you help people to know that
> they are creative and that they have a creative base upon which to
> build. Knowing what it is you are connected to is a very powerful
> rock to stand upon. When we sent out a group of kids from these
> programs they felt they had a place in this world. They were saying
> to the world, "Just move over, 'cause I'm here."

Bridge Building   After creating throughout the Black Belt many programs that link the study of culture with the development of people
and communities—music schools, workshops, and folk festivals—Jane
went on to become the director of the cultural program at the Highlander Center for Research and Education, in New Market, Tennessee.
Founded by Myles Horton, Highlander is the place that first supported
Septima Clark to develop the citizenship schools that Charles Payne
(1995), the historian discussed earlier, saw as so important to the civil
rights movement in the Black Belt.

As director of Highlander's cultural program, Jane worked with a variety of different cultural groups. Describing how her perspective expanded with the experience, Jane said, "Being at Highlander I got to make room in my family for other folks." At Highlander Jane was able to see other marginalized and silenced groups besides blacks becoming empowered as they reclaimed and built on their own cultural heritage. She could also feel how eye-opening cross-cultural collaborations can be when diverse groups of people open themselves up to each other. Furthermore, she became increasingly aware of the power inherent in the arts for creating social harmony:

> In a roomful of dissonant voices, a cultural worker takes the sounds and finds a space for them to work in harmony. In a community of many colors, a cultural worker finds a canvas for the colors to work beautifully together. A cultural worker brings cohesiveness to a flurry of movements. She creates a shared drama from the moments of very different lives. Cultural workers have the skills, imagination, and nature to put people with different shapes, sizes, ideas, and existences together in a way that makes a whole—a whole that creates an inspirational presence. If there was ever a time in this country for the artists it is now. We need to know how to take different colors and make them work together. We need to know how to take different textures and make a fabric. That is the instinct of the artist. It is what cultural work is about.

Since Highlander Jane has been traveling in the United States and abroad, looking for cultural workers who are reconnecting the people with their culture and finding a rock on which they can stand. Like Willie King, these local leaders were working with their neighbors to reestablish their community's tap roots, to call denigrating cultural stereotypes into question, and to develop a voice that others would heed. Because most of these local leaders were doing this work with the most meager of resources and little institutional backing, Jane decided to create the Center for Cultural and Community Development (CCCD). Like Ella Baker's In Friendship and SNCC, CCCD would create an ongoing mutual support system linking leaders from many different cultural communities. As part of a national network, even people working in small, isolated communities would be able to see their community's problems and solutions in the largest perspective possible. The network would also provide a range of the institutional supports they needed and were not getting in their local communities.

CCCD would help cultural workers establish relationships with foundations and government agencies and find audiences for the work they sponsor. The organization would sponsor a variety of institutes and forums, providing opportunities for cultural workers from diverse communities to learn from each other's history, culture, and struggles; to share resources, ideas, and strategies; and to provide further training in the philosophy and practices of cultural work. The institutes have been organized around such themes as "Youth as Makers of History and Culture," "Creativity as an Act of Resistance," and "Cultural Work as a Strategy for Social Change."

CCCD has worked with many different cultural communities in the United States and abroad. For example, it has worked with European groups trying to find ways that the immigrants flooding their countries could build bridges to the new culture without severing their ties to the old. The most electrifying of all: CCCD has sponsored cultural workers from Africa and the United States to crisscross the ocean so they might bolster each other's efforts to uplift their communities.

THE DREAM PROJECT

With her most recent project Jane seems to be creating a structure for children that has a lot in common with CCCD. At first, as she would move around the country giving workshops for children, Jane would get the children to add verses to each other's songs. Soon she had songs composed by Native American children from the Dakotas; children who were descendants of European immigrants growing up in rural New England; and descendants of involuntary African immigrants living in the rural South. When Jane filled a concert hall with the children's songs, audiences would be flooded with a sense of a common humanity and new possibilities for dialogue and connection.

Before long Jane was dreaming of bringing the children together in one place so they could make music together in a more literal sense. She called it her Dream Project. A first group of children met in the summer of 1996 and spent two weeks getting to know each other, developing their music, and recording their songs. The recording *We've All Got Stories: Songs from the Dream Project* (Sapp, 1996) is being distributed nationally by Rounder Records.

People in the communities where Jane had been working helped select the children who would participate. All of the candidates had some musical abilities. Beyond that, many of the children came from the margins of their own communities. They had had few opportunities to participate in local events much less to travel across the country to join other children in such a challenging and exciting enterprise.

By the end of their two weeks of work and play, all of the children were members of a national network that also became a tight and loving community—just like the experience of adults who participate in CCCD's activities. No doubt Jane will follow these young people, strengthening their ties to each other and backing them up, just as she has followed Ezora and Molly through their adult years, supporting them to continue developing themselves, their leadership abilities, and their communities.

Reflecting on the full array of projects developed by herself and the other cultural workers, Jane summarizes the essence of the work:

> As a cultural worker I am able to say I have a model of how to build an institution. I have a model of how you could build communities and schools where people feel included and respected. I have a model of how you respect and love yourself. I have a model of how you can work with and respect children and old people. I have a model of how you can make communities welcoming rather than alienating, discouraging places. I feel strongly committed to that model. I have a model and I have the courage to put my model out here beside your model. You have said to the rest of the world that only your model is important. That only your model can be valued. That only your model can bring true democracy, true happiness, true power, whatever. I dare to put my model of how to live beside your model. I dare to do that.

She speaks of the power of models like these and why they meet with so much resistance:

> When people latch on to models for living that they have created out of their own visions they are willing to change their lives. When the life becomes one with the vision it is very dangerous to the entrenched power structure. Business as usual can't go on. That is why this work meets the vehemence of resistance that it gets. They do not want the people to see new possibilities. They do not want the people to know they are able to act on those possibilities. They do not want the people to feel their own power to act. That is very dangerous.

Thinking about the Center for Cultural and Community Development, the Dream Project, and other public homeplaces where people from many different communities begin working together, Jane adds,

> Opening up possibilities between communities is a threat. It is one thing to see people change within a community but between communities! When people begin crossing all these barriers to band and bond together, that is a threat.

Rose Sanders.   In developing herself as a cultural worker and in developing the Center for Cultural and Community Development as an organization, Jane's closest collaborator over the years has been Rose Sanders. We detail Rose's work here because of its importance to the development of CCCD; it also gives us a broader view of the diverse approaches cultural workers assume.

Rose met with us twice. The first meeting began in her law office in Selma, Alabama. The second occurred a year later, at which time we were accompanied by a dozen community leaders from the African country of Mali. They were developing literacy programs in Mali around ideas that were remarkably similar to those of the African American cultural workers. Because Rose and her husband, Hank Sanders, now a senator in the Alabama legislature, incorporated all fourteen of us into their household, we were able to get quite a glimpse of how the Sanderses' family life blends with public life.

Waiting for the first interview in Rose's law office, we could not help but be impressed by the intensity of the work that was going on there. Phones rang, people bustled about, and piles of work cluttered every available surface. The walls of the corridors and waiting room were covered with plaques honoring the achievements of the law firm and its associates. When Rose arrived, this busy place seemed to bristle with even greater vitality. A regal, brown-skinned woman, African in appearance and dress, Rose filled the space with her presence. We immediately felt the warmest welcome. It was also clear from the start that Rose's fervent passion for her work was interlaced with a raucous sense of humor and an enormous zest for life. Only after meeting her does it seem possible that one person could work on so many fronts at once.

Rose studied law at Harvard University, she said, because she was told that black girls had to be teachers. She was the first black woman to be appointed as a judge in the state of Alabama. As lawyers, Rose and her colleagues have handled many cases important to the local community and some that have been vital to the nation. Rose is also a cultural worker par excellence. Whereas Jane travels from one community to another creating a variety of programs in the most out-of-the-way places, Rose has concentrated her efforts on Selma, Alabama. As a cultural worker, she has developed a countless number of projects and organizations that support the black community of Selma to have a voice in the way the town is run.

When Rose and her husband finished law school in the late 1960s, they, like the Sapps, decided to return to the Black Belt where they were raised. They wanted to throw themselves into the civil rights struggle and help develop the area for all its residents. It is fitting they chose Selma as it had been pivotal in the struggle for civil rights. When Selma's black community began a voter registration campaign in 1963, the reprisals were swift, massive, and brutal. While violence against blacks who were trying to exercise their rights was all too common in the South, it has been seldom documented. This time the national press came to Selma and pictures of vicious attacks on peaceful protesters were flashed on television screens across the world. The events in Selma continued to escalate until one Sunday afternoon hundreds of people were trapped on a bridge and mowed down by a massive force of police, firemen, and horses. The people were on their way to the state capital, where they had hoped to petition higher authorities for some sort of redress. That was a day of such violence it continues to be known as "Bloody Sunday" to those who follow the movement's history. When the nation watched the televised films of the assault by armed government officials on peaceful citizens, it was stunned. People from all corners of the country said, "Enough!" Four months later the U.S. Congress passed the Voting Rights Act. The right to vote was clearly established by the law of the land.

When Rose and Hank Sanders opened their law office they joined forces with J. L. Chestnut—a black lawyer who had been struggling against intense opposition to develop a legal practice in Selma for many years. The law firm they established was a hybrid: part legal service, part defense fund, part civil rights organization, part headquarters for political organizing, and part youth-development agency (Chestnut and Cass, 1990; Sanders, 1988). The Sanderses and their law firm have played a key role in reorganizing political life in Alabama. Twenty-five years after the passage of the Voting Rights Act the state of Alabama enjoys the highest rate of black political participation in the United States with more black elected officials than any other state in the nation (Sanders, 1988).

Rose has participated in this struggle as both a lawyer and a cultural worker; her law firm has backed both approaches with equal vigor. As a cultural worker, Rose has exercised her considerable abilities as a storyteller, playwright, and songwriter for drawing out and dramatizing the people's statements about their struggles and aspirations. She created the Black Belt Arts Center (B'BAC) so children could develop themselves as performing artists and have their voices heard throughout the community. At B'BAC children study the music of their people, compose their own songs, and write and produce original plays. Jane gives us a sense of Rose's approach:

> The way Rose Sanders runs the Black Belt Arts Center in Alabama everyone is included. She'll be doing a play with kids. If some new kids just happened to walk in, she will teach them the song and put them into the play. You should see Rose just raking these children in. Now some of them can really sing, some can really act, and some of them can't. Either way, nobody lost anything. They only gained something. Even the kids that weren't as talented found a community; they found a place where they be-

longed; they found friends; they found a woman who loves them with the biggest heart; they found themselves traveling to places they'd never been to.

Because of B'BAC the black children of Selma have had many opportunities to reflect their experiences through art-making; they have become remarkably articulate about their lives and their dreams. Through B'BAC they have cultivated large and devoted audiences who have become very interested in hearing what young people have to say about growing up black in Selma. Rose also developed the 21st Century Youth Leadership Training Project—a program for teenagers that brings potential leaders from Selma together with youth from across the nation to develop themselves as community-focused leaders.

Yet another of Rose's projects, Mothers of Many (MOM), organized the women of Selma into a political force dedicated to improving the lives of the community's children. The organization's name suggests its purpose: it is an organization to support the community othermothers of Selma who are interested in all the children of the community—not just those in their own family. MOM provides much of the leadership and volunteer labor needed to run B'BAC, 21st Century, and all the other community projects Rose and her friends dream up.

Rose and her colleagues have also turned the buildings that overlook the Edmund Pettus Bridge in Selma—the site of Bloody Sunday—into the National Voting Rights Museum. The museum has become a public homeplace in Selma where people of all colors gather to study their history and find ways to continue the development of their communities.

Combining cultural programs for children and adults with the law firm's work in the courts and legislature has led to many changes in Selma and the state of Alabama. One of the more recent efforts has been the reform of Selma's educational system (Applebome, 1994). In the face of court-ordered desegregation, Selma—like many other school districts throughout the nation—has kept the races segregated within a school building by grouping the students on the basis of "ability." While the *school system* as a whole is said to be desegregated, the *school buildings* have been almost completely segregated.

In Selma, as elsewhere, the students' abilities were determined by the teachers' subjective judgments (Oakes, 1985). Because most of the teachers equated intelligence with race and social class, black children were judged to be low in ability while white children were given high ratings. By the end of the 1980s, 90 percent of the white children were being educated in the high-ability track while only 3 percent of black children were seen fit to join them (Chestnut and Cass, 1990). This practice enabled the schools to continue segregating the children on the basis of race, even though race was no longer mentioned as a criterion.

Because lower-track students were not allowed to take standard high school courses such as algebra and biology, black students who did go on to college found themselves severely disadvantaged. When the black students came home from college for the holidays, they told the high school students about the inadequacies in Selma's educational system. When the high school students approached Rose in 1990 with their fears for the future, they decided they would form an organization with the sole purpose of dismantling the tracking system. Opposition to their efforts from the white community was so intense that school officials would not even discuss the issue with them. The black community saw no choice but to organize a school boycott and a series of nonviolent demonstrations. Rose was one of many jailed for their peaceful protests. In addition, a myriad of other charges were filed against her in the courts. Moves were also made to have her disbarred from the practice of law in the state of Alabama.

Rose's law firm played a number of different roles in this fight. Not only did the firm provide Rose with support for her cultural work with the children and parents, but it provided the legal services necessary to mount the students' case in the courts, and it raised thousands of dollars to cover the expenses involved.

All of the legal proceedings and charges against Rose have been dismissed. The federal courts ruled that the policies of the Board of Education did systematically discriminate against the black children of Selma. Negotiations are now taking place to decide how Selma will go about educating all of the children more adequately. Needless to say, the Sanderses and many others are insisting that Selma's black community play a role in designing the town's school reorganization plan. Although many white children have transferred to the newly constructed private schools that now dot the area, the black children of Selma now have a better chance of getting an adequate education (Applebome, 1994). The children's papers and other materials from this struggle are already being gathered and housed in Selma's National Voting Rights Museum so this and future generations can learn from their efforts.

The children of Selma became an important force for change within the schools. Rose links the students' success with the 21st Century leadership camps, B'BAC, and the many other programs they had developed for the youth of Selma over many years. She says,

> We were able to end these discriminatory practices in the schools because students provided leadership. We'd been working with those young people on developing the kinds of leadership skills that uplift the community: leadership that is community-focused leadership, as opposed to self-focused. Most programs and schools train for leaders that will be self-focused—focused on their own self-excellence, on their self-development—not on community development, not on community excellence. So when it came time to deal with the tracking issue, we had a cadre of young people in place in that school system who could take a leadership role on behalf of the whole community.

The children who had spent years with B'BAC and 21st Century had strong public voices. They could articulate the humiliations that black students experienced in the schools so well that many of the adults who had been sitting on the sidelines felt compelled to act. The children had also developed a full range of skills in leadership and community building. They were able to create a solid support system when their classmates stepped forward, helping their peers to work together and to take strong clear stands.

The black women of Selma were also an important force in this mammoth undertaking. When the school fight began, many were already confident, well organized, savvy political actors. Years of involvement in Mothers of Many (MOM) had created a cadre of women who were highly skilled at bringing the perspective of mothers into the public arena.

Jane, Rose, and the other African American cultural workers have at least two practices that are not widely shared by the homeplace women from European-based cultures. The African American cultural workers build on ancient cultural traditions that place art-making at the center of daily life of ordinary people. They encourage people to participate in the art-making, so the mirror that is constructed will reflect their most passionate statements about themselves and the world in which they live. The art-making also loosens the mind, opens the heart, and leads to dialogue. People begin to imagine that things could be otherwise. They dream of the world as it should be. They realize they share a common vision. Together the people begin reaching for goals that everyone agrees are of the utmost importance.

The aspirations are first expressed in art-making; they often evolve into concrete projects, like ending "ability grouping" that resegregated the children's schools. When the artwork is polished enough to reflect the fullness of the people's visions it is presented to the larger community. By presenting themselves to the public in the most vivid terms of their own choosing, people cut through the stereotypes that had obscured the reality of themselves, the world, and visions of better ways to live. The cultural workers understand that when a public dialogue is elevated by an art form, a chain of events is likely to be unleashed. The community is apt to broaden its perspective on the world as it is and as it could be, to arrive at a new place of understanding, to find new possibilities for growth and transformation. The improvised and evolving song itself becomes a metaphor for the community dialogue the cultural workers seek. The ability to compose one's own music becomes a metaphor for the ability to compose a life for one's self and one's community. (See Maxine Greene [1988, 1995] for compelling descriptions of the role of the arts in unleashing the moral imagination.)

Whatever else they are doing, Jane and Rose always seem to have at least one project directed toward art-making with young people. As Jane says, "they are always raking in the kids" so they can participate in one more musical event or theater production. Cultural workers are especially concerned to draw in the invisible and silent children standing in the margins of their community. The children find themselves members of a community where people talk together and care for each other. Through the art-making the young people begin talking to each other in the most serious way; they develop their statements to the world through the songs and plays they write. The art is often so powerful that adults begin looking at their community through the eyes of the children and decide something must be done. The cultural workers try to pick from the throng of young people those who have the potential of "seeing beyond what others see" and becoming the next generation's leaders. They are especially interested in identifying potential leaders who will strengthen the whole community by supporting the development of the most vulnerable. By looking for potential leaders among the children who stand in the margins, they hope to find those who will remember what it felt like to be pushed out, to be seen as less than others, to be unheard, to have one's uniqueness ignored.

Once the potential leaders are identified, the cultural workers back the young people up, nudging them to take their leadership potential very seriously. They talk with them about the serious issues facing the community. They encourage them to apply for scholarships and the like. They give the young people so many tasks that benefit the whole community one could say the youth were being thrust into an apprenticeship program. The cultural workers also help each other create summer camps and other programs where the skills of community-focused leadership are systematically taught. They are quite aware that most formal educational institutions teach only the skills of self-focused leadership and pay little attention to the development of silenced and vulnerable members of society and of community-focused leaders.

CHAPTER 10

THE PHILOSOPHY AND PRACTICE OF DEVELOPMENTAL LEADERSHIP

I want to lift my sister up. She is not heavy.
If I don't lift her up I will fall down.

I want to lift my brother up. He is not heavy.
If I don't lift him up I will fall down.

I want to lift my people up. They are not heavy.
If I don't lift them up I will fall down.

ROSE SANDERS

We now return to the questions that have driven our study of public homeplaces: Why have the Mothers' Center movements, the National Congress of Neighborhood Women, and the Center for Cultural and Community Development been so effective and enduring? Why have so many of the participants emerged as powerfully voiced people who speak up for both themselves and their communities? What has enabled these organizations to respond to diverse and changing needs yet remain cohesive and stable over long periods of time? How have they enabled their members to imagine that things could be different and to develop the skills to realize their dreams? Why have most been able to bridge vast differences of social class, ethnicity, age, and race so well?

We have sought answers to these questions by identifying the philosophies and practices the founders of public homeplaces hold in common. We believe these commonalities provide important clues about learning environments that enable even marginalized and silenced people to claim the powers of their minds and fight for the right to participate in the life of the larger society. The number of commonalities we were able to identify are striking, especially considering the differences between these organizations in terms of focus, populations served, and short-term goals.

METAPHORS TO LIVE BY

While we began our search for commonalities by looking at the home-place founders' philosophies and practices, we found similarities on a level that seemed even more basic. When the women tried to describe themselves and their work, they used similar metaphors suggesting embodied actions: lifting up, drawing out, drawing in, drawing from, bringing out, gearing up, connecting, caring, nurturing, growing, building, networking, bridging, uplifting, and raising up. All had devoted their lives to righting injustices, but when they talked about what that meant they were much more likely to speak of growth interrupted than a right denied.

When the homeplace women reach for words to describe what is most important about their particular organizations, they continually evoke metaphors suggesting home and family. A few examples include: "We are like a family." "I am really at home here." "This is a place where I can be who I am." "You make friends here and they become part of your extended family, the family that you are actually living in." "It was like a constant coffee klatch, night and day. Before we got an office we just moved from one kitchen table to another. Actually we still do, even though the new office is quite nice." "We think of our center as a public living room." "In this family everyone has a say and every voice is important. This is not anything like the family I grew up in, that is for sure!" "We're like the kind of family where people can fight fearlessly but no one ever even thinks of leaving—well, hardly ever." "When we have differences we keep struggling until we find a way that is pretty much okay for everybody. Some people call this 'reaching consensus,' some call it a 'win/win' approach. We are just trying to see that everyone in the family has a voice in the way things are run." "People were here for me yesterday; they will be here for me tomorrow, next year, ten years from now, whatever."

When Jan Peterson is asked how ordinary neighborhood women can build so many highly complex programs in a poor and deteriorating community, she invariably says something like, "We are like a family; we have made a lifelong commitment to each other. People who know they are going to be together over the long haul can take on something that might take ten years or more to accomplish." Notions of family and home are so central to all of these organizations that we think of them as the root metaphors that have shaped all aspects of the women's thinking about the institutions they have established.

Indeed, the consistent use of metaphors suggesting nurturing and growth also indicates that either the homeplace founders were working out of a long established cultural tradition of women's developmentally oriented leadership or they were in the process of instituting the tradition in their community. The passion and commitment these women bring to developmental work is attested to by Rose Sanders's song "I Want to Lift My People Up."

Psycholinguists George Lakoff and Mark Johnson (1980) maintain that metaphors suggesting embodied actions play a powerful role in the way we live. This is so, they argue, because human reason is imaginative, metaphorical, and intrinsically linked with the human body. Metaphorical thinking is often the first step in the development of a complex set of ideas. Such ideas seem easier to grasp when illustrated by metaphors suggesting more easily understood concrete experiences.

Lakoff and Johnson argue that the development of complex ideas is often facilitated by metaphorical maps organized around prototypical social roles as well. They call metaphorical figures "canonical persons" because they set a standard against which others are judged. Warrior, ruler, patriarch, and mother are common canonical figures that shape our thinking.

When the warrior is the canonical reference point, Lakoff and Johnson (1980, p. 4) say that all sorts of behaviors are likely to be comprehended and expressed in terms of war-making. Some examples they give of how the construction of ideas can be construed include: "His criticisms were *right on target.*" "I *demolished* his argument." "You disagree? Okay, *shoot!*" "He *shot down* all my arguments."

Fathers, warriors, and leaders are seen as canonical persons associated with actions that involve "ruling over" in many of the world's cultures. Mothers are typically linked with activities associated with "raising up." If men's thinking is rooted in notions of fathers, warriors, and "ruling over," and women's thinking is more often grounded in experiences of mothers and "raising up," it is likely due to the universal division of labor that permeated premodern societies. In her recent summary of the research on gender differences, Sandra Bem (1993) argues that even highly diverse cultures are actually very consistent in their treatment of men and women. A universal division of labor developed on the basis of sex, she holds, because of universal characteristics of premodern cultures. Without the means for effectively controlling fertility and adequate substitutes for mothers' milk, women typically had little choice but to organize their lives around mothering. Without the technology for extending the strength of the human body it was important for men to take advantage of the superior prowess that was generally available to their sex. Women everywhere were assigned the care of children while men were responsible for hunting and defending the group against intruders. Bem suggests that political power was developed by males because it is they rather than females who were assigned the task of defending the group. "[T]hat role assignment," Bem (1993, p. 31) writes, "may lead those warrior-males to see themselves—and to be seen by others—as the most important and powerful members of the group."

Given this persistent pattern, it makes sense that when women finally began developing leadership roles in society many would organize their thinking around maternal metaphors more than those generated by centuries of male experience. Most of the homeplace women we studied rejected leadership organized around patriarchal notions. Most were very critical of using the doctor-patient relationship as a model for working with people. They also avoided the language of the social services and the helping professions. To them people were neither "patients" to be "treated" or "cured" nor "clients" to be "serviced" or "helped." Instead, the homeplace women see themselves more like mothers who create nurturing families that support the growth and development of people and communities.

Even if there is an association between gender and the use of basic organizing metaphors, the association is not a consistent one. If you look carefully at the embodied actions suggested by the metaphors actually used by men and women in different social roles, you can see wide variations in the ways they depict themselves and their work. When speaking of their children, mothers often evoke images of "ruling over" rather than "raising up." Some fathers are so intent on "ruling" their families that even the eldest son has no hope of establishing himself as an adult while his father is alive. Yet other fathers begin lifting both sons and daughters up into relations of full equality from the moment of birth onward. Although warriors can be conquering heroes who subdue and enslave their neighbors, they can also be liberators who would free a vanquished people from bondage, like Harriet Tubman. Whenever Monika Jaeckel, Jan Peterson, and Rose Sanders are called warriors and fighters—and they often are—the images evoked are of liberation. Some leaders—both male and female—never think of themselves as ruling over or as leading their flock. Instead, they see themselves as drawing out the people's voices so that everyone can have a say in the way things are run. Because such leaders typically depict themselves as coaching the labors of people who are giving birth to their own ideas, we have come to think of them as "midwife leaders" who work out of the developmental tradition.

The Human Family   When we looked at the images of family and home that shape the public homeplaces we studied we found three major themes: (1) we are all members of the human family, (2) the family should maintain a warm and supportive homeplace where the development of all the members is nurtured, and (3) everyone should be responsible for home maintenance and developing the broader community that sustains the family.

While the founders of public homeplaces liken their particular organization to a family, they also see themselves and everyone else as members of the larger human family. As a birthright, everyone is included. The first obligation of the human family is to care for those least able to care for themselves: to raise up the young, to nurse the ill into health, to nurture the dying. When people are left out, pushed out, or retreating, special efforts must be made to lift them up and bring them back into the family circle.

The birth of each of the public homeplaces came about when the founders decided to do something about the exclusion of one group or another from society. At the same time, with the possible exception of the Mothers' Center movement in the United States, each organization has brought together people from many different racial, cultural, and class backgrounds. Even though the suburban U.S. Mothers' Centers may have been too isolated geographically and psychologically to forge significant connections between people from different walks of life, they do provide a common meeting ground for the whole range of women who live in these relatively homogeneous communities. Not only do the homeplace founders reject the separatist politics characteristic of many minority advocacy groups (Bargad and Hyde, 1991) but almost all of these women refer to themselves as "bridge builders." No doubt "bridge building" is a metaphor commonly found among those who are convinced that we are all members of one basic family.

The Family Supports Its Members   The homeplace women envision a family where everyone is welcomed and their development is well supported. They are constantly asking: Who is this person? Where is she now and where is she trying to go? What are the strengths she can build on? What kinds of experiences and challenges would support her development? How can we help her achieve her goals? The homeplace women try to see that the organization offers each member more and different responsibilities as the individual's capacities and interests grow.

Few noneducational social institutions take this kind of approach. More typically an institution's managers will set goals, create a job description, and select a person to fulfill the role. If the match between the person's interests and needs no longer fits the institution's job description, the individual is likely to move on (or be moved out) and someone else will be hired to fill his or her place (Howell, 1977).

Everyone Supports the Family   That public homeplaces model themselves after families that try to support the development of all its members is only half of the story. Family members, in turn, are expected to support the development of the family and the larger society that sustains it. The homeplace women are always asking: What are the problems facing this family (or this community, this movement, or this project)? What is it that we need now? What are your dreams for this community? How can we work together to see that these dreams are realized? What kind of contribution would you like to make? Are you ready to join this particular committee and help direct the project?

What kinds of statements do you think the world needs to hear from us? And the art-making cultural workers add: What art forms would speak to these problems and articulate our visions?

It is a commonplace notion in contemporary society that some specialized institutions, like families and schools, should see promoting the development of individuals as their central goal. The parallel notion—that individuals should be committed to the social institutions that support them—has lost a good deal of ground in modern times (see, for example, Bellah, Madsen, Sullivan, Swidler, and Tipton, 1985). Contemporary families speak of being "child centered," schools as "student centered," and therapies as "client centered." These same institutions seldom ask children, students, and clients to reciprocate and take responsibility for a larger social unity.

No doubt a sense of the individual's responsibility to the larger whole has withered, in part, because of the complexities of modern life. Children are no longer needed to feed chickens, gather firewood, weed the gardens, and do a myriad of other chores that make a visible, concrete contribution to the whole. Young and old alike participate in such large, competitive, hierarchically organized institutions that they are apt to have little experience with the sort of ongoing collaborative efforts required by democratic institutions. Consequently, they are unlikely to develop the mindset and skills involved in working together for the common good (Berman, 1997). The cultural commitment to individualism is now so extreme that many Americans believe a commitment to anything larger than the self not only handicaps the individual but also constrains the development of the society. The common good, many believe, is best created by the free play of individual self-interest and market forces—not by people who devote themselves to the creation of caring communities.

The homeplace women we interviewed are always trying to balance the intricate interrelationships between the development of people and the development of their organization. The constant interplay between meeting the needs of many individuals who are always developing and meeting the needs of an ever-evolving community undoubtedly accounts for much of the flexibility and vitality of these long-lived organizations. It also helps explain why so many of the involved individuals have become such creative, outspoken, and responsible participants in the larger society. (For a different example of this process, see Traub, 1995.)

Decrying the separation of public and private life, the homeplace women argue that women should be free to enter into public life on an equal footing with men. They also argue that both men and women should be encouraged to bring into public life the philosophy and practices that make private homes nurturing places to live. As Hildegard Schoos, from the German Mothers' Center movement, says, overcoming the schism between public and private is key:

> Mothers' Centers are not mainstream—that is for sure. Profession-
> als here in Germany are very fascinated by us. Try as they might,
> they can't seem to replicate the mode. They cannot do it because
> they keep the public and the private separated. We actually try to
> merge the Mothers' Centers into one whole cosmos of work *and*
> private life. That is our secret. Professionals can't make the model
> work because they do not integrate what they value in their per-
> sonal life with their professional offerings.

By creating public spaces that are the moral equivalent of an in-
clusive, egalitarian, nurturing family, full of socially responsible people, the homeplace women have created a working model of the kind of world they yearn for in their dreams. Day in and day out, the homeplace women get hands-on, practical experience in building the kind of world they long to have. As the members watch each other develop, their understanding of the importance of this kind of moral commitment deepens, their efforts intensify, and their successes multiply. The possibility of a world where all humanity is well nourished is kept alive in the face of overwhelming evidence to the contrary.

We see quite the opposite scenario taking place among many of the silenced standing at the margins of society who model themselves after a warrior who would "rule over" rather than "raise up." Instead of seeing the world as a nurturing place, bursting with life, these people see the death and destruction. They align themselves with "Author-
ity/Right/We" and form themselves into militia groups to fight the "Illegitimate/Wrong/Other." They prepare for Armageddon, where the final and conclusive battle between the forces of good and evil will be fought—and won.

The moment that one embraces the idea that we are all members of one family, the dualisms that pit the We against the Other become ludicrous. If the smallest child and the most silenced of the excluded are viewed as having the capacity to be thinking, contributing members of the family, there can be no Authority and no We that holds a monopoly on Truth and Goodness. There is no Other responsible for all the world's evil.

DIALOGUE

Undoubtedly the practice that most sets homeplace founders apart from traditional leaders has to do with the balance the homeplace women establish between speaking and listening. While most public leaders are highly articulate spokespersons (Gardner, 1995), their conception of the listening process can vary widely. Democratic leaders feel ethically bound to listen to their constituents so that they might represent their concerns accurately and fairly. Authoritarian leaders want their followers to be seen but not heard. Some burn books and control the press when they feel it necessary to silence alternative voices. They have their minions rewrite history when the standard versions are not to their liking. All too often they jail or execute dissidents who insist on having a say (Orwell, 1946/1984).

All leaders who develop great power to influence and control others do listen, although they may never acknowledge the process. Even the most ruthless dictators must be in tune with their followers' anxieties, values, and goals, or the people will withdraw support and the regime will collapse.

The homeplace women are all highly articulate leaders—indeed, most are extraordinarily gifted storytellers and spokespersons. Even so, when the homeplace women talk about their own leadership styles they invariably emphasize listening at least as much as speaking. While only a few of the homeplace women like to think of themselves as spokespersons, all of them—without exception—see themselves as the kind of leader who draws out the voices of people so that they might speak for themselves.

Monika Jaeckel, one of the German Mothers' Center founders,

describes the shift that allowed her to see the importance of listening in her own development as a leader:

> In the political movement I was first involved with I was one of the few women who were accepted as leaders. It was really a boys' club and I was one of the boys. My trip then was to be as good as any man. They accepted me as one of them. I was received into the inner circle.

Looking back on that experience, Monika analyzes the ways they silenced any voices that might intrude on theirs:

> We were all very intellectually oriented but in a highly competitive way. To win out you had to bring your argument across, not only in content but in style. You had to be very charismatic to be able to be heard at all. You had to put down what someone else was saying to make any kind of dent. Not only did you need to have a loud voice, but you needed to speak fast. You silenced others by putting them down.

Monika sees important differences between traditional academic discourse and the mode these political leaders employ:

> To pick apart what someone else was saying was also a university style. But in this political movement we were more involved in manipulating people than in dissecting their arguments. To get people to agree, we would talk in such a way that no other thought but ours could arise in a person's mind. We were always on a soap box giving propaganda speeches. You did not say what you had to say and then give the other person space to say what they thought. You were out there to convince, not to discuss.

Eventually Monika grew bored with this way of working, primarily because it did not allow her—or anyone else—to develop their thinking:

> This way of talking made many things taboo. If you weren't convincing enough you were shot down. It meant that you could not explore things that you were not so sure about.

Like many of the other homeplace women, Monika discovered a more collaborative way of talking when she joined the women's movement:

> The C-R [consciousness-raising] groups that I was involved with had this exploratory quality where you could just talk without making it a campaign. You could just let ideas evolve.

The C-R groups developed a process for dialogue that invited everyone's participation. Women—mostly white and middle class—all over Western Europe and North America began meeting regularly in small groups. The groups were welcoming and safe places where people could think about the unthinkable: for example, about social arrangements that are so much a part of everyday life they are beyond one's conscious awareness. Women drew out each other's thinking and raised these issues into awareness. They let the ideas evolve by listening to each other speak and by pooling their insights. The new ideas that had explanatory power spread like wildfire, zigzagging from one group to the next, from one continent to another. In this manner masses of white middle- and upper-class women were able to construct a much broader understanding of their status in modern society than any group of experts could ever have assembled for them. Needless to say, the civil rights movement provided very similar opportunities for African Americans from all socioeconomic levels throughout the society.

That the homeplace women have developed a style of public discourse and public leadership that emphasizes listening and calls forth a highly collaborative dialogue is not surprising. This is quite consistent with the kinds of communication patterns that many women tend to establish. Summing up the research on conversational styles among men and women, sociolinguist Deborah Tannen (1990) says that from early childhood on, girls are apt to see themselves as individuals in a network of sustaining connections. The conversations girls and women have with each other are more like negotiations for closeness, with people seeking and giving support and confirmation. Boys and men, on the other hand, are more apt to view themselves as separate autonomous individuals struggling to preserve their status in a hierarchical social order. Their same-sex conversations are like negotiations in which people try to achieve and maintain the upper hand and protect themselves from others' attempts to put them down and push them around. While girls discuss and reach for consensus, boys argue and strive to be the ones who come out on top. Highly collaborative discourse patterns—"improvisations"—are also found throughout the African Diaspora. They have made all genres of black music a vibrant and ever-evolving form (Levine, 1978).

As their primary goal is to bring the silenced into voice, the homeplace women are always on the lookout for those who are hanging back, always figuring out ways that these people might be drawn into the conversation. Their most basic tool for generating a dialogue is the kind of open-ended question that invites discussion, reflection, and careful listening.

The centrality of this kind of question posing is made evident by the fact that all of the public homeplaces studied (like the Listening Partners project) grew out of one kind of an interview study or another. Each of the founders, concerned that a particular group of people was not being heard, decided she would listen to them in a sustained and systematic way. She would hear what these people had to say; she would learn from what they had to contribute. Although some of these stories were touched on in earlier chapters, here we highlight the commonalities.

Jane Sapp first began a formal study of the folkways and music of her people in college. With or without funding, Jane is always studying the music and folkways of the African Americans. She has conducted a series of systematic studies of the music and the culture in two areas of the rural South where blacks were maintaining many of the ways of their African ancestors: the coastal Sea Islands and the Black Belt that cuts across the Deep South. As part of her research process she creates music groups and folk festivals where people can develop their art together and present it to a wide variety of audiences. Jane's projects always evolve into a public dialogue, albeit one often conducted largely in song. She says,

> My aim was not really to have, quote, "a music program," but to have a place where people could come and talk to each other and share their experiences through music. You teach them to sing. When you shake people out with the singing, they build a relationship between

each other. Then you start talking about what you're singing about. You keep asking, "Why do you sing?" and "What's important about that?" and exploring the meaning of the songs in terms of their lives and their history. You want them to know why they're singing and what they're singing. You want them to use the music to develop their own statements to the world.

The art-making provides a mirror that allows a community to see beyond demeaning stereotypes and behold the fullness of their humanity. When Jane saw people blossom in the course of these events, she realized there was a need for public spaces where people could continue this kind of art-making together. The Center for Cultural and Community Development was born in that realization.

Although Jan Peterson did not have a formal grant to study the Brooklyn neighborhood she intended to organize, she conducted an extensive community study on her own. Drawing on her college training as a history major, Jan helped the women document how the community was being run. When they saw that community women were systematically excluded from the formal governance structures, they began looking at the informal structures women had created for themselves. Jan documented and mirrored the strengths she found in the Neighborhood Women as politically committed leaders, as a historian might. She says,

> I'm very good on history. I am very good at tying together and articulating the kinds of political involvements that most women forget. Women are always saying, "I'm not political." You can see that they are actually the most political people in the world: they are out there speaking up, organizing, pressuring, and advocating! And then they say, "I'm not political!" I could just roar! They want to erase their own history! I keep track of the history because I am very big that women should know what they have done, that they should see the impact of their work. Women's lack of awareness of the way they impact public space is one of the major problems in terms of women's voice today.

Jan draws on her skills as a historian to document the leadership of women in the community. Even though Jan has earned a master's degree in social work and is a licensed therapist, she worries about the ultimate impact of social service–oriented disciplines and professions. She is concerned that all too often social workers and therapists encourage people to focus on the personal and ignore the societal. People become clients and patients who are helped to adjust to their culture rather than active citizens who work to transform the society that diminishes the potential of so many lives. In Jan's hands, "doing history"—that is, making a very careful account of women's experiences in the community and the community's responses—is a powerful tool for developing a responsible group of community activists.

Jan was particularly interested in the ways the many Italian and African American women in the neighborhood were drawing on their cultural and family traditions to re-create a sense of community in what could have been a very barren urban landscape. She apprenticed herself to these women, some she said were "old enough to be my mother," to learn more about these traditions. Together the women reinstated the best of these cultural variations as they sought ways to create a caring community. Immigrant women who might have felt ashamed of their newcomer status began to realize they had important knowledge to contribute to the neighborhood and the nation.

The neighborhood women themselves began to "do history." In a long series of conversations the women articulated how things really *did* work in their neighborhood, how they *had* worked in other times and places, and how they *should* work. It wasn't long before the women were "making history." To bring the community more in line with the common visions they had articulated to each other, the women began developing one action project after another. As we have seen, the list of their projects is a long one.

The seed for the German Mothers' Center movement was planted when Monika and her colleague Greta Tüllmann, both active in feminist politics and the university research community, got funding to study women who work at home raising young children. They chose to study housewives because women living this lifestyle were almost totally unknown to them and their political associates. Feeling the same dearth of information in the United States, social worker Patsy Turrini and her colleagues began conducting a series of focus group interviews with new mothers. They were swamped with calls from mothers desperate to talk about their experiences with researchers who might take them and their work seriously.

In both countries the researchers brought groups of mothers together, listened, and recorded what they heard with care. In both cases the researchers and the mothers shared their stories. They found the conversations so fruitful they decided to establish a public meeting place where mothers could continue to meet and reflect together on the conditions of their lives. Once they had envisioned a better way, women in both countries supported each other to change the conditions of their lives, their families, and their communities.

In summary, all of the public homeplaces were begun by researchers who apprenticed themselves to their so-called research subjects. Yet the researchers were like students; their "subjects" were the authorities who would teach them what they needed to know. In the give and take of the two-way conversation that ensued, "the researched" soon began to ask questions of their own. Everyone—researchers and "subjects"—became collaborators, analyzing their situations and imagining alternatives. Discussions continued until a consensus was formed. Common dreams became a group's goals and another public homeplace would be instituted.

While the founders of the public homeplaces are all women who hold strong convictions with enormous passion, they are also unusually open-minded. They are always reexamining their old assumptions and habits, they adopt new strategies, and they take up unexplored challenges. They are always questioning, reevaluating, and trying to see things from a different vantage point; they get others to do the same. They are such good listeners, because they see themselves learning from everyone, no matter how young, inexperienced, or silenced a person might be. Homeplace women listen with particular care to those who are just coming into voice. They know that the contributions that the young and the silent might make to the whole are too often lost because no one listens. Jane Sapp puts it this way:

I'm always afraid that I am going to miss a treasure that got thrown away because somebody didn't value them, because someone didn't like the color of their skin or thought they were too fat or too skinny. I am afraid that I'm going to miss some new answer to some important problem that got thrown away because no one took the time to listen. I'd rather bring everybody in, rather than to have missed something really wonderful. I can't help but believe that when you bring everybody in, that something really important will happen. There might be new knowledge, insights, and strategies. There might be new bonds that will give people more courage and strength for the resistance.

Undoubtedly, the public homeplaces are such vital, intellectually stimulating places because they bring very dissimilar people into a highly reflective dialogue. When people with different points of view listen to each other with care, the discussions cannot help but be eye-opening.

PRAXIS

While dialogue is of the utmost importance to the homeplace women, they are also committed to putting the ideas under discussion into action. The homeplace women are forever developing and testing their ideas through art-making and action projects in the community. Whether they are launching a new community service, a folk festival, or a theater piece, the ultimate aim of their projects is the development of people and communities.

When Jan Peterson started working on a doctorate several years ago, she realized how important it was to her and the Neighborhood Women that they act on their ideas:

> I feel so out of place at the university. How can all of these people be so excited simply talking about ideas, without ever seeing them go someplace? Some people love sitting through meetings, talking about ideas. Then they walk away and never think about it again. They feel no responsibility for carrying out the ideas—not one bit. Maybe it's because I am very working class. Working-class people are very hands-on. They want to do things with their hands that they can see. If there is an idea, I want to try to carry it out; I want to see where the ideas are going to go; I want to see if they are practical or not.

The practice of moving back and forth between generating and implementing ideas has many important consequences. The never-ending series of projects creates a multiplicity of new roles and demanding responsibilities for everyone; people tend to live up to the responsibilities. People have a high level of commitment because they have been involved in the conversations that generated the projects. When people push their ideas into action, they see that their words and ideas can have important consequences. They develop a vested interest in having plans that are well conceived. They work hard and try to do their best. Not only will individuals contribute the skills they have, but they stretch themselves and develop new ones as they are needed. When a project's overriding goal is important to everyone, people work collaboratively, trying to bring out the best in each other. Any rivalry that existed between individuals and subgroups is likely to recede into the background.

The homeplace women approached their projects as if they were experiments from which to reflect and learn. No one, not even the group's leaders or any other authority, can be certain how things will work out. There are no sure answers to be found in the back of any book. When the group embarks on a new project, everyone steps into the unknown and risks failure, but they take the risk together (see Welch, 1990). When things go well, the groups take the success as a model to be improved upon. The women continue developing their prototype, pushing it in as many directions as possible. They look on this process as an experiment when things go poorly. They try to figure out what went wrong and why; they tinker with the model and try again.

When diverse people collaborate on solving common problems, they see each other looking at the issues from many different angles. Individuals begin to realize they have a viewpoint and that their point of view is valuable. They see the oldest, most experienced members of the group learning from the youngest and the least experienced. They see people just like themselves working hard, disciplining themselves, and developing an area of real expertise. They think, "If she can do that, why can't I?"

Many of the public homeplace's projects are also scrutinized by a larger public. This is true whether the project is a new program for the community or an art performance. When the public responds well, the group members think, "Oh, what we have to say really is important!" They find allies who help them further the work. When the audience fails to respond, the women ask each other, "Why can't we get people to understand the importance of these ideas?" "What is it that we don't understand?" and they return to the drawing board. After the home-place women have carried out a number of successful projects in the larger community, they realize that not only can they have a voice in how things are run, but it can be a public voice. It is often at this point that the idea that they and people like themselves could be Others is called into question.

The homeplace women not only sponsor action projects in their local communities, they each have built an extended network, bringing to-gether many different people from around the globe who are engaged in similar action projects in their local communities. The homeplace women get hands-on practical experience *and* a larger world perspec-tive; they become comfortable moving back and forth between the particular and the abstract; they see that problems in the local commu-nity have roots that extend into the broader society and beyond. They find women from around the world looking at similar issues from very different perspectives; they also find very different women arriving at remarkably similar analyses. Either way, bridging the local with the global seems to bring with it an explosion of thinking on everyone's part. Most importantly, these national and international networks re-confirm the homeplace women's most basic conviction—that we are all members of one family; we are all integral to the larger whole.

TWO APPROACHES TO DEVELOPMENTALLY ORIENTED LEADERSHIP

When we scrutinized the ways the homeplace leaders were actually drawing people out and supporting them to become creative, collabora-tive thinkers, we realized they used two different approaches. These approaches parallel the two modes of procedural knowledge in *Women's Ways of Knowing:* separate and connected knowing. Both—described in Chapter 2—modes provide powerful tools for drawing out people's thinking and helping them refine their ideas. Both modes provide a coherent set of procedures for drawing out and developing ideas. Both involve asking good questions, careful listening, and trying to conceptu-alize the frameworks people bring to their meaning-making. Although both modes encourage people to reflect on their experiences and artic-ulate what they think and why, the two modes are quite distinct.

The Separate Approach

Leaders working out of the separate mode ask good questions, listen, and try to conceptualize the other person's frame of mind. They play the devil's advocate, countering people's thoughts with questions and countersuggestions that are designed to point out inconsistencies, er-rors, and gaps in logic. They see conflict, challenge, and disequilibrium as a spur for developing well-thought-out ideas. The separate knower's ability to play this kind of doubting game is made easier by a stance that remains detached, impersonal, analytic, and divorced from feeling. Leaders who draw on the separate mode hope that their questions and counterexamples will goad people's development as critical thinkers. They want people to become adept at analyzing the weaknesses of their own reasoning. They want people to learn to question the logic of others—even that of established authorities.

Many people mistakenly assume individuals like the men in Monika's "boys' club" are good examples of procedural knowers in the separate mode. Monika's former associates most certainly were skilled at debating and dismantling other people's ideas, but they were *not* good procedural knowers because they were not interested in develop-ing and testing new ideas. By Monika's own account, she and her asso-ciates used argument, conflict, and fast talk to squelch the thoughts of others. They had no intention of drawing out others so they might be-come creative, independent thinkers in their own right.

The Connected Approach

When the leaders are operating out of the connected mode they invite people to tell their personal stories, and they draw out their thinking by asking good questions. They try to enter into another's frame of mind through a process of empathic role-taking. They listen intently. They put themselves in the person's shoes and try hard to understand and appre-ciate the logic *and* the feelings that inform the person's story line. They struggle to see the world as the person sees it, without biasing their perceptions by their own views. If the other person's ideas and emotions are still embryonic and vaguely formed, they refrain from criticizing. Instead, they play the "believing game" until they have achieved a good understanding of why a person might think a certain way. They look for and document the person's strengths rather than his or her errors and limitations. They try to create warm, nurturing environments where people's ideas will flow freely. They focus on the growing edge by trying to see where the person wants to go and the steps they already have taken. They lodge themselves at that brink. Like a bridge person, they provide the support people need as they move into the unknown.

Combining the Approaches While the founders of the public home-places we studied seldom take an adversarial stance with an individual struggling to find a voice, they model and teach the skills of separate knowing in a variety of other ways. First and foremost, they are always taking a critical stance toward unjust authorities and societal arrangements. And they are willing to bring their righteous anger to bear to fight against such injustices. They encourage others to raise questions, to articulate their anger, and to battle against the injustices that would put them in a diminished state. In so doing, they step beyond the social conventions that define the good woman as always loving, accepting, and passive—never angry, fighting, and powerful.

As the philosopher Elizabeth Spelman (1989) notes, anger is the one emotion superordinates regularly deny the Other, even though superordinates usually depict subordinates as emotional rather than intelligent. Superordinates appropriate anger for themselves, although they generally see themselves as thinking people who are unswayed by emotion. In her discussion of this anomaly, Spelman quotes Aristotle, who says, "The man who does not get angry when there is reason to be angry, or does not get angry in the right way at the right time and with the right people, is a dolt" (p. 263). To Aristotle, anger is embedded in reason; anger is a reasonable response of a person facing injustice. Spelman goes on to explain why Aristotle saw anger as a valued emotion for free men but not for slaves or free women. She writes,

> [Anger] is a judgment. To be angry at [another person] is to make myself, at least on this occasion, his judge—to have, and to express,

a standard against which I assess his conduct. If he is in other ways regarded as my superior, when I get angry with him I at least on that occasion am regarding him as no more and no less than my equal. So my anger is in such a case an act of insubordination: I am acting as if I have as much right to judge him as he assumes he has to judge me. So I not only am taking his actions seriously but by doing so I am taking myself seriously, as a judge of the goodness or badness of his actions. (p. 266)

Spelman calls anger the essential political emotion, and argues that "the systematic denial of anger can be seen as a mechanism of subordination, and the existence and expression of anger as an act of insubordination" (p. 272). She writes,

Anything resembling anger [in women] is likely to be redescribed as hysteria or rage instead. . . . Blacks have been typically depicted by whites as in any case full of emotion—but *not* full of anger. In fact, the emotion of anger seems positively to be excluded by the image of the shuffling step-and-fetchit or the field hand ecstatic to be working under a friendly sun. (p. 264)

The swift and massive reaction to the black power advocates of the civil rights movement lends credence to Spelman's argument. Indeed, some argue that this reaction brought an end to the war on poverty and unleashed the war on the poor (see, for instance, Freedman, 1996).

Homeplace women, like Rose Sanders, Jan Peterson, and Monika Jaeckel, are such fearless and avid fighters against injustice that they are widely known as warriors to friend and foe alike. All three relish a good fight. One of Jan Peterson's many stories suggests the zest she brings to a confrontation: The Neighborhood Women had saved the old hospital from being demolished but were still struggling to get the buildings developed for housing much needed by the local community. Just as the women and their allies were close to finally securing all the permits and funding, the evangelist minister Jimmy Swaggert appeared on the scene. He wanted to buy the buildings for the Assembly of God church's new international headquarters. Of course, Jan rose to the occasion:

After years of effort we now had to compete with the Assembly of God church. They didn't even have a base in our neighborhood; they had no interest in the neighborhood. The Assembly of God is a fast-growing, right-wing religion that is against everything we have been struggling to achieve. They confine women to the home; they expect women to accept anything and everything their husbands tell them. So there we are, having now to fight a whole different battle. That took us another year. Many people in the community sided with Swaggert. Even if they didn't, they were too respectful of the priest to fight back. It's not that they love the priest; they just don't fight the priest. They go around the priest. Zan [a Protestant minister Jan would later marry] and I led the battle against the Assembly of God because we weren't afraid to fight a religious leader. People were actually shocked 'cause we took them on so ferociously. They were also shocked because we were also Protestants and the people from the Assembly of God were from my ethnic group. It was the most humorous thing to battle a church *and* your own ethnic group in the middle of this community! People couldn't get over it. [She roars with laughter.]

While the homeplace founders often tell stories of being drawn into battle, Rose's story best illustrates the process:

I am driven by injustice. What do I mean when I say I am driven? Let me give you an example. Every time I see something that isn't fair I feel driven to act, whether I want to do it or not. Sometimes I really do not want to do what I have to do. When you are driven it is hard to be sidetracked.

Rose illustrates her point with a story about an event that occurred a few days earlier in Centerville, a little town some distance from her home in Selma, Alabama:

Let me tell you about Saturday night. I was coming home from my sister-in-law's funeral. I just hated to leave the family, so I stayed long after everyone else had already gone on. I ended up driving by myself. When I came through Centerville I saw these cops beating up on this man. I said, "Oh, my God! I've got to do something!" Then I said to myself, "I'm probably going to get abused. There is nothing to protect me. There are no lights. There is no one who would help me. But I can't let them just beat that man. There is no way to avoid this." I was really scared. I was scared because I knew the consequences were not going to be good for me in this little predominantly white town. Even so, I just knew I couldn't pass there without stopping.

As Rose drew closer she realized she had been given a last-minute reprieve. She continues:

> When I got really close I could see that the men were laughing and cutting up. The cops weren't beating up on anybody! They were playing! I was so happy! I was so relieved. I said, "Thank you God!"

We flood the room with our laughter, amazed that Rose had been saved in spite of herself. Reflecting on her own story, Rose goes on to say she has become less impulsive with age. Now she looks a lot further before she leaps. Still, this greater reflectivity does not prevent the leaping. She says,

> In my younger days I would not have thought of the consequences. I would have just stopped. This night I thought of the consequences. I was frightened by the consequences. Even so, I knew I would stop the car. It's this sense of injustice that drives me. Once I am brought into it, I can't go around it. If I hold myself back from doing something I know I should be doing, it would be like chipping away at my physical constitution.

While some of the homeplace women never enter into the melee as directly as Jan, Monika, and Rose, they are ardent about everyone's right to resist the injustices they face. This sense comes through in one of Jane Sapp's stories. Jane had been working hard to get a group of her college students in Birmingham to compose their own musical statements to the world.

> I asked these young people to write a song about what they really feel. Weeks went on and nothing was being written. I finally said, "I'm tired of this. I want you to take just a half an hour. Talk to each other, find out what is really up there at the top of your

thinking, write about that, and then put some music to it. I am going to leave, and when I return in a half an hour, I want a song." So they wrote the song, "Die, Die Mr. Charlie." Mr. Charlie, of course, is a name for whites. The song went like this:

Working in the fields all day long.
Told Mr. Charlie I wanta go home.
Sun shinning hot,
Like a burning hell
A longing for some water from that old well.

Die Mr. Charlie.
Die, die Mr. Charlie.
Because we are going to be free.

If I had a hammer,
I'll tell you what I'd do.
I'd hit Mr. Charlie and his bull dog too.

If I had a match,
I'll tell you what I'd do.
I'd burn all these acres and his big house too.

The song greatly angered the school's administrators, who said Jane had been wrong to encourage the students to say what they thought. She disagreed:

These young people were from Alabama. They were children of sharecroppers. They were singing about their own experiences and their parents' experiences working in the fields. I thought that we shouldn't run away from the rage of these young people.

The freedom to counter injustice with anger, Jane argues, provides the motor for change:

Can you imagine what African American people went through in their history? That rage had to go somewhere but people had been denied that rage. If you showed rage you were considered very dangerous; things would happen to you if you gave any indication of your rage. The black power movement created possibilities for the rage. There were places for it to go. It went into that song. It went into the poetry. It went into the plays that were being performed. And it went into the demands for justice. It went into the creation of freedom schools. White people were looking at one kind of thing, but we were looking at freedom schools where our children would be treated with dignity. The freedom schools were a way that our kids could feel the sense of possibility in their lives. It went into the creation of political campaigns and black people's own political party as we sought equality in the electorate.

Then thinking again of "Mr. Charlie," Jane continues,

What did we do with the rage that these young people from Alabama experienced from sharecropping? What do we do with the rage that comes from living in a racist, segregated, and violent society? It went into the creation of cooperatives for farmers. The Federation of Southern Cooperatives grew out of that. They said, "Let's define for ourselves where we are going to put this rage. If you couldn't pay us fairly, we will form our own farmers' cooperatives." This was a way of people banding together and finding self-determination. The possibilities were endless. It was a time of great creativity.

The public homeplaces trigger constant discussions, mostly of a moral nature; these in turn spur the development of individual members and the group as a whole. Participants talk about the conditions of the lives they are leading. They look at what is and ask, "Is this how it should be?" They articulate the problems and try to figure out what can be done to improve things. Sometimes they design a project to actually change the situation; other times they write a song or produce a play and bring the issue to a public conversation.

In short, public homeplaces are ideal settings for silenced people to acquire the skills of separate knowing and take a critical stance toward an unjust society. Every homeplace has among its members people who are particularly comfortable and skilled at analyzing, that is, taking things apart. They provide good models for the rest. When many people work together developing a critique of the status quo, it helps even those who have been well trained to be seen but not heard to stand back and say, ' This is wrong and something should be done about it."

When the homeplace women put their ideas into action, they also learn to take a critical stance toward themselves and their own work. The women are always standing back and asking such questions as, "What are we trying to say?" "What are our principles here?" "Is this consistent with our long-term goals?" "How can we persist without compromising our values?" "Can't we ask for more?" "Let's play the devil's advocate, and look for all the flaws in the things we did." "How could we redesign the project so next time it will come even closer to those things we value?'

The discussions that questions like these generate are often heated. When organizations are as diverse as most of the public homeplaces we studied are, people are likely to have very different perspectives and goals. The issues under discussion are also likely to be of great personal and social importance. When moral conflicts over issues of real concern arise between people who have a cooperative and trusting relationship, the debates and disagreements can be especially productive (Weinstock, 1993). When people argue with each other, they are not trying to outdo each other. They want the group to develop better ideas and more coherent goals that everyone will be able to embrace. When the discussions get heated people are apt to feel that it is the ideas that are under attack and not the individuals. Evaluation sessions do not degenerate into the kind of blaming that often occurs between people who are in a competitive relationship. When goals are not met or if someone's performance is less than hoped for, the homeplace women simply ask, "Why didn't this work?" "What went wrong?" "How could we have supported you to do a better job?" "What should we do the next time?"

People who work well together find this kind of collaborative critical process invigorating. Everyone learns that when things are not good enough they can be improved. Everyone will pitch in and help. In this way, the homeplace women get many opportunities to observe how conflicts and debates can provide a creative force, pushing participants to develop their ideas far more fully than anyone would have ever imagined before the conflict arose.

When the homeplace women find themselves locked in battle with each other or with people outside of the group, they have no interest in manipulating others into following them blindly. They try to get those they disagree with to broaden their thinking by dissecting their arguments. They point out the contradictions and flaws in their opponents' logic and they assess the moral ground on which their arguments rest. The homeplace women also try to develop and articulate their own case well, backing up their arguments with data, explaining why their position is morally stronger.

The U.S. Mothers' Center women confronted hospital personnel to bear witness to the inadequacies of their services. When they exposed the flaws in the medical establishment's approach, they backed up their case with a wealth of carefully documented evidence. They also took a moral stance that demanded that the mothers' point of view be honored. As the conflict unfolded, it became clearer and clearer that the hospital's administrators and physicians had scarcely considered the perspectives of the women and families they were supposed to be serving.

Jan Peterson had to battle many neighborhood women who wanted the organization they were developing to serve only women from their particular ethnic group. Because Jan battled long, hard, and well for the idea that all the women in the neighborhood be included, most members began to work hard for a goal they had not even considered before Jan came to town. Those who did go off to form an organization expressly for their own group were far more articulate about their goals and plans because they had been tangling with Jan.

When Jan Peterson and Rose Sanders first began organizing local people to have a voice in how things were being run in Brooklyn and Selma, respectively, the traditional leaders in both communities were outraged. Even so, Jan and Rose led their forces in battle after battle. In the end the traditional leaders of both communities began to listen with care to the voices of people whom they previously had thought unworthy of participating in public life.

Even though the public homeplaces we studied have supported their members to engage in conflict openly and effectively, some of the women are ambivalent about this aspect of their work. They do not always acknowledge the potential benefits of engaging in conflict, nor do they clearly explicate the processes they use. Some of the organizations even put forth policies that seem to rule out engaging in conflict altogether. When the U.S. Mothers' Center movement decided to become a national organization it adopted a policy that local chapters should avoid "social advocacy actions . . . that would serve to divide a community, would cause social unrest and create distance. . . . Programs or practices that offend a specific community group are also to be avoided" (Zimmerman, 1980, p. 38). Although the policy was instituted out of fear that a national movement for mothers could be destroyed if drawn into the abortion debate, the policy is stated in very broad terms. Many women in the movement feel that the policy perpetuates gender stereotypes and keeps some of the Mothers' Centers from engaging in political struggles.

The Neighborhood Women have articulated and codified a whole series of "agreements" or "rules" that essentially teach the skills of connected knowing and have made the group such an accepting and supportive homeplace for its members. Even though it is one of the most feisty of the organizations we studied, its members have not articulated so clearly the practices that enable them to take strong critical stances and handle conflict so creatively—practices that have made the Neighborhood Women such a spirited and effective organization.

When the most renowned thinkers in the Western world have theorized about the sources of evolution and development, they have focused their attention almost exclusively on the role played by conflict, competition, and disequilibrium. Darwin (1896) looked to competition and the survival of the fittest to explain the evolution of the species; Marx (1933) saw class struggle giving rise to higher forms of social organization; Freud (1927) saw personality structures developing out of the clash of intrapsychic forces; Piaget (1985) and Kohlberg (1984) attributed the development of an individual's cognitive structure and moral thought to conflict and disequilibrium. The list could go on and on.

The homeplace founders we studied have little doubt that conflict—well handled—can spur the development of people and communities. Many of them engage in conflict with zest and skill, winning battle after battle. Even so, when the homeplace founders set out to promote the development of individuals and communities, they looked to factors almost universally ignored by the eminent thinkers who have shaped Western intellectual discourse. The women have no doubt that harmony, nurturing, mutuality, and reciprocity are at least as important for fostering growth and development as competition, conflict, disequilibrium, and dominance.

At the turn of the twentieth century Jane Addams and the women at Hull House in Chicago straddled both of these poles, as well. They too engaged in conflict with zest and profit. Not only were they regularly fighting politicians unresponsive to the needs of the most vulnerable members of society, they battled each other, as a letter from a Hull House resident to a friend attests:

> We were a kind of a family group together—a very argumentive family group, for we often disagreed. Our personal opinions varied widely, and our arguments not infrequently began at the breakfast table; and during the day the various participants in the current controversy seemed to have sharpened their weapons and prepared for the new arguments that were sure to be heard at the dinner table—with Ms. Addams often serving as mediator and laughing as verbal shots were fired. And in the late evening hours the arguments were still going on. (Deegan, 1988, p. 48)

While Addams and the Hull House women engaged in conflict with gusto and competence, they also rejected the notion that conflict, competition, and dominance are *the* key to social progress. They believed that holding a conflict model of society actually reinforces and perpetuates adversarial relations. Conflict, competition, and dominance often lead to chaos and the decline of individuals and society. In their minds, mutual support was at least as important as mutual struggle. The Hull House women argued that social progress was more sure if one held up a model of development built around a collaborative, democratic process of discussion involving all members of society.

This is why Addams, like the homeplace women we studied and the Black Belt community othermothers who preceded them, was always holding up a model of society where harmony, collaboration, and caring relationships are seen as the springboard to personal and community development. This is why Addams employed a maternal metaphor when writing in 1879 to Ellen Starr, her closest friend and collaborator, to articulate a vision that was realized ultimately in the creation of Hull House:

> Back of it all . . [is] a great Primal cause—not nature, exactly, but a *fostering* Mother, a necessity, brooding and watching over *all* things, above every human passion. (Addams, 1965, pp. 3–4)

Like the Hull House women, the homeplace women are optimists who believe that human beings are fully capable of creating a loving and nurturing society. They aim for nothing less—even though they can be certain that it will not happen in their lifetime.

As midwife leaders sponsoring the development of the excluded and the silenced, the homeplace women search for the strengths rather than the flaws of individuals and communities; they affirm what they see (Clinchy, 1996 . They look for the "growing edge," trying to see people at their very best trying to see where they are hoping to go, and then trying to find ways to document and mirror what they have seen. The word *trying* keeps coming to the fore as it is hard to see things that are still just coming into being.

The singing group Sweet Honey in the Rock captures the essence of this process of affirmation in Ysaye Barnwell's song "No Mirrors" (Barnwell 1991). The inspiration for the song came from a friend's story of growing up in a house with no mirrors.

No Mirrors

> There were no mirrors in my nana's house
> No mirrors in my nana's house
> And the beauty that I saw in everything
> the beauty in everything
> was in her eyes.
>
> . . . So I never knew that my skin was too Black
> I never knew that my nose was too flat
> I never knew that my clothes didn't fit
> And I never knew there were things that I missed
> and the beauty in everything was in her eyes.

(Barnwell, 1991)

A character in Toni Morrison's *Beloved* speaks of a friend who is gifted at mirroring people's strengths:

> She is a friend of my mind. She gather me, man. The pieces I am, she gather them and give them back to me all in the right order. It's good, you know, when you got a woman who is a friend of your mind. (1987, pp. 272–273)

By all accounts, Patsy Turrini, Lorri Slepian, and many other founding members of the U.S. Mothers' Centers were experts at playing "the believing game"—seeing, documenting, and mirroring the strengths of the women who joined them. One of the original members still marvels at Patsy's approach and the impact it made on her twenty-some years later:

> Patsy believed in me at a time I did not believe in myself. All the time she would sit there and go, "You can do it. You can do it!" After a while you begin to think, "Well, I respect her and she's saying I can do it. Well, maybe I can do it. Well, why not give it a try?"

The Mothers' Center founders held up many different kinds of "mirrors" for participants. They made audio- and videotapes of the group interviews so the women could see for themselves how thoughtful their conversations were. They helped the women turn their observations about the hospitals' treatment of maternity patients into a successful reform effort. Then they helped the women transform the process they generated into a well-articulated working model of research-service-advocacy groups that guided the development of Mothers' Centers all around the country.

From the beginning Monika Jaeckel and Hildegard Schoos thought that German housewives were better able to design programs that would support women's development than were professional educators who knew little about housewives and the lives they were leading. They gathered and mirrored the women's aspirations for themselves and their community until a coherent plan for a Mothers' Center emerged. Once a center was established they focused on each new member's strengths and goals, helping the woman figure out where she was trying to go and what she wanted to contribute to the center. They even secured the resources so each woman could be paid a salary for the contributions she made, like most workers in the society. Instead of writing the book on the first three successful centers, Monika and her colleagues got the members to author the book themselves. The process of helping the women develop their ideas into a book-length manuscript was long and arduous. They continued the work, draft after draft, until the book reflected the women's best thinking quite beautifully. Monika and Greta did the final editing and the book was published (Jaeckel and Tüllmann, 1988). When the book became a best-seller among mothers throughout Germany, the authors could not help but see themselves in a whole different light.

Jan Peterson uses her training as a historian to mirror the strengths she finds in Neighborhood Women. She documents with special care the abilities that others seldom acknowledge: women's leadership and their contribution to public life. When women and others in subordinate positions exercise creativity, authority, and power, they are often thought of as "shrill," "strident," "angry," and "egotistical," especially if they assert themselves in these ways in public. Women often hide their strengths and apologize for their achievements. Even women who have been profoundly active and powerful in public life tend to present their achievements as flowing from mere luck and the generosity of others rather than as the result of hard, concerted thought and action (Heilbrun, 1988).

Because of Jan's relentless documentation (and some say badgering), many Neighborhood Women have learned to avoid these denials and to demand public recognition from others for their accomplishments. Now whenever a major victory is achieved the Neighborhood Women stage some sort of public ceremony to mark the event.

Yet, it has always been an uphill battle to get traditional community leaders to honor the women's work in community ceremonies. At first the old leaders took all the credit for a successful project without even acknowledging the women's participation. Needless to say the NW's historian had gathered sufficient evidence to expose these errors and the practice has slowly abated. When a major community ceremony celebrated the groundbreaking for the housing complex in the old hospital, the mayor of New York City was invited and the neighborhood women were given center stage at the event. To listen to the women talk, getting the mayor and other dignitaries to share the dais with them was as great a victory as developing the housing complex itself. A longtime NW member described the battle:

> When we had to meet up with the forces of all these men we stayed unified. We became a very formidable force. Every single time one of them tried to circumvent us we said, "No, you're not!" and we pushed ourselves back in. Every time one of them pushed himself forward we pushed another woman forward. They were not going to have that stage all to themselves. We earned the right to speak with all the work that everyone did when things were really tough. We earned that right!

Not only do these very tangible, publicly celebrated achievements enable the women to feel like an effective force in their community, but there is widespread agreement that the community has come to view the Neighborhood Women in a similar light.

As with the other homeplace women, the cultural workers begin with a very careful detailed study of people, where they have been, what they care about, and where they are trying to go. Jane Sapp says,

> You have to hang out in the community. You have to walk around in the community, look, and listen. You are looking for the knowledge the people have created for themselves. It is always there. You have to walk and look. But you have always to keep looking with "new eyes" so that you see things beyond what people usually look for.

The cultural workers look with "new eyes," mirroring strengths others fail to see. Jane continues:

> Your way of being with others must say, "I believe in you. I'm open to you. You can be whatever you want to be around me. You don't have to have a great voice in this singing group. You can just be you." I try to carry myself in such a way that people will know that whatever they let come forth is accepted, is cherished, is valued, is validated.

Jane says that once cultural workers have seen "things beyond what people usually look for," they try to share what they have learned:

> I was learning so much but it wasn't enough for just me to be having that information. What I was learning had to also be learned by others from that community. Others in the community had to know and hear the same things that I was hearing. I wanted the people to have the resources that would enable them to tell these stories to each other. If you see that the people care about quilting, you might get them to help you give classes for young people on quilting. When you start from what is most important to people, it says, "I think you are important." To go to a woman who quilts and say, "Would you come share your quilting?" it says, "I honor you." And people respond to your coming to those things that are most precious to them.

Cultural workers do the things that human beings everywhere do to reflect on the condition of their lives: they stage plays, build museums, write histories, compose songs, give concerts, and organize festivals. In these ways, Jane says,

> Cultural workers hold up a mirror for people to look at themselves, their lives and their communities. Our work as cultural workers is to show you what we see. The reflections help people inventory their culture, their history, their stories, and their social relationships. At our best we are your mirrors. Sometimes artists are the only people who can announce to you that you are okay.

Seeing themselves and their people's ways reflected in the cultural workers' eyes and in all the art-making, people get a greater sense of their own and their culture's worth. They get a clearer picture of who they are, how they have been able to overcome obstacles in the past, their dreams for the future, and how to overcome the obstacles that lay ahead. Jane says,

> Taking stock, a community finds that it already has a great deal in place to build on. They come to see their community as a place of power rather than a place of powerlessness.

Most importantly, cultural workers radiate a sense of hope. As Jane says,

> By picking up on the light that radiates on everything, we try to develop ourselves in terms of our capacity to radiate light. Sometimes you get the feeling that your very hope is all that is holding someone up. You just got to keep holding the hope. You can't let down. It's like with babies. You just have to keep holding that neck until they can hold their head up on their own. You got to keep holding it no matter how much the baby is squirming and spitting. If you stand there and just keep holding the hope, eventually they too will believe.

CHAPTER 11

PASSING THE TRADITION ON

That which touches me most
Is that I had a chance to work with people
Passing on to others
That which was passed to me.

"ELLA [BAKER]'S SONG"
BY BERNICE JOHNSON REAGON (GRANT, 1986)

A leadership tradition rooted in maternal practice and maternal thinking has gone unnamed, just as women's traditional work has been uncounted when governments assess a nation's wealth (Waring, 1988). Whereas developmentally focused leadership is seldom acknowledged, models of leadership organized around paternal metaphors and practices have been meticulously described throughout all of recorded history. Mary Helen Washington, a scholar who has played a key role in revealing the literary traditions of black women, helps us understand why a tradition would have no name and why a people's contribution would not be counted:

> The creation of [a] tradition is a matter of power, not justice, and
> that power has always been in the hands of men—mostly white
> but some black. Women are disinherited. Our "ritual journeys,"
> our "articulate voices," our "symbolic spaces" are rarely the same as
> men's. . . . The appropriation by men of power to define tradition
> accounts for women's absence from our records. (1990, p. 32)

We put it more boldly. Whenever people are cast as Other, they are largely unseen and unheard. The language used to describe them and their contributions is apt to be impoverished, inaccurate, and demeaning.

When a tradition has no name people will not have a rich shared language for articulating and reflecting on their experiences with the tradition. Poorly articulated traditions are likely to be fragile. Without a common language the tradition will not become part of a well-established, ongoing dialogue in the larger society. Institutional supports to develop and refine the tradition's philosophy and practices will not be developed. Leaders' efforts to pass the tradition on to the next generation will be poorly supported. Existing educational institutions will not hire faculty who are experts in the tradition; appropriate curriculum and apprenticeships will not be developed. This situation is increasingly problematic as more and more of society's caring work is now being carried out by professionals who receive all of their professional training within the formal educational system (see McKnight, 1995).

When the developmental tradition has no name, people hoping to build such an organization will be hard-pressed to find a leader. By the same token, a public homeplace's ability to search for a successor to the founding leader will be severely limited when there is no in-house candidate. Many will give up before the search even starts. Some will assume that it was the founder's personality and charisma that made the organization such a generative place for its members. These, they argue, are unique and can never be replicated. Others assume that a nurturing stance in public life is achieved through intuition, just as good mothering in private life is credited to a woman's biology. They do not realize that the founder had a philosophy and a set of practices that were well designed for creating nurturing environments and promoting the development of people. They do not understand that the approach was achieved through study, engaged practice, dialogue, and reflection.

Because conventional notions of leadership and organizational structures are so different from those of the developmental tradition, others will not even recognize the founder as a real leader, nor will they see the underlying structures that made the public homeplace so empowering. They are likely to argue against leaders and organizational structures altogether. They simply do not understand that creating organizations where people can be their best requires a powerful form of leadership and the most intricate of structures.

Without a common language to articulate this alternative notion of leadership, a search committee would not even be able to write up an adequate job description listing the various leadership qualities needed if the institution is to begin or continue its developmental work. It would be difficult to ask the candidates the kinds of questions that might reveal expertise in the tradition such as the following:

- How would you go about promoting the growth of this organization while also nurturing the development of all its members?
- What practices have helped you draw out people's voices and best thinking? How have you and your colleagues documented and represented people's strengths, so they might be more able to reflect on their accomplishments and build on foundations already in place?
- What do you do to encourage people to take a collaborative, experimental approach to the problems they face? By an experimental approach we mean analyzing situations; articulating questions, problems, and visions for the future; brainstorming new approaches; drawing up well-thought-out action plans; studying the results; and going back to the drawing board whenever a need is perceived.
- Can you think of a metaphor that would give us a good sense of the kind of organization you would most like this to be? How would that play itself out?

As it now stands, most of the colleges and universities that help people develop leadership in government, corporations, and civic organizations are only beginning to teach the philosophy and practices of developmental leadership in a systematic and coherent way (see, for instance, Argyris, 1985; Chrislip and Larson, 1994; Lipman-Blumen, 1996; Osborne and Gaebler, 1992; Schon, 1983; Senge, 1990). Very few of the leaders of public homeplaces said the schools they attended were important sources of their leadership training. Instead, they credited the civil rights and/or the women's movement for most of their education. They were, as Barbara Omolade (1994) put it, among Ella Baker's many daughters.

The African American cultural workers said their involvement in the civil rights movement was only one source of their leadership training—albeit an important one. They were also well trained by women leaders from the Black Belt hometowns where they grew up. Most of these teacher/mentors were members of their own families.

This was not a pattern found among women from European-

based cultures. None of the white founders of public homeplaces mentioned women leaders among their female relatives and neighbors who
mentored them in the developmental tradition. Instead, they described
themselves and their age-mates inventing the form as they worked on
one project or another in the women's and/or the civil rights movement. These memories were intensely infused with a sense of creativity
and the excitement of discovery. Mothers and grandmothers were often
valued for their abilities to create warm nurturing relationships in the
extended family and the immediate neighborhood, but not in the
larger community. Even without elaborate models and educational programs showing them the way, the white women are integrating into
their public work many values and skills their mothers and grandmothers cultivated in the home.

THE TRAINING OF DEVELOPMENTAL LEADERS IN THE AFRICAN DIASPORA

From the stories that Jane Sapp and Rose Sanders tell, it is clear that the
training of women leaders in black communities of the rural South was
largely an informal, mentor-based effort. Their mentors were community leaders—mothers, grandmothers, and neighborhood women—
who usually worked without support from any well-recognized social
or educational institutions. The stories of these mentors help us imagine how educational and other kinds of social institutions might be
constructed to pass on the philosophy and practices of developmentally
oriented leadership to subsequent generations in a coherent, systematic
fashion.

The community leaders who played key roles in Jane Sapp's development included her grandmother (Sister Bailey) and the women in
her grandmother's circle of friends. Sister Bailey had been born into
slavery as, undoubtedly, were many other women who worked to make
Jane's hometown—the Bottom—a nurturing and vibrant community.

In describing her mentors and models, Jane begins by describing
the women's skills as homemakers:

My grandmother and her group of old women were people who
threw a great protective net over everything. They would touch

you. They would never let you be a stranger. They wouldn't allow it, even if you wanted it. They were always saying, "Come into my house. Be a part of my family." When they took your hand the whole world seemed to glow. They were people who could pat you on the shoulders and make you feel so special. They had a magnificent force that binds us and holds us. When you were in their presence, you felt the essence of life. You felt love in its highest sense. The earth just glowed with their presence.

Like all kinds of highly successful public leaders (Gardner, 1995), these women were gifted storytellers who helped others see the big picture and gain a larger view of the world. Jane says:

People like my grandmother had poetry in their voices. They were able to bring deep meaning to the spoken word. It's like they nurtured their words. They would embrace and savor the words they sent out—taste them even. I can hear and see those women's voices in my mind. They were able to put out the spoken word in ways that made the words seem visual. You could both hear and see the words when they spoke. You could taste and feel the words. That is what a fine storyteller does.

These highly articulate women were also fine listeners, as Jane says:

People like my grandmother lived their lives with a heightened awareness, sensitivity, and ability to connect. Every person and every experience is given a lot of attention. It's like living your life with all of your pores open so everything is coming in. Everything is intensely felt, looked at, and reflected upon.

Jane's mother also listened and gave her space for reflection.

My mother protected me. She helped me have the space I needed for thinking. She'd tell others, "Let her be quiet," "Let her sing," "Let her be, she's playing the piano." She understood my heart. She anchored herself in her family and went about taking care of us with the passion of a lioness. She found a way to protect us and yet to prepare us for the world. After every trial and tribulation, she really listened and helped us understand what we had been through.

Gifted storytelling and gifted listening are the two capacities most needed for creating an ongoing dialogue that gives rise to powerful personal and collective statements that people who are just coming into voice can give to the world.

Jane always refers to her grandmother and her grandmother's friends as this "group" or "circle of old women." The images of "group" and "circle" suggest the collaborative nature of their collective endeavor. The emphasis on "old" implies these women have achieved the highest levels of wisdom and power that, Jane says, comes from their moral core. Indeed, Sister Bailey had garnered so much moral authority that people saw her "as a godlike ruler of the universe." Jane said, "Sometimes my grandmother was called the Empress because she had that sense of ruling the whole wide world. People jumped when she spoke."

The focus of these powerful black women was intensely concentrated on promoting the development of their families, their neighbors, and the community as a whole. Jane describes how these women kept her and the other children immersed in a full array of their developmental projects: raising vegetables, flowers, chickens, and the smaller children. Jane explains her involvement in this early apprenticeship:

> I've always loved to watch things grow. I loved planting the garden with my grandmother. I wanted to be there when the seedlings came up through the ground. I would go to the garden right after a rain because I knew the rain speeded up the growth. I wanted to see it go from seed to plant. I was like a time-frame photographer. I like to see things blossom. I like to see children grow. I can't stand to see anything that stops that growth.

Jane's interest in nurturing development became a driving force even in her earliest years:

> Many times I was the last one to go to sleep at night because I wanted to make sure everybody was all right. I was not the mama of that house, by no means. Nevertheless, I would tiptoe around, looking in on everyone, and they would be sleeping soundly. They'd look good and I would be at peace. As a kid I did this. I am

still doing this. I want everybody to be all right. I want everybody to be included. I want this circle. I want a whole. But let me tell you, it's not easy.

Sister Bailey's developmental projects extended far beyond her garden. She and her circle of old women were always working to make the community a more just and caring place, especially for children and others least able to fend for themselves. Jane says,

> My grandmother and her group of old women dealt with big, big issues—voting issues, school board issues, zoning issues. This group of women fought like hell for the black community. Today, the women who I am most comfortable with are women who create big spaces and deal with big issues.

These fearless fighters would turn issues that no one else would touch into political campaigns. One story among many: When Jane was thirteen years old, a classmate—impregnated by their schoolteacher—came to Jane for help. Jane was overwhelmed at her friend's predicament. She was further distressed to find that the adults she and her friend first turned to ignored the situation in silence. It was different when Jane appealed to her grandmother for aid. The Empress put on her hat, rounded up her friends, and marched downtown. She and the other old women confronted everyone from the head of the school board on down. The teacher never again set foot in the school and the community began rallying around the child.

Jane said her grandmother and her group of old women were always on the lookout for young girls who might become qualified to be one of the next generation's developmental leaders—a leader who could go beyond the given, a leader who would not be afraid to take on the big issues, a leader powerful enough to lift up a whole community:

> They would identify you early on in life as someone who is going to be able to see beyond what others see. There is a saying that "the seventh child is the child that has a special ability to see beyond what others can see," or that "a child born with a veil over the eyes has this gift." In reality those sayings are too literal and formulaic. Those women thought the number of people who could have those gifts was limitless, not just the seventh child. They

looked everywhere for such strengths. Wherever they saw the potential they would nurture it.

Clearly, Jane was one of those who emerged. She describes the
process:

> My mother was like the teacher who would provide you with all
> the things you needed to become who you wanted to be—even if
> she did not quite understand what it was that you were trying to
> do. My grandmother was not like that. She was not the kind of
> teacher who would wait for you to decide what you wanted to be.
> She would put you on the path. She was the leader type with clear
> goals and a clear agenda. She would snatch you up to that agenda
> and say what she thought you should be doing.

Although Sister Bailey had no qualms about snatching Jane up
and telling her what she ought to be doing, she was also insistent that
Jane dream her own dreams and follow her own light.

> My grandmother was always asking me, "What did you dream?"
> "What do you see?" "What do you hear?" My grandmother and
> her circle of old women anchored us in a vision of what the world
> could be. You know you have to anchor your dreams and beliefs
> like a rock or they will just get washed away.

Clearly, Jane decided to "be snatched up." She would carry on in
her grandmother's footsteps. She would try to see "beyond what others
can see," she would work to uplift her people, and she would help identify and train the next generation of developmental leaders. The Center
for Cultural and Community Development is simply Jane's way of
drawing together her generation's circle of old women from around the
country into a leadership support group. In these homeplaces—as in her
grandmother's kitchen—the cultural workers, the young, and the
excluded all work together developing the vision and courage it takes to
march downtown and tackle "the big issues." The Dream Project—the
children's musical groups—is one of many projects that enables Jane to
identify young people who might develop the capacity to see beyond
what others see and become a leader in the developmental tradition.

★ ★ ★

When Rose Sanders speaks about her development as a community leader driven by a passion for justice, she does not mention the years she spent studying law at Harvard University. Instead, her stories mostly revolve around three mentors: her own mother, a neighbor who turned her home into a schoolhome, and her grandmother who ran a schoolhome out of her backyard.

Rose's mother was also the kind of community leader who worked hard to see that a "great protective net" was covering everyone. The following story, Rose says, is the main story she tells whenever she tries to explain why she does the work she does:

> My mother was a terribly outspoken woman—always independent, always willing to stand up to personal injustices. For example, in my community there was only one white family. They were as poor as poor can be. I have not, to this day, seen anybody any poorer. My mother required me to take food to this man and his wife every day. I had to go all the way down this hill, in this dark little valley, to take them this food. I used to have nightmares about them. I know I was reacting to physical appearances. He was so scary. They were so malnourished. His wife looked like Popeye's wife—she was so skinny. They never bathed. I didn't know this till later but they [white people] just threw 'em into the black community 'cause they were totally unwanted. Total rejects. So my mother took it upon herself to feed this family. She used to make me go down there every day!

Rose's mother, it seems, thought that all of the excluded—even the pariahs from the white community—should have the care they need.

Rose's parents named her after a neighborhood woman who took it upon herself to provide black girls with something the town fathers had no intention of supplying: a first-rate education. Rose says,

> I was born right across the street from the woman's house who I'm named after—Aunt Rose. She was another whole story. She was a powerful woman. She sent scores of black women to college. She educated them right in her own house.

Rose's grandmother, Mama Mitchel, also ran a schoolhome out of her place in downtown Mobile, Alabama. She raised Rose and twenty or so other children. Some, like Rose, came in summertime because they wanted to spend time with Grandmother Mitchel; others who came were orphans of some storm or another and needed a home in the world.

Like Jane's grandmother, Mama Mitchel placed the highest priority on creating a safe and nurturing place where people would feel at home. She encircled her house and garden with a tall fence. She wanted the children to feel safe even in the midst of the social disarray that surrounded the neighborhood. The garden was so inviting everyone in town called her place "the yard." Rose (Sanders, 1988) writes in an autobiographical essay,

> She defined the world so we weren't in any way threatened by it. . . . That tall, tall fence . . . forbade evil to enter, or forbade me to exit to places where evil resided. (p. 137)

Whenever any of the children would ask to leave the yard, Mama Mitchel would decline, saying, "Too much evil in the world." Rose explains:

> She didn't like for us to go beyond that fence. That was her way of protecting us from what was beyond the fence. It is like, "I can't control what is out there, but I know what is out there is bad for you. So I am going to try to protect you from it as long as I can." (p. 138)

Mama Mitchel had to be a powerful fighter if she were to have any hope of protecting the children growing up in the yard. Rose (Sanders, 1988) also remembers her grandmother as a godlike ruler of the whole universe:

> It was as if [my grandmother] ruled the whole wide world. As far as I was concerned, Grandma Mitchel was everywhere. [Wherever I went] I could hear her talking to me. . . . I thought she was something between an angel and a saint, not that I knew the difference between the two. (p. 135)

Rose now believes that her grandmother had aspired to be a preacher but put the dream aside. Musing on the exclusion of such women from the pulpit, Rose (Sanders, 1988) writes:

I never thought of her as a preacher, though. Never saw a woman preacher in those days. Funny, it was easier to fantasize about her being an angel than to grasp the possibility that she could be one of those ministers called by God himself to preach the gospel. (p. 135)

Conventional warriors, empresses, gods, and goddesses often derive power from their potential to wreak harm. Their authority is based on a permanent imbalance of power. They are always the supreme leader, surrounded by those who pay homage.

The strength of leaders like Sister Bailey and Mama Mitchel is different. Their power is firmly rooted in their abilities to lift up, not to tear down. While the imbalance of power between these women and others can be vast, as with a small child, it is a temporary imbalance. The thrust is always to raise the lesser one upward.

Children growing up under the tutelage of Mama Mitchel or the Empress may never develop the audacity to imagine themselves as equals to such women. Nevertheless, Jane and Rose saw their mentors operating out of relationships of reciprocity, mutuality, and equality all the time. Whereas ordinary rulers place themselves at the apex of a line of command, these women moved in a circle with other powerful old women. They surrounded themselves with equals, not underlings. Most of these powerful women also established long-term marriages with strong men as coequals and collaborators. These women even demanded and achieved the respect of many whites, enabling them to build some sorely needed bridges between the two communities. Even if these women were seen as godlike to their mentees, they were gods who lived among equals and sponsored the capacities for dialogue, mutuality, and reciprocity in others.

Rose came to understand that her grandmother ruled the world with such a fierce hand because she was utterly determined that all the children from the yard would achieve the dreams that she and her forebears had been denied.

I grew to understand that the dream wouldn't be achieved until all the folks in the yard achieved it. That's what Grandma Mitchel's yard was all about. In her own way she was trying to make sure that everybody in the yard achieved the dream.

Mama Mitchel had an unshakable belief that Rose was fully capable of achieving her dreams. Rose (Sanders, 1988) writes that her grandmother was always saying to her,

> You gonna be somebody, gal. The Lord done already worked it
> out. Just keep your eye on your dreams and hold on. (p. 139)

Rose entered adolescence with such confidence in herself she could declare, "It was too late for me to fail" (p. 139). She attributes her self-assurance to Mama Mitchel's insistence that "she was going to be somebody."

Equally important to Rose's development, no doubt, was her grandmother's insistence that she keep her eyes on her own dreams and look inward for signs of her own goals. Although Rose's future was already assured by the powers above, she would have to guide her own life in accordance with the dreams she held for herself and for her community.

The insistence that people and communities be guided by their own dreams undoubtedly plays an important role in developing the sense of courage, independence, and clarity of purpose that is so characteristic of Jane, Rose, and the other cultural workers. A navigator with clear goals in mind and a good sense of direction is clearly able to drive farther and faster than a person who is always waiting for someone else to point the way.

The importance of dreams, hope, and courage for people cast as Other cannot be overestimated. Jane says of her grandmother and her group of old women:

> These were women who have had *hard, hard* times. I will never
> know the hard times that they have had. Yet, they still loved life.
> You know what I mean? They still *loved!* There was something
> about them that said, "I still love. I still care. Life never beat out for
> me the beauty that is yet here. I still trust that there will be a to-
> morrow and that there will be something good about tomorrow. I
> can't wait for tomorrow to come." They had the courage not to
> run away from tomorrow.

Rose says women like her grandmother coped with dreams deferred without giving up hope. "Dreams deemed unattainable were placed on hold and quietly transferred to the next generation." Jane echoes Rose's observation:

> You know how the old folks always say, "I don't know if I will ever get there, or if my children will get there, but you just have to keep on." It's this will, this courage, this strength to keep on fighting, even though you are never sure what the outcome will be. You don't even know if your children will get there but you must keep trying. Something inside says you must keep chipping away at this stone. You have to keep the hope of the possibility alive.

No doubt the art-making that permeates the African diaspora also plays a key role in keeping dreams alive. The arts flourished in Mama Mitchel's yard as they did at Sister Bailey's, although Rose's childhood stories are more about theater than music. Rose says when she and her playmates were prevented from venturing beyond the fence, they invented the larger world in their imaginations and in the many theatrical productions they created and performed in the yard. Rose writes,

> The yearning to venture beyond the yard remained strong. So we fantasized. Many days were spent creating plays and skits that we acted out as seriously as Broadway's best. Very little was reduced to writing, but the make-believe worlds we created gave us a sense of freedom that transcended that tall fence and the "evil" beyond its bounds. Much of my compassion for life was born in that yard. (p. 138)

The yard has served Rose as a metaphor for homeplaces that nurture the development of everyone, but most especially those straggling along the wayside. All of Rose's homeplaces like the Black Belt Arts Center, the 21st Century Youth Leadership Training Project, and the National Voting Rights Museum are places where young people can gather to articulate their experiences through art-making. Drawing on the whole range of cultural arts—theater productions, singing, storytelling, and studying the community's carefully collected artifacts—young people in Rose's homeplaces document their own experience and develop their vision of the world. In the process they are supported to create a make-believe world that transcends the "evils" that exist in the real world, just as the children had done in Mama Mitchel's yard. Whenever people develop a vision that transcends the evil, Rose—the activist—goads them to bring the real world into alignment with the dream.

Jane and Rose have been highly successful in their efforts to develop the leadership skills of the next generation. A serious illness recently forced Rose to cut back on most of her projects in Selma. As Rose stepped back, a cadre of young leaders was ready to step forward. Her daughter, Malika Sanders, became the director of the 21st Century Youth Leadership Movement in 1995. It now has twenty-three chapters in five states and abroad. Each of Rose's other organizations has continued in her absence with strong able leaders, well trained to work within the developmental tradition. All of the new leaders began schooling themselves as cultural workers early in their childhood years through apprenticeships in B'BAC and/or the 21st Century. Although most have graduated from first-rate colleges and could have gone anywhere, they have chosen to return to Selma and carry on the work. All reports suggest that this new generation of leaders has the deepest understanding of the goals, philosophy, and practices of leadership in the developmental tradition. They will carry the tradition forward during their watch, maybe pushing it to a new level. When their time has passed it is likely that a new group of well-trained community leaders oriented to development will be there to step in and fill their shoes, as well. Needless to say, MOMS, CCCD, and many other groups of old women whom Rose and Jane helped to form are standing in the wings ready to support this new group of young leaders whenever the occasion arises.

Jane says cultural outsiders have had a hard time understanding the tradition of "passing it on" to the next generation of community leaders and the importance of this tradition to the survival of the black community:

> Funders never understood that this was what we were working for all this time. They thought we were just giving a play or a folk festival. They couldn't see that we were lifting up the community and a new generation of leaders who would carry on the work after us. They could see our short-term goals but they couldn't imagine the long-term ones.

No doubt people from the mainstream are so used to thinking that leadership training occurs in schools and universities that many find it difficult to imagine it happening in other settings.

SCHOOLS THAT PASS THE TRADITION ON

All modern governments establish specialized institutions—schools—where the traditions and knowledge believed to be important to the society are taught in a systematic way to each subsequent generation. Schoolchildren are introduced to aspects of these traditions at an early age; the curriculum grows in complexity and scope as the students mature. What would schools look like if society were committed to passing on the tradition that has no name—creating public homeplaces and nurturing the development of all people, but most especially the people who have been excluded and unsupported?

We believe such schools would be shaped by philosophies and practices similar to those that have guided Listening Partners, the Mothers' Center movements, the National Congress of Neighborhood Women, and the Center for Cultural and Community Development. First and foremost, schools for all socioeconomic classes and every age group would be welcoming places where everyone is made to feel at home. The scale and design of the schools would be such that every voice could be heard and savored. As in well-functioning families, the development of each student would be nurtured. The students, in turn, would be expected to take real responsibility for the development and governance of the school family. In short, schools would be worthy of the name "schoolhome" (Martin, 1992).

Schoolhomes would demand that all students become active collaborative participants in community life for two basic reasons: (1) the process of creating and maintaining the community is a powerful stimulus for the development of engaged, articulate, collaborative, and creative people committed to the common good, and (2) the schoolhomes themselves would model the kind of caring, democratic society that is the ultimate goal of the developmental tradition.

Development would be central to the curriculum of schoolhomes. Students would be given responsibilities for raising many forms of living things: plants, animals, and the younger children at the school.

These activities would be an integrated part of an ongoing study of developmental processes and the creation of nurturing ecosystems. The school itself would be studied by students and teachers as a environment for sponsoring the development of all the participants. People would be constantly looking for ways of making the school a more nurturing place and evaluating the results.

In schoolhomes, the teachers would be skilled at drawing out the students' questions and reflections; they would listen with care so they could better understand their students, their histories and cultures, their accomplishments, as well as their hopes and aspirations. They would document what they see and re-present their findings so the students could reflect on their strengths and dreams.

Teachers would teach students the skills of active listening and empathic role-taking. Students would be encouraged to look for and document each other's strengths and visions. They would be expected to work especially hard to draw out and understand any student who was standing back. With everyone engaged in these practices, all of the students would become quite knowledgeable about the capabilities they already have in place, articulate about their visions, and confident in their abilities to take the next step and move forward. Students who have done so much work to understand and support each other would be highly invested in each other's progress.

Students and teachers would also cultivate the tools of separate knowing—to stand back and take a critical stance toward their own work and the work of others. What were our goals? What happened? What did we achieve? What were our failures? Were there unintended consequences? Was the logic we used to analyze the situation adequate? Were our plans sufficient? Debate, playing the devil's advocate, and argumentation would be encouraged as tools for developing and testing ideas with others. Yet argumentation to control and limit the thinking of others would be ruled out. Homeplaces, after all, are predicated on an open and highly civil dialogue where even the most fragile of voices would be heard and valued.

Because the students and teachers would have such a good understanding of each other, they would be able to develop collaborative learning projects rooted in the group's most driving questions and concerns. These action projects would be like experiments. Students and teachers would work together posing questions and clarifying goals. They would brainstorm and utilize other techniques to encourage divergent thinking and open the mind to new possibilities. Students and teachers would gather the expertise that might shed new light on the issues under consideration. Plans for solving the problems posed would be drawn up and a division of labor mapped out. People's talents would be matched with the tasks to be accomplished. Sometimes a job would be assigned to someone who had the needed expertise; other times it might go to people who were ready to cultivate a new skill. When the projects were completed, students would conduct a very careful evaluation of the work. Does the project need to be redesigned and repeated? Is there a follow-up project we should institute? If so, what would be our goals? How would we accomplish them? And so on.

Because students would participate in designing the action projects, it is likely they would work together, stretching and reaching for goals that most everyone agreed were important. The older or more accomplished students would feel responsible for drawing out the voices of younger and more marginal students so all could make a fuller contribution to the projects and have a voice in the life at school.

Students would be encouraged to use a full range of languages (spoken and written words, mathematics, and all of the arts—including song, dance, story graphics, and theater) to explore their ideas, document their findings, and communicate with others. Because it takes time and careful feedback for ideas to ripen and bear fruit, school-homes would encourage even very young students to work their way through many drafts, sharing each draft with their collaborators, and considering the responses carefully each time they reworked the material. Once the students' ideas developed coherence and power, they would be encouraged to present the work to the broader community. In this way the students begin to develop a public voice and the community gets to see the best work that the young people have to offer.

Whatever the discipline under study, even the very young would be expected to use the tools of the discipline to actively construct knowledge. When students read the works of historians they would also "do" history. For instance, they might piece together historical narratives from interviews and fragments of data collected from their own people. When students studied social and natural sciences, they would "do science": posing questions, making observations, running tests, and presenting their findings to peers. When students would read the great poets they would also write poetry, making their own statements to the world. The same would be true of theater, music, and painting.

Students who have been marginalized as Other would be given special opportunities to explore their personal and collective histories with others who share their marginalization. People are freer to explore ideas that run counter to conventional expectations and stereotypes if they do not have to deal with anyone who might represent the controlling elites. The students would be encouraged to pay particular attention to the strengths and contributions cultivated by each other and the group as a whole, that is, to identify the individual and collective "growth stories." This work is not easy. It demands that students become creative and thoughtful researchers who can examine received knowledge, see things that others seldom notice, and find names for things that are rarely articulated.

Once the students began to think of themselves as potential agents of their own history, they would be encouraged to build collaborative networks with others, especially with those who operate out of very different cultural perspectives. When very dissimilar people begin working toward common goals, they are apt to construct a vastly enlarged picture of the world and its possibilities. Not only will the students be more able to envision a world where disparate people cooperate with each other, but they also will have many of the skills needed to build such a world.

If a society were to provide young people of all ages and social classes with schoolhomes, we believe that most members of each new generation would become creative original thinkers, able to go beyond the given, they would also become skilled in collaboration, dedicated to the common good, and able to nurture these qualities in others. From such a broad base, each generation would go on to produce a new crop of leaders committed to the developmental tradition. Some will emerge as outstanding leaders exceptionally capable of moving the general populace to develop their capacities as human beings to an unusual degree. As Jane Sapp has said:

We as human beings see ourselves as so developed we don't think there is any more evolution to be done. We figure that everything else is still evolving but we are at the pinnacle. I feel that is wrong. We haven't begun to explore our capacity to care, to be concerned, the capacity to feel, to think, to know, to be open, to be connected, to be moved, to be just, to be aware of the light that radiates on everything.

APPENDIX A

PROTOCOLS OF THE LISTENING PARTNERS PROJECT INTERVIEWS AND ASSESSMENTS

LISTENING PARTNERS PARTICIPANTS   LP # _____

Name _____ Interviewer _____ Date _____

Address: Street & Box #   Town   State   Zip Code   Referred to LP by

Phone Number: Indicate own or a neighbor's name and number

Your Social Security #   Your Age   Date of Birth

Education Level—Last School Grade attended, GED, etc.

Study Child's Name   Age   Date of Birth   Sex

Father's name   Father's occupation   Ed. Level

Father's involvement (e.g., none, calls, visits, gifts, pays support, lives with, etc.)

2nd child's name   Age   Date of Birth   Sex

Father's name   Father's involvement   Ed. Level

3rd child's name   Age   Date of Birth   Sex

Father's name   Father's involvement   Ed. Level

| | | Check if more on back _____ |

4th child's name   Age   Date of Birth   Sex

Father's name   Father's involvement   Ed. Level

Your current marital status _____ Marital history _____
Your current source(s) of income (check *all* that apply):
none _____ boyfriend/husband/child's dad _____ own earnings _____ SSI _____
combo of yours & his _____ ANFC _____ Other (specify) _____

Jobs you have held (past and present)   Volunteer jobs (past and present)
Peer support groups-Past: _____ Present _____
Religious ident. (if any): _____ Parents' marital status _____
Your mother's: occupation _____ education level _____
Father's: occupation _____ education level _____

Name, address, and telephone number of someone who could always reach you in case we decide to track everyone down five years from now:
Name: _____ Relationship to you: _____

Address: Street & Box #   Town   State   Zip Code   Phone Number

THE LISTENING PARTNERS INTERVIEW
(General Outline)

I.   SELF-DESCRIPTION AND BACKGROUND INFORMATION

1.   Thinking back on your life for the past year or so, what stands out for you? (What kinds of things have been important?) (What stays with you?)

Tell me something of what your life is like right now.

2.   *Self-description:* How I'd like you to think about yourself. How would you describe yourself to yourself? (If you were to tell yourself who you really were, what would you say?)

How is the way you see yourself now different from the way you saw yourself in the past? How so?

What are things about yourself that you've come to appreciate more, things that you really like about yourself and don't want to change?

3.   *Relationships:* Now that you have described yourself, I would like you to think about the important people in your life. Who are the people you have really important relationships with right now?

Have your relationships with these people changed over the years? How so?

[If not covered]: Are you getting along with your kids differently now than before? How so?

4.   *Friendships:* All right now let's focus in on friendships. To help me understand what you think friendships are all about, why don't you finish this sentence: "A friend is someone who_____."

Has the way you think about friends and friendships been changing? How's that?

Has the way you get along with friends been changing? How so?

Do you have more friends now than you did a couple of years ago, or less, or about the same?

Are there people with whom you can talk about everything and anything?

Would you like to have more people you could talk with, or less, or is this about right?

Can you have more than one really good friend? Why?/Why not?

II. *THE EPISTEMOLOGICAL DEVELOPMENT INTERVIEW:
WAYS OF KNOWING* (adapted from Belenky, Clinchy, Goldberger,
and Tarule, 1986/1997).

We are trying to understand how women come to gain a voice and feel
the power of our minds more fully and you can help us by sharing your
experiences. Some of us grew up feeling kind of dumb while others of us
grew up feeling pretty good about ourselves as thinkers.

1.   How was that for you growing up? What has been your experience?

2.   How do you go about understanding new things? How would you
describe yourself as a thinker? (If they do not respond, ask: Think about the
times when you are trying to understand something new. How do you go
about it?)

3.   Now I would like you to think about times when you disagreed with
other people. Most of us have had disagreements or conflicts with other
people at some times.

  A) How do you handle situations like that?

  B) How do you think the way you handle them affects your relation-
     ships with these people?

  C) Do you feel differently about disagreeing with these people now
     than you did in the past?

  D) Okay, so when you and others disagree, what goes on in your
     mind? How do you figure out what you think? (If they do not re-
     spond, ask: How do you know what's true? In your own mind,
     what's going on?)

  E) What do you think you learn from such disagreements or conflicts?

[NOTE TO INTERVIEWER: IF IT IS LIKELY TO BE PRODUC-
TIVE, ASK THE ABOVE QUESTIONS ABOUT FRIENDS AND/OR
AUTHORITIES IF THESE HAVEN'T BEEN COVERED.]

4.   In thinking about disagreements or conflicts with others, can there be
more than one answer that is really right or true? Why?/Why not?
[Try to get an example.]

  A) How do you know what's right or true? (Would you explain what
     you mean by that?)

B) Can you say some answers or opinions are better than others? (Can you explain that?) What would make an opinion better than another?

5. In general, how do you think people get their knowledge and ideas? And you—in general, how do you usually get your knowledge and ideas?

6. Here are a few statements by other women. I would like you to comment on each of these. [These are conversation starters and give a chance to explore their thinking and their developmental history more. Find out whether or not and under what conditions the comment is true for the person. Try to get examples.]

A) SOMETIMES CLASSROOM DISCUSSIONS ARE SO CONFUSING. I TEND TO TRUST MORE WHAT A TEACHER SAYS THAN WHAT A STUDENT SAYS. THE STUDENT IS GIVING HER OPINION; IT MIGHT NOT BE THE RIGHT ONE. THE TEACHERS ARE ALWAYS MORE OR LESS RIGHT.

B) I LIKE IT WHEN PEOPLE *SHOW* YOU, NOT *TELL* YOU WHAT'S WHAT. I FIND IT REALLY HARD TO LEARN JUST FROM WORDS.

C) WHEN I NEED TO LEARN SOMETHING, I LIKE TO JUST LISTEN TO THE PEOPLE WHO REALLY KNOW ABOUT IT.

D) I CAN COUNT ON MY GUT TO TELL ME THE TRUTH— THE TRUTH FOR *ME*.

E) WHEN I HAVE A PROBLEM TO SOLVE, I USE MY MIND. I LIKE TO REALLY THINK THINGS THROUGH CAREFULLY BEFORE I MAKE A DECISION.

7. How have you changed as a learner or a thinker over the past year or so? What led to the changes?

III. *THE PARENT-CHILD COMMUNICATION STRATEGY
    INTERVIEW* (adapted from McGillicuddy-DeLisi, Johnson, Sigel,
and Epstein, 1980)

Now I would like to read you some stories about some other mothers and
their children who are all about four years old. Then I'll ask you some
questions about the stories that will help me understand your ideas about
how children learn and how parents can best help them.

1. BILLY WAS PLAYING WITH HIS LINCOLN LOGS. A COU-
   PLE OF PIECES WOULDN'T FIT TOGETHER, AND BILLY
   STARTED THROWING THEM AROUND THE ROOM.

A. *What* do you think is the best way for a parent to handle such a situation?
[Or]   (*What* is the best response for a parent to make in this situation?)

B. *Why* do you think that this response is the best response in this situation?
[Or]   (What makes this response the best one?)
[If this does not elicit a codable answer, try these follow-ups:]
(What would you be trying to do? What would be your main goal?)

C. If that [name the response] doesn't work and Billy is (still) throwing his
toys around (again), what would you do next?

D. Why would you choose that?
[If this does not elicit a codable answer, try these follow-ups:]
(What would you be trying to do? What would be your main goal?)

2. ONE DAY JUDY'S FRIEND WAS INVITED OVER TO PLAY.
   JUDY HAD TAKEN OUT THE LEGO SET TO PLAY WITH
   IN THE LIVING ROOM. SHE WASN'T SHARING ANY OF
   THE LEGO PIECES WITH HER FRIEND.

A. *What* do you think is the best way for a parent to handle such a situation?
[Or]   (*What* is the best response for a parent to make in this situation?)

B. *Why* do you think that this response is the best response in this situation?
[Or]   (What makes this response the best one?)
[If this does not elicit a codable answer, try these follow-ups:]
(What would you be trying to do? What would be your main goal?)

C. If that [name the response] doesn't work and Judy (still) won't share
her toys (again), what would you do next?

D. Why would you choose that?
[If this does not elicit a codable answer, try these follow-ups:]

(What would you be trying to do? What would be your main goal?)

3. MOTHER WAS GIVING ERIC A BATH. ERIC WAS PLAY-ING WITH HIS PLASTIC BOWL AND SOME OTHER THINGS IN THE TUB. ERIC WANTED TO KNOW IF HIS METAL SPOON WOULD FLOAT LIKE HIS BOWL.

A. *What* do you think is the best way for a parent to handle such a situation?
[Or] *(What* is the best response for a parent to make in this situation?)

B. *Why* do you think that this response is the best response in this situation?
[Or] (What makes this response the best one?)
[If this does not elicit a codable answer, try these follow-ups:]
(What would you be trying to do? What would be your main goal?)

C. If that [name the response] doesn't work and Eric still is not satisfied, what would you do next?

D. Why would you choose that?
[If this does not elicit a codable answer, try these follow-ups:]
(What would you be trying to do? What would be your main goal?)

4. DOROTHY KEPT ASKING HER MOTHER TO PLAY WITH HER. MOTHER TOLD DOROTHY THAT SHE WAS VERY BUSY RIGHT NOW. BUT DOROTHY KEPT ASKING HER TO PLAY

A. *What* do you think is the best way for a parent to handle such a situation?
[Or] *(What* is the best response for a parent to make in this situation?)

B. *Why* do you think that this response is the best response in this situation?
[Or] (What makes this response the best one?)
[If this does not elicit a codable answer, try these follow-ups:]
(What would you be trying to do? What would be your main goal?)

C. If that [name the response] doesn't work and Dorothy still is not satis-fied, what would you do next?

D. Why would you choose that?
[If this does not elicit a codable answer, try these follow-ups:]
(What would you be trying to do? What would be your main goal?)

5. BEFORE MOVING ON TO THE NEXT SECTION, LET ME ASK YOU: HAS THE WAY YOU'VE BEEN RAISING YOUR KIDS—TEACHING AND DISCIPLINING THEM—BEEN CHANGING? HOW SO?

IV. *THE HYPOTHETICAL MORAL JUDGMENT INTERVIEW*
(adapted from Colby, Kohlberg, Speicher, Hewer, Candee, Gibbs, and Power, 1987)

Now I would like to read you a little story and ask you some questions about it.

THE HEINZ DILEMMA: In Europe, a woman was near death from a rare disease. There was one drug that the doctors thought might save her. It was a drug that a druggist in the same town had recently discovered. The drug was expensive to make, but the druggist was charging *10* times what the drug cost him. He paid $200 for the materials, but he was charging $2,000 for the prescription. The sick woman's husband, Heinz, went to everyone he knew to borrow the money, but he could only get about $1,000—which is half of what he needed. He told the druggist that his wife was dying, and asked him to sell it cheaper or to let him pay later. But the druggist said, "No, I discovered the drug and I'm going to make money from it."

1. What do you think the problem is here?

   A) What should be done about it?

2. Should Heinz steal the drug? Why or why not?

   A) Would that be right or wrong? Why?

3A: [Ask only if she said it is *right* to steal. Otherwise, go to 3B; if she says it's right and wrong, ask questions from both A and B.]

   A1) If Heinz no longer loves his wife, should he still steal the drug? Why or why not?

   A2) Suppose the person dying is not his wife, but a stranger. Should Heinz steal the drug for a stranger? Why or why not? (Suppose it's a pet animal that he loves, should Heinz steal to save the pet animal?)

   A3) It is against the law for Heinz to steal the drug. What is to be said for following the law in this situation? What is the best reason you could give for Heinz to obey the law in this situation?

   A4) Now you've said you think Heinz should steal the drug. Can you tell me, kind of to summarize what you've been saying, what's the best reason you could give for Heinz to break the law and steal the drug?

3B: [Ask only if she said it is *wrong* to steal]:

   B1) Would it make a difference if he really loved his wife?

   B2) Heinz's wife will die if she does not get the drug. What is to be said in favor of stealing to save her life?

   B3) Now you've said it's wrong to steal and you've talked some about it. Could you just summarize your thinking for me on that by telling me what's the best reason you could give for Heinz to obey the law in this situation?

4.   Suppose Heinz does steal the drug. He is caught and brought to trial. The jury finds him guilty of stealing and the judge has to decide on the sentence. Should the judge sentence him or let him go free? Why or why not? [Try to get the participant's best reasons for sentencing Heinz *and* for letting him go free.]

CLOSING QUESTIONS

1.   What will your life be like in the future? Say, five years from now?

2.   Is there anything else that you want to add to help us understand you and how you have been changing during the past year or so?

Rosenberg Self-Esteem Scale
(Rosenberg, 1979)

LP # _____ Time _____ Name _____ Date _____

I will read 10 sentences to you. Think about each one and tell me whether you strongly agree, agree, disagree, or strongly disagree.

1. On the whole, I am satisfied with myself.
☐ Strongly Agree   ☐ Agree   ☐ Disagree   ☐ Strongly Disagree

2. At times I think I am no good at all.
☐ Strongly Agree   ☐ Agree   ☐ Disagree   ☐ Strongly Disagree

3. I feel that I have a number of good qualities.
☐ Strongly Agree   ☐ Agree   ☐ Disagree   ☐ Strongly Disagree

4. I am able to do most things as well as most people.
☐ Strongly Agree   ☐ Agree   ☐ Disagree   ☐ Strongly Disagree

5. I feel that I do not have much to be proud of.
☐ Strongly Agree   ☐ Agree   ☐ Disagree   ☐ Strongly Disagree

6. I certainly feel useless at times.
☐ Strongly Agree   ☐ Agree   ☐ Disagree   ☐ Strongly Disagree

7. I feel that I'm a person of worth, at least on an equal plane with others.
☐ Strongly Agree   ☐ Agree   ☐ Disagree   ☐ Strongly Disagree

8. I wish that I could have more respect for myself.
☐ Strongly Agree   ☐ Agree   ☐ Disagree   ☐ Strongly Disagree

9. All in all, I am inclined to feel that I am a failure.
☐ Strongly Agree   ☐ Agree   ☐ Disagree   ☐ Strongly Disagree

10. I take a positive attitude toward myself.
☐ Strongly Agree   ☐ Agree   ☐ Disagree   ☐ Strongly Disagree

The Family Social Support Scale
(adapted from Dunst, Jenkins, and Trivette, 1984)

LP # _____ Time _____ Name _____ Date _____

Listed below are people and agencies that oftentimes are helpful to members of families raising a young child. This questionnaire asks you to indicate how helpful each source is to *your family*. Please circle the response that best describes how helpful the sources have been to your family during the past *6 months*. *Cross out* any sources of help that have not been *available* to your family during this period of time.

	Not at All Helpful	Sometimes Helpful	Generally Helpful	Very Helpful	Extremely Helpful
1. My parents 1	2	3	4	5
2. Parents of the baby's father 1	2	3	4	5
3. My relatives/kin 1	2	3	4	5
4. Relatives/kin of the baby's father 1	2	3	4	5
5. Baby's father 1	2	3	4	5
6. My friends 1	2	3	4	5
7. Friends of baby's father 1	2	3	4	5
8. My own children . . . 1	2	3	4	5
9. Other people's parents 1	2	3	4	5
10. Church 1	2	3	4	5
11. Social groups/clubs .1	2	3	4	5
12. Co-workers 1	2	3	4	5
13. Parent groups 1	2	3	4	5
14. My family or child's physician 1	2	3	4	5
15. Professional helpers (social workers, therapists, teachers etc.) 1	2	3	4	5
16. School/day-care center 1	2	3	4	5
17. Professional agencies (public health, social services, mental health, etc.) 1	2	3	4	5
18. Other _____ 1	2	3	4	5

Checklist of Changes

LP # _____ Time _____ Name _____ Date _____

PLEASE CHECK ALL OF THE APPROPRIATE RESPONSES TO HELP US UNDERSTAND WHAT YOU'VE BEEN DOING SINCE THE LAST INTERVIEW, ABOUT NINE OR TEN MONTHS AGO.

WORK
Since the last interview, I worked outside the home: yes____;   no____.
        Describe:_____ .
Is this different from before: yes____;   no____.
Since the last interview, I got new ideas and plans for working outside the home in the future: yes____;   no____.
        Explain: _____ .

EDUCATION/TRAINING
Since the last interview, I worked on my education or training:
yes____;   no____.
If yes, did you:
        work on your GED   yes____;   no____.
        get your GED   yes____;   no____.
        sign up for or take a course   yes____;   no____.
        Describe:_____ .
        enroll or participate in a training program:
                                yes____;   no____.
        Explain: _____
                _____ .
Other: _____ .

Since the last interview, I got new ideas and plans for learning new things:
yes____;   no____.
        Describe:_____ .
Any other changes: _____ .

HEALTH AND HEALTH CARE
Since the last interview, my health is:
the same____;   better____;   worse____.
        Explain _____ .
Since the last interview, my child's health is:
the same____;   better____;   worse____.
        Explain _____ .
The way I take care of myself is:
the same____;   better____;   worse____.

Explain _____ .

Since the last interview, I smoke:

    the same____;   more____;   less____;

    I quit smoking since the last interview____;   I don't smoke____.

Since the last interview, I exercise:

    the same____   more____;   less____.

Since the last interview, my eating habits are:

    the same____;   better____;   worse____.

    Explain _____ .

CHECK ALL THAT APPLY:

Since the last interview, I looked into: improving my eyesight____;

improving my hearing____;   getting dental work done____;   other____.

    Explain: _____ .

Since the last interview, I actually did things to improve my eyesight:____.

Since the last interview, I actually did things to improve my hearing:____.

Since the last interview, I did things to improve my dental care:____.

Other: _____ .

Any other changes in your health care: _____ .

HOUSING

Since the last interview, our housing situation is:

the same____;   better____;   worse____.

    Explain _____ .

Since the last interview, our heating is:

the same____;   better____;   worse____.

Any other housing changes this year: _____ .

TELEPHONE

Do you have a phone?   yes____;   no____.

If yes, how long have you had one? _____ .

If no, how long have you been without one? _____ .

TRANSPORTATION

Please check all the responses that apply to you:

Since the last interview, I got a driver's permit____.

Since the last interview, I got a driver's license____.

I had my license before the last interview____.

Since the last interview, I lost my license____.

Since the last interview, I got a car____.

Since the last interview, I have more access to a car____.

Since the last interview, it's easier for me to get rides____.

Overall, since the last interview, I get around:

the same____;   better____;   worse____.

SUPPORT GROUPS/FRIENDS

Since the last interview, I thought about joining a support group or groups:
yes_____;   no_____.
     Describe:_____ .
Since the last interview, I joined a support group or groups (other than LP):
yes_____;   no_____.
     Describe:_____ .
Since the last interview, I thought about making new friends or spending more time with my friends: yes_____;   no_____.
Since the last interview, I made a new friend (or friends):   yes_____;   no_____.
Since the last interview, I've spent more time with my friends:
yes_____;   no_____.

Videotaped Mother-Child Interaction Coding Categories
(adapted from Flaugher and Sigel, 1980)

CODING CATEGORY	DEFINITION
Child Management	Parental efforts at stopping or modifying a behavior of the child that the parent does not approve of.
Task Management	Specific directions the parent gives the child that are related to facilitating the task.
Mental Operational Demand (MOD)	Level of cognitive demand placed on the child.
Low MOD	Closed questions or parent statements that may or may not require a response from the child; very little information processing is required of the child.
Medium MOD	Parent questions or statements that require the child to retrieve information in order to respond to the parent. These questions necessitate that the child go beyond the information given and manipulate it in some fashion.
High MOD	Parent questions or statements that require the child to not only retrieve information but also to organize and integrate it in order to respond to the parent. The child is generating her or his own thoughts, ideas, methods.

APPENDIX B

Characteristics of participants at preintervention, by cohort and experimental group: numbers reflect means/frequencies (range) unless otherwise noted.

	LP Group Participants (n=59)		Control Group (n=61)	
Age of mother (yrs.)	24.3	(17–34)	24.3	(18–34)
# children	1.9	(1–5)	2.2	(1–4)
Gender of study child # females (% female)	25	(42%)	26	(43%)
# (%) Intact (legal) nuclear families	29	(50%)	27	(44%)
# (%) Families on welfare	33	(58%)	36	(63%)
# (%) Families with some religious affiliation	34	(58%)	39	(64%)
Mother's education (yrs.)	11.4	(8–15)	10.8	(6–14)
Father's education (yrs.)	11.4	(6–18)	10.6	(4–14)★
Maternal grandmother's ed. (yrs.)	10.5	(4–16)	10.5	(6–16)
Maternal grandfather's ed. (yrs.)	10.1	(5–14)	10.4	(4–16)
Socioeconomic status (Hollingshead)				
Family of origin	23.1	(8–48)	23.7	(8–58)
Family of procreation	20.8	(8–51)	19.1	(8–45)
Family support				
Total helpfulness (sd) of supports				
–All supports (out of 85)	34.1	(10.3)	39.0	(11.7)★
–Informal supports only (of 55 possible)	23.0	(7.1)	25.4	(7.9)
–Formal supports only (of 30 possible)	11.1	(5.3)	13.7	(6.3)★
Mean helpfulness (sd) of available supports: 1 (not helpful) – 5 (extremely helpful)				
–Total supports	2.7	(.7)	2.8	(.7)
–Informal supports only	2.6	(.7)	2.7	(.7)
–Formal supports only	3.1	(1.0)	3.1	(1.0)
Number of supports at least generally helpful				
–Total	6.3	(0–17)	7.2	(1–15)

-Informal support only	4.1	(0–11)	4.7	(1-9)
-Formal supports only	2.2	(0-6)	2.6	(0-6)
Maternal self esteem (s.d.)	2.8	(.40)	2.9	(.34)
Maternal Ways of Knowing	6.0	(1-10)	4.8	(1-10)**

Note. T-tests were performed on all variables by experimental/control group within cohorts and overall, except the following, where Chi-square (2×2) tests were performed: gender of study child, # (%) intact (legal) nuclear families, # (%) families on welfare, and # (%) families with some religious affiliation.

*p < .05
**p < .001

NOTES

INTRODUCTION: OTHERNESS AND SILENCE

1. Words printed in uppercase letters indicate the interviewer's comments and questions. Some quotes from interviews we conducted have been edited to preserve the meaning of verbatim speech. The names of participants of the Listening Partners program and some facts have been altered to protect the women's identities.

2. We use the terms *white, black,* and *people of color* because these phrases are used by many of the people we interviewed to describe themselves and their counterparts. We understand these terms to suggest different cultural communities, not fixed biological entities as implied by conventional but unscientific notions of race. To suggest the ambiguous nature of these concepts, we have chosen to use lowercase letters. A similar notion about cultural communities undergirds our thinking about gender differences. When we speak of women's ways of knowing, maternal thinking, maternal practice, and women's leadership traditions (as we often do), we refer more to the cultural achievements of women than to the biology of their sex. Women's ability to create public homeplaces and nurture the development of people, families, and communities is rooted in the work of raising up the most vulnerable members of society, generation after generation, throughout human history. Even though biology contributes to the ways in which many social roles are assigned to men and women, we believe that these roles and abilities grow out of engaged practice more than biology. We are quite certain that men are as capable as women of developing similar approaches. Indeed, many have.

3. Omolade and many other African American women use "womanist" to distinguish their approach from "feminist" visions more common among European Americans. (See Walker, 1983.)

CHAPTER 2: CONFRONTING OTHERNESS: PREVIOUS RESEARCH

1. In *Women's Ways of Knowing* this outlook was named "silence." We have taken the liberty of changing it to "silenced." The added "d" helps distinguish this way of knowing from the approaches others have observed in several non-Western cultures (Goldberger, 1996), where silence gives rise to powerful modes of connecting with and apprehending the world that do not depend on language.

CHAPTER 3: THE LISTENING PARTNERS PROJECT

1.   All quotations in this chapter come from participants of the Listening Partners program unless otherwise noted; names and other identifying information have been changed to protect participants' privacy.

2.   This pilot project was funded by an award from the A. L. Mailman Family Foundation, Inc. (White Plains, New York), to Lynne A. Bond and Mary Field Belenky, from September 1985 to July 1986.

3.   Grant MCJ–500541 was awarded to Lynne A. Bond and Mary Field Belenky, The University of Vermont, by the Maternal and Child Health Bureau, Department of Health and Human Services, Public Health Service, October 1, 1986, to June 1, 1991.

CHAPTER 4: WHAT WAS LEARNED

1.   More complete information regarding the research design, analyses, and interpretation is available from the authors, c/o Lynne A. Bond, Department of Psychology, John Dewey Hall, The University of Vermont, Burlington, VT 05405–0134. See also Appendix A for the protocols of the interviews and assessments that were used.

2.   All intervention participants resided in one county. As each intervention participant was successfully recruited into the program, we then identified a control-group participant from the neighboring county who was the same age and had a child of the same gender and age; control-group members were selected so that their educational, family, employment, and financial backgrounds and present living situations were similar to those of the intervention participants. Statistical comparisons of the characteristics of the intervention and control groups confirmed that they were virtually identical on all of these variables at the onset of the project (see Appendix B).

3.   In our initial conversations with each woman whom we invited to join Listening Partners, we clarified whether she would have the opportunity to participate in the intervention group or the control group. All intervention participants resided in one county, while the control participants resided in the neighboring county.

4.   Robert K. Merton began asking the question, "What stands out for you about . . . ?" in the 1940 (see Merton and Kendall, 1946; see also Merton, Fiske, and Kendall, 1956). Adapting Merton's question, William Perry (1970) began each of his annual interviews of undergraduate students with, "Why don't you start with whatever stands out for you about the year?" Belenky, Clinchy, Goldberger, and Tarule (1986/1997) adapted the question for their study, as did we. The question suggests the interviewer is interested in understanding the interviewee in her own terms and that she will be expected to reflect actively on her experience, articulating the aspects most relevant to her.

5.   The 82 percent refers to the eighty of the ninety-seven women who provided the information necessary to calculate the socioeconomic status of the households in which they were raised.

6.   Statistical comparisons revealed that the mean epistemology score was slightly higher for members of the intervention group than the control group at the onset of the project. We believe that the most silenced women we contacted were more likely to agree to participate in the project when we were asking them only to complete interviews rather than to complete interviews *and* weekly peer-group intervention sessions. In subsequent analyses comparing the intervention and control groups on epistemological perspectives and change, we worked exclusively with "change scores," that is, the change in a woman's score from one assessment period to the other, in order to control for the slight differences between the groups at the onset of the project.

7.   Stepwise multiple regression analyses were performed to examine predictors of attendance at the intervention sessions. The independent or predictor variables included the preintervention Ways of Knowing scores, level of education, age, and one of two pairs of assessments for informal and formal social support at preintervention (Family Support Scale ratings of total helpfulness of all informal supports and total helpfulness of all formal supports, or ratings of the number of informal supports and number of formal supports considered by the respondent to be both available to her and at least generally helpful). The dependent or outcome variable was the total number of intervention sessions attended.

8.   We expressly excluded the Listening Partners program as a social support in our statistical analyses so that any calculations of an intervention effect would not reflect the mere presence of our program.

9.   Three-way Multivariate Analyses of Variance (Time × Intervention Group × Epistemological Perspective at onset of the project) were used to examine the change in epistemological perspectives from pre- to postintervention and follow-up. A statistically significant three-way interaction effect revealed that intervention participants who entered the program as silenced or received knowers showed greater epistemological gains than comparable members of the control group. These differences were significant at postintervention and even stronger at follow-up.

10.   A series of stepwise multiple regression analyses was performed to examine maternal predictors of epistemological change from preintervention to follow-up. The independent or predictor variables included preintervention epistemological score, level of education, age, number of intervention sessions attended (as a measure of the predictive value of the intervention itself), and one of two pairs of assessments for informal and formal social support at preintervention (Family Support Scale ratings of total helpfulness of all informal supports and total helpfulness of all formal supports, or ratings of the number of informal supports and number of formal supports considered by the respondent to be both available to her and at least generally helpful). The dependent or outcome variable was the *change* in epistemology score from preintervention to follow-up (defined as follow-up score minus preintervention score).

CHAPTER 5: MOTHERS AND CHILDREN

1.   Our Epistemological Development interview was adapted from the interview used by Belenky, Clinchy, Goldberger, and Tarule (1986/1997). The complete coding manual for our adapted version of the interview is presented in Weinstock (1989).

2.   A full description of the scoring strategy is included in L. A. Bond, M. F. Belenky, and J. S. Weinstock (1991), *Listening Partners: Psycho-social Competence and Prevention*, Final Report of #MCJ-500541 (10/1/86–6/1/91) to the Maternal and Child Health Bureau, HRSA, PHS, DHHS. Copies are available from the authors, c/o Lynne Bond, Department of Psychology, John Dewey Hall, The University of Vermont, Burlington, VT 05405-0134.

3.   This category is a modification of one that McGillicuddy-DeLisi, Johnson, Sigel, and Epstein (1980) called *distancing* and originally defined as "responses by the parent which attempt to influence the child through the use of a procedure intended to induce the child's active verbal participation centered on a problem defined in the situation. This type of communication places a mental demand on the child and functions as an inquiry directed at the child from the parent" (p. 9).

4.   This category was adapted from a category referred to as *activity* by McGillicuddy-DeLisi, Johnson, Sigel, and Epstein (1980).

5.   See, for example, A. V. McGillicuddy-DeLisi (1982); see also, McGillicuddy-DeLisi, Johnson, Sigel, and Epstein (1980).

6.   For a detailed description, see Bond, Belenky, and Weinstock (1991), available from the authors, c/o Lynne Bond, Department of Psychology, John Dewey Hall, The University of Vermont, Burlington, VT 05405-0134. See also Monsey (1990).

7.   Detailed descriptions of statistical analyses and interpretations of these research findings are included in Bond, Belenky, and Weinstock (1991), available from the authors, c/o Lynne Bond, Department of Psychology, John Dewey Hall, The University of Vermont, Burlington, VT 05405-0134.

   For the purpose of quantitative statistical analyses, the Ways of Knowing interviews were read and analyzed for evidence of one of five major epistemological positions as well as evidence of more minor epistemological assumptions that suggested the emergence of more complex understandings or the continued embeddedness in less complex understandings. Therefore, individuals could be coded into one of seventeen theoretically possible ordinal levels based on a major and minor epistemological code.

8.   One-way Analyses of Variance were used to examine whether women's average use of each communication strategy in the hypothetical scenarios varied with the women's epistemological perspectives. Analyses of mean levels for endorsing each of the communication strategies revealed that women with more complex epistemological perspectives endorsed more intellectual facilitation, more parent activity, and less authoritarian communication.

9.   To analyze statistically the relationship between mothers' epistemologies and their modal communication response in the hypothetical scenarios, a rank num-

ber was assigned to each modal communication strategy based on the amount of parent control involved in the strategy as well as the amount of intellectual challenge placed on the child. On a dimension from high parent control/low intellectual demand to low parent control/high intellectual demand, an authoritarian modal response was ranked first, followed by direct authoritative, parent activity, rational authoritative, and finally intellectual facilitation (as described earlier in this chapter). A one-way analysis of variance confirmed that women with any silenced epistemological assumptions endorsed a more directive, less intellectually demanding communication strategy compared with women with more complex epistemologies.

10. Pearson Product-moment Correlation analyses were used to examine the relationship between mothers' epistemological perspectives (revealed through the Ways of Knowing Interview) and their use of child management strategies. A significant negative correlation emerged, revealing that more complex epistemological perspectives were associated with less frequent use of child management strategies. In addition, a Two-way Multivariate Analysis of Variance (Epistemological Perspective × Teaching Task) examined the ways in which women's use of child management strategies varied with epistemological perspective and teaching task. Analyses revealed that women whose epistemological perspective included silenced knowing used more child management strategies than women whose epistemological perspective reflected received or subjective knowing.

11. A two-way Multivariate Analysis of Variance (Epistemological Perspective × Teaching Task) was used to examine whether women's use of intellectually challenging statements to their children varied with the women's epistemological perspective and the teaching task (intellectual challenge was coded using an adaptation of the Parent-Child Interaction Observation Schedule, developed by Flaugher and Sigel, 1980; see Appendix A). Analyses revealed that, on the Lego task, women with any silenced knowing used fewer intellectually challenging statements with their children than women with received or subjective knowing.

12. From the *Parent-Child Communication Strategy Interview* of McGillicuddy-DeLisi, Johnson, Sigel and Epstein (1980); see Appendix A.

⬙ BIBLIOGRAPHY ⬙

Adams, F., with M. Horton (1975). *Unearthing Seeds of Fire: The Idea of Highlander.* Winston-Salem, NC: J. F. Blair.

Addams, J. (1965). *The Social Thought of Jane Addams*, C. Lasch (ed.). Indianapolis: Macmillan.

Adorno, T. W., E. Frenkel-Brunswik, D. J. Levinson, and R. N. Sanford (1950). *The Authoritarian Personality.* New York: Harper.

Adorno, T. W., E. Frenkel-Brunswik, D. J. Levinson, and R. N. Sanford (1982). *The Authoritarian Personality*, abridged edition. New York: W. W. Norton.

Allport, G. (1958). *The Nature of Prejudice.* Garden City, NY: Doubleday Anchor Books.

American Association of University Women (1991). *Shortchanging Girls, Shortchanging America: A Call to Action.* Washington, DC: American Association of University Women.

Applebome, P. (1994). New South and old: In Selma, everything and nothing changed. *New York Times*, August 2, pp. A1 and B6.

Argyris, C. (1985). *Strategy, Change, and Defensive Routines.* Boston: Pitman.

Asante, M. K. (1987). *The Afrocentric Idea.* Philadelphia: Temple University Press.

Ascher, C., L. DeSalvo, and S. Ruddick (eds.) (1984). *Between Women: Biographers, Novelists, Critics, Teachers, and Artists Write About Their Work on Women.* Boston: Beacon Press.

Auerbach, A. B. (1968). *Parents Learn Through Discussion: Principles and Practices of Parent Group Education.* New York: John Wiley & Sons.

Badger, E. D. (1971). A mothers' training program—the road to a purposeful existence. *Children* 18: 168–73.

Badger, E. D. (1973). *Mother's Guide to Early Learning.* Paoli, PA: McGraw Hill.

Bakan, D. (1966). *The Duality of Human Existence: An Essay on Psychology and Religion.* Chicago: Rand McNally & Company.

Baker, E. (1973). Developing community leadership. In G. Lerner (ed.), *Black Women in White America: A Documentary History.* New York: Pantheon.

Bakhtin, M. M. (1986). *The Dialogic Imagination.* Austin: University of Texas.

Bambara, T. C. (ed.) (1970). *The Black Woman.* New York: New American Library.

Bargad, A., and J. S. Hyde (1991). Women's studies: A study of feminist identity development in women. *Psychology of Women Quarterly* 15: 181–201.

Basseches, M. (1984). *Dialectical Thinking and Adult Development.* Norwood, NJ: Ablex.

Baumrind, D. (1989). Rearing competent children. In W. Damon (ed.), *Child Development Today and Tomorrow.* San Francisco: Jossey-Bass.

Baumrind, D. (1991). Parenting styles and adolescent development. In R. Lerner, A. C. Petersen and J. Brooks-Gunn (eds.), *The Encyclopedia of Adolescence.* New York: Garland Press.

Baxter Magolda, M. B. (1992). *Knowing and Reasoning in College: Gender-Related Patterns in Students' Intellectual Development*. San Francisco: Jossey-Bass.

Belenky, M. F. (1978). *Conflict and Development: A Longitudinal Study of the Impact of Abortion Decisions on Adolescent and Adult Women*. Unpublished doctoral dissertation. Cambridge, MA: Harvard University.

Belenky, M. F., B. McV. Clinchy, N. R. Goldberger, and J. M. Tarule (1986/1997). *Women's Ways of Knowing: The Development of Self, Voice, and Mind*, 10th anniversary edition. New York: Basic Books.

Bellah, R. N., R. Madsen, W. M. Sullivan, A. Swidler, and S. M. Tipton (1985). *Habits of the Heart: Individualism and Commitment in American Life*. Berkeley: University of California Press.

Bell-Scott, P., B. Guy-Sheftall, J. Royster, J. Sims-Wood, M. DeCosta-Willis, and L. Fultz (eds.) (1991). *Double Stitch: Black Women Write About Mothers and Daughters*. Boston: Beacon Press.

Bem, S. L. (1993). *The Lenses of Gender: Transforming the Debate on Sexual Inequality*. New Haven, CT: Yale University Press.

Berkowitz, M. W. (1985). The role of discussion in moral education. In M. W. Berkowitz and F. Oser (eds.), *Moral Education: Theory and Application*. Hillsdale, NJ: Lawrence Erlbaum.

Berman, S. (1997). *Children's Social Consciousness and the Development of Social Responsibility*. Albany: State University of New York Press.

Bond, L. A., M. F. Belenky, and J. S. Weinstock (1991). *Listening Partners: Psychosocial Competence and Prevention*. Final Report of Grant MCJ–500541 (10/86–6/91) to the Maternal and Child Health Bureau, Rockville, MD.

Bond, L. A., M. F. Belenky, J. S. Weinstock, and T. Cook (1996). Imagining and engaging one's children: Lessons from poor, rural, New England mothers. In S. Harkness and C. M. Super (eds.), *Parents' Cultural Belief Systems: Their Origins, Expressions and Consequences*. New York: Guilford Press.

Borish, S. (1991). *The Land of the Living: The Danish Folk High Schools and Denmark's Non-violent Path to Modernization*. Nevada City, CA: Blue Dolphin.

Bouvard, M. G. (1994). *Revolutionizing Motherhood: The Mothers of the Plaza de Mayo*. Wilmington, DE: Scholarly Resources Inc.

Branch, T. (1988). *Parting the Waters: American in the King Years*. New York: Simon & Schuster.

Broughton, J. (1983). Women's rationality and men's virtues: A critique of gender dualism in Gilligan's theory of moral development. *Social Research* 50: 597–624.

Brown, E. B. (1989). Womanist consciousness: Maggie Lena Walker and the Independent Order of Saint Luke. *Signs: Journal of Women in Culture and Society* 14: 610–33.

Brown, E. B. (1991). Mothers of mind. In P. Bell-Scott, B. Guy-Sheftall, J. Royster, J. Sims-Wood, M. DeCosta-Willis, and L. Fultz (eds.), *Double Stitch: Black Women Write About Mothers and Daughters*. Boston: Beacon Press.

Brown, G. W., and T. Harris (1978). *Social Origins of Depression: A Study of Psychiatric Disorders in Women*. New York: Free Press.

Brown, L. (in prep.). *Stones in the Road: Anger, Class, and Adolescent Girls*. Cambridge, MA: Harvard University Press.

Brown, L., D. Argyris, J. Attanucci, B. Bardige, C. Gilligan, K. Johnston, B. Miller, D. Osborne, M. Tappan, J. Ward, G. Wiggins, and D. Wilcox (1988). *A Guide to Reading Narratives of Moral Conflict and Choice for Self and Moral Voice*. Unpublished monograph. Cambridge, MA: GEHD Study Center, Harvard University.

Brown, L. M., and C. Gilligan (1992). *Meeting at the Crossroads: Women's Psychology and Girls' Development*. Cambridge, MA: Harvard University Press.

Brown, R. (1965). *Social Psychology*. New York: Free Press.

Bruner, J. (1986). *Actual Minds, Possible Worlds*. Cambridge, MA: Harvard University Press.

Buffalo, A. (1993, March/April). Sweet Honey in the Rock: A cappella activists. *Ms.* 3 (5): 24–31.

Bureau of the Census (1995). *American Women: A Profile*. Washington, DC: U.S. Department of Commerce, Economics, and Statistics Administration.

Cantarow, E., with S. G. O'Malley and S. H. Strom (1980). *Moving the Mountain: Women Working for Social Change*. Old Westbury, NY: Feminist Press.

Carothers, S. (1990). Catching sense: Learning from our mothers to be black and female. In F. Ginsberg and A. L. Tsing (eds.), *Uncertain Terms: Negotiating Gender in American Culture*. Boston: Beacon Press.

Chestnut, J. L., Jr., and J. Cass (1990). *Black in Selma: The Uncommon Life of J. L. Chestnut, Jr.* New York: Farrar, Straus and Giroux.

Chodorow, N. (1978). *The Reproduction of Mothering: Psychoanalysis and the Sociology of Gender*. Berkeley: University of California Press.

Chopin, K. (1899/1972). *The Awakening*. New York: Avon Books.

Chrislip, D. D., and C. E. Larson (1994). *Collaborative Leadership: How Citizens and Civic Leaders Can Make a Difference*. San Francisco: Jossey-Bass.

Christian, B. (1990). The highs and the lows of black feminist criticism. In H. L. Gates, Jr. (ed.), *Reading Black, Reading Feminist: A Critical Anthology*. New York: Meridian Books.

Clark, S. (1990). *Ready from Within*. C. S. Brown (ed.). Trenton, NJ: Africa World Press.

Clinchy, B. McV. (1993). Ways of knowing and ways of being: Epistemological and moral development in undergraduate women. In A. Garrod (ed.), *Approaches to Moral Development: New Research and Emerging Themes*. New York: Teachers College Press.

Clinchy, B. McV. (1996). Connected and separate knowing: Toward a marriage of two minds. In N. R. Goldberger, J. M. Tarule, B. McV. Clinchy, and M. F. Belenky (eds.), *Knowledge, Difference, and Power: Essays Inspired by Women's Ways of Knowing*. New York: Basic Books.

Clinchy, B. McV. (in press). A plea for epistemological pluralism. In B. McV. Clinchy and J. K. Norem (eds.), *A Reader in Gender and Psychology*. New York: New York University Press.

Clinchy, B. McV., and C. Zimmerman (1982). Epistemology and agency in the development of undergraduate women. In P. Perun (ed.), *The Undergraduate Woman: Issues in Educational Equity*. Lexington, MA: D. C. Heath.

Colby, A., and W. Damon (1992). *Some Do Care: Contemporary Lives of Moral Commitment*. New York: Free Press.

Colby, A., L. Kohlberg, B. Speicher, A. Hewer, D. Candee, J. Gibbs, and C. Power (1987). *The Measurement of Moral Judgment: Volumes 1 and 2*. New York: Cambridge University Press.

Collins, P. H. (1991a). *Black Feminist Thought: Knowledge, Consciousness, and the Politics of Empowerment*. New York: Routledge.

Collins, P. H. (1991b). The meaning of motherhood in black culture and black mother–daughter relationships. In P. Bell-Scott, B. Guy-Sheftall, J. Royster, J. Sims-Wood, M. DeCosta-Willis, and L. Fultz (eds.), *Double Stitch: Black Women Write About Mothers and Daughters*. Boston: Beacon Press.

Cooper, A. J. (1892/1988). *A Voice from the South/by a Black Woman of the South*. New York: Oxford University Press.

Crawford, V. L., J. A. Rouse, and B. Woods (1990). *Women in the Civil Rights Movement: Trailblazers and Torch Bearers, 1941–1965*. New York: Carlson.

Daloz, L. A. P., C. H. Keen, J. P. Keen, and S. D. Parks (1996). *Common Fire: Lives of Commitment in a Complex World*. Boston: Beacon Press.

Damon, W., and M. Killen (1982). Peer interaction and the process of change in children's moral reasoning. *Merrill-Palmer Quarterly* 28: 347–67.

Darwin, C. (1896). *The Origin of Species by Means of Natural Selection, or, The Preservation of Favored Races in the Struggle for Life*. New York: D. Appleton.

Davis, A. Y. (1981). *Women, Race, and Class*. New York: Random House.

de Beauvoir, S. (1957). *The Second Sex*, H. M. Parshley (trans. and ed.). New York: Knopf.

Debold, E., M. Wilson, and I. Malave (1993). *Mother Daughter Revolution: From Betrayal to Power*. Reading, MA: Addison-Wesley.

Deegan, M. J. (1988). *Jane Addams and the Men of the Chicago School, 1892–1918*. New Brunswick, NJ: Transaction Books.

Dewey, J. (1916/1966). *Democracy and Education*. New York: Free Press.

Dill, B. (1987). The dialectics of black womanhood. In S. Harding (ed.), *Feminism and Methodology*. Bloomington: Indiana University Press.

Dix, T., D. N. Ruble, and R. J. Zambarano (1989). Mothers' implicit theories of discipline: Child effects, parent effects, and the attribution process. *Child Development* 60: 1373–91.

Dunst, C. J., V. Jenkins, and C. M. Trivette (1984). Family Support Scale: Reliability and validity. *Journal of Individual, Family, and Community Wellness* 1: 45–52.

Ede, L., and A. Lunsford (1990). *Singular Texts/Plural Authors: Perspectives on Collaborative Writing*. Carbondale: Southern Illinois University Press.

Edwards, C., L. Gandini, and G. Forman (eds.) (1995). *The Hundred Languages of Children: The Reggio Emilia Approach to Early Childhood Education*. Norwood, NJ: Ablex.

Eisenberg, N., and B. Murphy (1995). Parenting and children's moral development. In M. H. Bornstein (ed.), *Handbook of Parenting: Vol. 4. Applied and Practical Parenting.* Mahwah, NJ: Lawrence Erlbaum.

Elbow, P. (1973). *Writing Without Teachers.* New York: Oxford University Press.

Elbow, P. (1986). *Embracing Contraries: Explorations in Learning and Teaching.* New York: Oxford University Press.

Elias, D. G. (1993). *Educating Leaders for Social Transformation.* Unpublished doctoral dissertation. New York: Teachers College Press.

Elshtain, J. B. (1995). *Democracy on Trail.* New York: Basic Books.

Evans, S. M. (1979). *Personal Politics: The Roots of Women's Liberation in the Civil Rights Movement and the New Left.* New York: Knopf.

Evans, S. M. (1989). *Born for Liberty: A History of Women in America.* New York: Free Press.

Evans, S. M., and H. C. Boyte (1986). *Free Spaces: The Sources of Democratic Change in America.* New York: Harper & Row.

Feuerstein, R., with Y. Rand, M. B. Hoffman, and R. Miller (1980). *Instrumental Enrichment: An Intervention Program for Cognitive Modifiability.* Baltimore: University Park Press.

Feuerstein, R., Y. Rand, and J. Rynders (1988). *Don't Accept Me As I Am: Helping "Retarded" People to Excel.* New York: Plenum Press.

Fine, M. (1991). *Framing Dropouts: Notes on the Politics of an Urban Public High School.* Albany: State University of New York Press.

Flaugher, J., and I. Sigel (1980). *Parent-Child Interaction Observation Schedule.* Princeton, NJ: Educational Testing Service.

Flavell, J. (1988). The development of children's knowledge about mind: From cognitive connections to mental representations. In J. W. Astington, P. L. Harris, and D. R. Olson (eds.), *Developing Theories of Mind.* New York: Cambridge University Press.

Forman, J. (1972). *The Making of Black Revolutionaries.* New York: Macmillan.

Freedman, S. G. (1996). *The Inheritance: How Three Families Moved from Roosevelt to Reagan and Beyond.* New York: Simon & Schuster.

Freire, P. (1970). *Pedagogy of the Oppressed,* M. B. Ramos (trans.). New York: Herder & Herder.

Freud, S. (1927). *The Ego and the Id.* London: Hogarth Press.

Fromm, E., and M. Maccoby (1970). *Social Character in a Mexican Village: A Sociopsychoanalytic Study.* Englewood Cliffs, NJ: Prentice-Hall.

Gamson, W. A. (1992). *Talking Politics.* New York: Cambridge University Press.

Gamson, W. A. (1995). Hiroshima, the Holocaust, and the politics of exclusion: 1994 Presidential Address. *American Sociological Review* 60: 1–20.

Gamson, W. A. (1996). Safe spaces and social movements. *Perspectives on Social Problems* 8: 27–38.

Gans, H. (1995). *The War Against the Poor: The Underclass and Antipoverty Policy.* New York: Basic Books.

Garcia Coll, C. T., E. C. Meyer, and L. Brillon (1995). Ethnic and minority parenting. In M. H. Bornstein (ed.), *Handbook of Parenting: Vol. 2. Biology and Ecology of Parenting.* Mahwah, NJ: Lawrence Erlbaum.

Gardner, H. (1985). *The Mind's New Science: A History of the Cognitive Revolution.* New York: Basic Books.

Gardner, H. (1991). *The Unschooled Mind.* New York: Basic Books.

Gardner, H. (1995). *Leading Minds: An Anatomy of Leadership.* New York: Basic Books.

Gergen, K. J. (1991). *The Saturated Self: Dilemmas of Identity in Contemporary Life.* New York: Basic Books.

Gilbert, S. M., and S. Gubar (1979). *The Madwoman in the Attic: The Woman Writer and the Nineteenth-Century Literary Imagination.* New Haven, CT: Yale University Press.

Gilbert, S. M., and S. Gubar (1994). *No Man's Land: The Place of the Woman Writer in the Twentieth Century: Vol. 3. Letters from the Front.* New Haven, CT: Yale University Press.

Gilligan, C. (1977). In a different voice: Women's conceptions of the self and morality. *Harvard Educational Review* 47: 481–517.

Gilligan, C. (1982/1993). *In a Different Voice: Psychological Theory and Women's Development,* 2nd edition. Cambridge, MA: Harvard University Press.

Gilligan, C. (1990). Joining the resistance: Psychology, politics, girls, and women. *Michigan Quarterly* 29: 501–536.

Gilligan, C., and M. F. Belenky (1980). A naturalistic study of abortion decisions. In R. L. Selman and R. Yando (eds.), *Clinical-Developmental Psychology.* San Francisco: Jossey-Bass.

Gilligan, C., N. P. Lyons, and T. J. Hanmer (eds.) (1990). *Making Connections: The Relational Worlds of Adolescent Girls at Emma Willard School.* Cambridge, MA: Harvard University Press.

Gilligan, C., J. V. Ward, and J. M. Taylor (eds.) (1988). *Mapping the Moral Domain: A Contribution of Women's Thinking to Psychological Theory and Education.* Cambridge, MA: Harvard University Press.

Gilligan, C., and G. Wiggins (1988). The origins of morality in early childhood relationships. In. C. Gilligan, J. V. Ward, and J. M. Taylor (eds.), *Mapping the Moral Domain.* Cambridge, MA: Harvard University Press.

Goldberger, N. R. (1996). Cultural imperatives and diversity in ways of knowing. In N. R. Goldberger, J. M. Tarule, B. McV. Clinchy, and M. F. Belenky (eds.), *Knowledge, Difference, and Power: Essays Inspired by Women's Ways of Knowing.* New York: Basic Books.

Goldberger, N. R., J. M. Tarule, B. McV. Clinchy, and M. F. Belenky (eds.) (1996). *Knowledge, Difference, and Power: Essays Inspired by Women's Ways of Knowing.* New York: Basic Books.

Grant, J. (1970). Mississippi politics: A day in the life of Ella Baker. In T. C. Bambara (ed.), *The Black Woman.* New York: New American Library.

Grant, J. (1986). *Fundi: The Story of Ella Baker* (Videorecording). New York: First Run/Icarus Films.

Greene, B. (1990). Sturdy bridges: The role of African-American mothers in the socialization of African-American children. *Women and Therapy* 10: 205–230.

Greene, M. (1988). *The Dialectic of Freedom.* New York: Teachers College Press.

Greene, M. (1995). *Releasing the Imagination: Essays on Education, the Arts, and Social Change*. San Francisco: Jossey Bass.

Grusec, J. E., and J. J. Goodnow (1994). Impact of parental discipline methods on the child's internalization of values: A reconceptualization of current points of view. *Developmental Psychology* 30: 4–19.

Hansen, R. D., and V. E. O'Leary (1985). Sex-determined attributions. In V. E. O'Leary, R. K. Unger, and B. S. Wallston (eds.), *Women, Gender, and Social Psychology*. Hillsdale, NJ: Lawrence Erlbaum.

Harding, S. (1986). *The Science Question in Feminism*. Ithaca, NY: Cornell University Press.

Harding, S. (1996). Gendered ways of knowing and the "epistemological crisis" of the West. In N. R. Goldberger, J. M. Tarule, B. McV. Clinchy, and M. F. Belenky (eds.), *Knowledge, Difference, and Power: Essays Inspired by Women's Ways of Knowing*. New York: Basic Books.

Harkness, S., and C. M. Super (eds.) (1996). *Parents' Cultural Belief Systems: Their Origins, Expressions and Consequences*. New York: Guilford Press.

Harkness, S., C. M. Super, and C. H. Keefer (1992). Learning to be an American parent: How cultural models gain directive force. In R. G. D'Andrade and C. Strauss (eds.), *Human Motives and Cultural Models*. New York: Cambridge University Press.

Haste, H. (1994). *The Sexual Metaphor*. Cambridge, MA: Harvard University Press.

Hayden, D. (1984). *Redesigning the American Dream: The Future of Housing, Work, and Family Life*. New York: Norton.

Hayden, D. (1995). *The Power of Place: Urban Landscapes as Public History*. Cambridge, MA: MIT Press.

Haywood, T. L. (1983). College for neighborhood women: Innovation and growth. In C. Bunch and S. Pollack (eds.), *Learning Our Way: Essays in Feminist Education*. Trumansburg, NY: Crossing Press.

Heilbrun, C. (1988). *Writing a Woman's Life*. New York: Ballantine.

Hinsdale, M. A., H. M. Lewis, and S. M. Waller (1995). *It Comes from the People: Community Development and Local Theology*. Philadelphia: Temple University Press.

Hirsch, E. D., Jr., J. F. Kett, and J. Trefil (1993). *The Dictionary of Cultural Literacy*, 2nd edition. Boston: Houghton Mifflin.

Hirsch, M. (1989). *The Mother/Daughter Plot: Narrative, Psychoanalyses, Feminism*. Bloomington: Indiana University Press.

Hirsch, M. (1990). Maternal narratives: "Cruel Enough to Stop the Blood." In H. L. Gates, Jr. (ed.), *Reading Black, Reading Feminist: A Critical Anthology*. New York: Meridian Books.

Hollingshead, A. B. (1975). *Four Factor Index of Social Status*. Unpublished manuscript. New Haven, CT: Yale University Press.

hooks, b. (1990). *Yearning: Race, Gender, and Cultural Politics*. Boston: South End Press.

Horton, M. (1990). *The Long Haul: An Autobiography*, H. Kohl and J. Kohl (eds.). New York: Doubleday.

Howell, M. (1977, December). Just like a housewife: Delivering human services. *Radcliffe Alumnae Magazine,* pp. 5–7.

Hull, G. (1984). Alice Dunbar-Nelson: A personal and literary perspective. In C. Ascher, L. DeSalvo, and S. Ruddick (eds.), *Between Women: Biographers, Novelists, Critics, Teachers and Artists Write About Their Work on Women.* Boston: Beacon Press.

Hurston, Z. N. (1937/1991). *Their Eyes Were Watching God.* Urbana: University of Illinois Press.

Hurston, Z. N. (1979). *I Love Myself When I Am Laughing . . . and Then Again When I Am Looking Mean and Impressive: A Zora Neale Hurston Reader,* Alice Walker (ed.). New York: Feminist Press.

Ibsen, H. (1879/1950). *A Doll's House.* New York: Modern Library.

Jack, D. C. (1991). *Silencing the Self: Women and Depression.* Cambridge, MA: Harvard University Press.

Jacobs, H. A. (1861/1987). *Incidents in the Life of a Slave Girl: Written by Herself.* J. F. Yellin (ed.). Cambridge, MA: Harvard University Press.

Jaeckel, M., and G. Tüllman (eds.) (1988). *Mutter im Zentrum/Mütterzentrum.* Munich, Germany: DJI Verlag Deutsche Jugendinstitut.

James, W. (1910/1970). The moral equivalent of war. In R. Wasserstrom (ed.), *War and Morality.* Belmont, CA: Wadsworth.

Jordan, J., Kaplan, A., Miller, J., Stiver, I., and Surrey, J. (1991) *Women's Growth in Connection: Writings from the Stone Center.* New York: Guilford Press.

Kaltoft, G. (1988). Unpublished interview with Jane Sapp.

Kaltoft, G. (1990). *Music and Emancipator Learning in Three Community Education Programs.* Unpublished doctoral dissertation. New York: Teachers College Press.

Katz, M. (1989). *The Undeserving Poor: From the War on Poverty to the War on Welfare.* New York: Pantheon.

Kegan, R. (1982). *The Evolving Self: Problems and Process in Human Development.* Cambridge, MA: Harvard University Press.

Kegan, R. (1994). *In Over Our Heads: The Mental Demands of Modern Life.* Cambridge, MA: Harvard University Press.

Keller, E. F. (1985). *Reflections on Gender and Science.* New Haven, CT: Yale University Press.

Kimball, M. M. (1995). *Feminist Visions of Gender Similarities and Difference.* New York: Haworth Press.

Kohlberg, L. (1981). *Essays on Moral Development: Vol. 1. The Philosophy of Moral Development: Moral Stages and the Idea of Justice.* San Francisco: Harper & Row.

Kohlberg, L. (1984). *Essays on Moral Development: Vol. 2. The Psychology of Moral Development: The Nature and Validity of Moral Stages.* San Francisco: Harper & Row.

Kohn, M. (1977). *Class and Conformity: A Study in Values, with a Reassessment,* 2nd edition. Chicago: University of Chicago Press.

Kohn, M., and C. Schooler, with J. Miller, K. Miller, C. Schoenback, and R. Schoenberg (1983). *Work and Personality: An Inquiry into the Impact of Social Stratification.* Norwood, NJ: Ablex.

Labouvie-Vief, G. (1994). *Psyche and Eros: Mind and Gender in the Life Course.* New York: Cambridge University Press.

Ladner, J. A. (1971). *Tomorrow's Tomorrow: The Black Woman.* Garden City, NY: Doubleday.

Ladner, J. A., and R. M. Gourdine (1984). Inter-generational teenage motherhood. *SAGE: A Scholarly Journal on Black Women* 1 (2): 22–24.

Lagemann, E. C. (ed. (1985). *Jane Addams: An Educational Biography.* New York: Teachers College Press.

Lakoff, G., and M. Johnson (1980). *Metaphors We Live By.* Chicago: University of Chicago Press.

Lappe, F. M., and P. M. Du Bois (1994). *The Quickening of America: Rebuilding Our Nation, Remaking Our Lives.* San Francisco: Jossey-Bass.

Leibowitz, H. (1989). *Fabricating Lives: Exploration in American Autobiography.* New York: Knopf.

Lerner, G. (1973). *Black Women in White America: A Documentary History.* New York: Pantheon.

Lerner, M. (1996). *The Politics of Meaning: Restoring Hope and Possibility in an Age of Cynicism.* Reading, MA: Addison-Wesley.

Lever, J. (1976). Sex differences in the games children play. *Social Problems* 23: 478–87.

Levine, L. W. (1978). *Black Culture and Black Consciousness: Afro-American Folk Thought from Slavery to Freedom.* New York: Oxford University Press.

LeVine, R. A., P. M. Miller, A. L. Richman, and S. LeVine (1996). Education and mother–infant interaction: A Mexican case study. In S. Harkness and C. M. Super (eds., *Parents' Cultural Belief Systems: Their Origins, Expressions and Consequences.* New York: Guilford Press.

LeVine, R. A., P. M. Miller, and M. M. West (1988). Parental behavior in diverse societies. *New Directions in Child Development, 40.* San Francisco: Jossey-Bass.

Levinson, D. J., and N. Sanford (1982). Preface to the abridged edition. In T. W. Adorno, E. Frenkel-Brunswick, D. J. Levinson, and R. N. Sanford (eds.), *The Authoritarian Personality,* abridged edition. New York: W. W. Norton.

Lightfoot, S. L. (1983). *The Good High School: Portraits of Character and Culture.* New York: Basic Books.

Lipman-Blumen, J. (1996). *The Connective Edge: Leading in an Interdependent World.* San Francisco: Jossey-Bass.

Loevinger, J. (1976). *Ego Development: Conceptions and Theories.* San Francisco: Jossey-Bass.

Loevinger, J., and B. Sweet (1961). Construction of a test of mothers' attitudes. In J. C. Glidewell (ed.), *Parental Attitudes and Child Behavior.* Springfield, IL: Thomas.

Lyons, N. (1983). Two perspectives: On self, relationships, and morality. *Harvard Educational Review* 53: 125–145.

Maccoby, E. E., and J. A. Martin (1983). Socialization in the context of the family: Parent–child interaction. In E. M. Hetherington (ed.), *Handbook of Child*

Psychology: Vol. 4. Socialization, Personality, and Social Development. New York: John Wiley & Sons.

Marshall, P. (1983). The making of a writer: From the poets in the kitchen. In P. Marshall, *Merle and Other Stories.* London: Virago Press.

Martin, J. R. (1992). *The Schoolhome: Rethinking Schools for Changing Families.* Cambridge, MA: Harvard University Press.

Marx, K. (1983). *The Portable Karl Marx.* New York: Viking Press.

Mayhew, K. C., and A. C. Edwards (1936). *The Dewey School.* New York: Appleton-Century.

McAdams, D. P. (1990). Unity and purpose in human lives: The emergence of identity as a life story. In A. Rabin, R. Zucker, and S. Frank (eds.), *Studying Persons and Lives.* New York: Springer.

McFadden, G. J. (1993). Clark, Septima Poinsetta. In D. C. Hine, E. B. Brown, and R. Terborg-Penn (eds.), *Black Women in America: An Historical Encyclopedia.* Bloomington: Indiana University Press.

McGillicuddy-DeLisi, A. V. (1982). The relationship between parents' beliefs about development and family constellation, socioeconomic status, and parents' teaching strategies. In L. M. Laosa and I. E. Sigel (eds.), *Families as Learning Environments for Children.* New York: Plenum Press.

McGillicuddy-Delisi, A. V., J. E. Johnson, I. E. Sigel, and R. Epstein (1980). *Communication Strategy Administration and Coding Manual.* Princeton, NJ: Educational Testing Service.

McGillicuddy-DeLisi, A. V., and I. E. Sigel (1995). Parental beliefs. In M. H. Bornstein (ed.), *Handbook of Parenting: Vol. 3. Status and Social Conditions of Parenting.* Mahwah, NJ: Lawrence Erlbaum.

McKnight, J. (1995). *The Careless Society: Community and Its Counterfeits.* New York: Basic Books.

McLaren, J., and H. Brown (1993). *The Raging Grannie Songbook.* Philadelphia: New Society Publishers.

Meier, D. (1995). *The Power of Their Minds: Lessons for America from a Small School in Harlem.* Boston: Beacon Press.

Merchant, C. (1980). *The Death of Nature: Women, Ecology, and the Scientific Revolution.* New York: Harper & Row.

Merton, R. K., and P. L. Kendall (1946). The focused interview. *American Journal of Sociology* 51: 541–55.

Merton, R. K., M. Fiske, and P. L. Kendall (1956). *The Focused Interview: A Manual of Problems and Procedures.* New York: Free Press.

Miller, J. B. (1976/1987). *Towards a New Psychology of Women,* 2nd edition. Boston: Beacon Press.

Miller, J. B. (1988). Connections, disconnections, and violations. *Work in Progress,* No. 33. Wellesley, MA: Stone Center Working Paper Series.

Mishler, E. G. (1986). *Research Interviewing: Context and Narrative.* Cambridge, MA: Harvard University Press.

Monsey, T. V. C. (1990). *Why Parents Parent as They Do: Relationships Between Mothers' Epistemologies and Their Communication Strategies with*

Their Children. Unpublished master's thesis. Burlington: University of Vermont.

Montessori, M. (1917/1965). *Spontaneous Activity in Education.* New York: Schocken Books.

Morgan, D. L. (1993). *Successful Focus Groups: Advancing the State of the Art.* Newbury Park, CA: Sage.

Morris, A. D. (1984). *The Origins of the Civil Rights Movement: Black Communities Organizing for Social Change.* New York: Free Press.

Morrison, T. (1983). Interview with Claudia Tate. In C. Tate (ed.), *Black Women Writers at Work.* New York: Continuum.

Morrison, T. (1987). *Beloved: A Novel.* New York: Knopf.

Morrison, T. (1992). *Dancing in the Dark: Whiteness and the Literary Imagination.* Cambridge, MA: Harvard University Press.

Moses, R., R. Kamii, S. Swap, and J. Howard (1989). The algebra project: Organizing in the spirit of Ella Baker. *Harvard Educational Review* 59: 423–43.

Moulton, J. (1983). A paradigm of philosophy: The adversary method. In S. Harding and M. Hintilla (eds.), *Discovering Reality: Feminist Perspectives on Epistemology, Metaphysics, Methodology, and Philosophy of Science.* Boston: D. Reidel.

Muncy, R. (1991). *Creating a Female Dominion in American Reform 1890–1935.* New York: Oxford University Press.

National Congress of Neighborhood Women (1993). *The Neighborhood Women's Training Sourcebook.* New York: The National Congress of Neighborhood Women.

Noddings, N. (1989). *Women and Evil.* Berkeley: University of California Press.

Oakes, J. (1985). *Keeping Track: How Schools Structure Inequality.* New Haven, CT: Yale University Press.

Ogbu, J. (1987). Variability in minority responses to schooling: Nonimmigrants vs. immigrants. In C. Spindler and L. Spindler (eds.), *Interpretive Ethnography of Education at Home and Abroad.* Hillsdale, NJ: Lawrence Erlbaum.

Oliner, P. (1995). *Toward a Caring Society.* New York: Praeger.

Oliner, S., and P. Oliner (1988). *The Altruistic Personality: Rescuers of Jews in Nazi Europe.* New York: Free Press.

Olsen, T. (1961/1978) *Tell Me a Riddle.* New York: Delacorte Press.

Omolade, B. (1994). *The Rising Song of African American Women.* New York: Routledge.

Orenstein, P. (1994). *Schoolgirls: Young Women, Self-Esteem, and the Confidence Gap.* New York: Doubleday.

Orwell, G. (1946/1984). *Nineteen Eighty-Four.* New York: Oxford University Press.

Osborne, D., and T. Gaebler (1992). *Reinventing Government.* Reading, MA: Addison-Wesley.

Owen, U. (ed.) (1985). *Fathers: Reflections by Daughters.* New York: Pantheon.

Pagels, E. (1995). *The Origin of Satan.* New York: Random House.

Paley, G. (1994). *Collected Stories.* New York: Farrar, Straus, and Giroux.

Palmer, P. J. (1983). *To Know As We Are Known: A Spirituality of Education.* San Francisco: Harper & Row.

Parks, S. D. (1989). Home and pilgrimage: Companion metaphors for personal and social transformation. *Soundings* 72: 297–315.

Payne, C. (1989). Ella Baker and models of social change. *Signs: Journal of Women in Culture and Society* 14 (4): 885–99.

Payne, C. M. (1995). *I've Got the Light of Freedom: The Organizing Tradition and the Mississippi Freedom Struggle*. Berkeley: University of California Press.

Perry, W. G., Jr. (1970). *Forms of Intellectual and Ethical Development in the College Years: A Scheme*. New York: Holt, Rinehart and Winston.

Piaget, J. (1965). *The Moral Judgment of the Child*. New York: Free Press.

Piaget, J. (1985). *The Equilibration of Cognitive Structures: The Central Problem of Intellectual Development*. Chicago: University of Chicago Press.

Piirak, E., L. A. Bond, and M. F. Belenky (1995). *Variations in Women's Expression of Self-Reflection*. Unpublished manuscript. Burlington: Department of Psychology, University of Vermont Press.

Polkinghorne, D. (1988). *Narrative Knowing and the Human Sciences*. Albany: State University of New York Press.

Pomerleau, A., G. Malcuit, and C. Sabatier (1991). Child-rearing practices and parental beliefs in three cultural groups of Montreal: Quebeçois, Vietnamese, Haitian. In M. H. Bornstein (ed.), *Cultural Approaches to Parenting*. Hillsdale, NJ: Lawrence Erlbaum.

Power, C., A. Higgins, and L. Kohlberg (1989). *Lawrence Kohlberg's Approach to Education*. New York: Columbia University Press.

Putnam, R. D. (1995). Bowling alone: America's declining social capital. *The Responsive Community* 5 (2): 18–23.

Pyle, L. (1996). *We Are the Leaders: A Look at the World Through Grassroots Women's Eyes*. Videotape. L. Pyle, 75 W. Mosholu Parkway, Bronx, NY, 10467.

Ransby, B. (1993). Baker, Ella Josephine. In D. C. Hine, E. B. Brown, and R. Terborg-Penn (eds.), *Black Women in America: An Historical Encyclopedia: Vol. 1*. Bloomington: Indiana University Press, 1: 70–74.

Rath, A. (1995). *Moving Out While Staying Put: A Psychological Analysis of Poor Irish Women's Perspectives on Transformation and Change*. Unpublished doctoral dissertation. Cambridge, MA: Harvard University.

Rawls, J. (1971). *A Theory of Justice*. Cambridge, MA: Belknap Press of Harvard University Press.

Reagon, B. J. (1983). Coalition politics: Turning the century. In B. Smith (ed.), *Home Girls: A Black Feminist Anthology*. New York: Kitchen Table: Women of Color Press.

Reagon, B. J. (1990). Foreword: Nurturing resistance. In M. O'Brien and C. Little (eds.), *Reimaging America: The Arts of Social Change*. Philadelphia, PA: New Society Publishers.

Reagon, B. J., and Sweet Honey in the Rock (1993). *We Who Believe in Freedom: Sweet Honey . . . Still on the Journey*. New York: Doubleday.

Reinharz, S. (1992). *Feminist Methods in Social Research*. New York: Oxford University Press.

Reinharz, S. (1994). Toward an ethnography of "voice" and "silence." In E. J.

Trickett, R. J. Watts, and D. Birman (eds.), *Human Diversity: Perspectives on People in Context*. San Francisco: Jossey-Bass.

Rich, A. (1976). *Of Woman Born: Motherhood as Experience and Institution*. New York: W. W. Norton.

Richards, D. (1985). The implications of African-American spirituality. In M. K. Asante and K. W. Asante (eds.), *African Culture: The Rhythms of Unity*. Westport, CT: Greenwood Press.

Rogoff, B. (1990). *Apprenticeship in Thinking: Cognitive Development in Social Context*. New York: Oxford University Press.

Rose, M. (1995). *Possible Lives: The Promise of Public Education in America*. New York: Houghton Mifflin.

Rosenberg, M. (1979). *Conceiving the Self*. New York: Basic Books.

Rossiter, A. (1988). *From Private to Public: A Feminist Exploration of Early Mothering*. Toronto, Ontario: The Women's Press.

Ruddick, S. (1994). *Maternal Thinking: Towards a Politics of Peace*. Boston: Beacon Press.

Ruddick, S. (1996). Reason's "femininity": A case for connected knowing. In N. R. Goldberger, J. M. Tarule, B. McV. Clinchy, and M. F. Belenky (eds.), *Knowledge, Difference, and Power: Essays Inspired by Women's Ways of Knowing*. New York: Basic Books.

Rushing, A. B. (1987). God's divas: Women singers in African American poetry. In R. Terborg-Penn, S. Harley, and A. B. Rushing (eds.), *Women in Africa and the African Diaspora*. Washington, DC: Howard University Press.

Ryan, W. (1971). *Blaming the Victim*. New York: Random House.

Sadker, M., and D. Sadker (1994). *Failing at Fairness: How America's Schools Cheat Girls*. New York: Scribners.

Sanders, R. A. (1988). Mobile, Alabama. In E. Sullivan and M. Stokes Jennison (eds.), *An Alabama Scrapbook: 32 Alabamians Remember Growing Up*. Huntsville, AL: Honeysuckle Press.

Sanford, N. (1962). The developmental status of the entering freshmen. In N. Sanford (ed.), *The American College*. New York: Wiley.

Sanford, N. (1982). Social psychology: Its place in personology. *American Psychologist* 37: 896–903.

Sapp, J. (1996). *We've All Got Stories: Songs from the Dream Project*. Audio recording. Cambridge, MA: Rounder Records.

Sarbin, T. R. (1986). *Narrative Psychology: The Storied Nature of Human Conduct*. New York: Praeger.

Sartre, J. (1948). *Anti-Semite and Jew*, G. J. Becker (trans.). New York: Schocken Books.

Schon, D. (1983). *The Reflective Practitioner: How Professionals Think in Action*. New York: Basic Books.

Schoolboys of Barbiana (1970). *Letter to a Teacher*, J. Holt (ed.), N. Rossi and T. Cole (trans.). New York: Random House.

Seeger, P., and B. Reiser (1989). *Everybody Says Freedom: A History of the Civil Rights Movement in Songs and Pictures*. New York: Norton.

Seifer, N. (1976). *Nobody Speaks for Me*. New York: Simon Schuster.

Seigfried, C. H. (1996). *Pragmatism and Feminism: Reweaving the Social Fabric*. Chicago: University of Chicago Press.

Seitz, V. R. (1995). *Women, Development, and Communities for Empowerment in Appalachia*. Albany: State University of New York Press.

Sen, G., and C. Grown (1987). *Development, Crises, and Alternative Visions: Third World Women's Perspectives*. New York: Monthly Review Press.

Senge, P. (1990). *The Fifth Discipline: The Art and Practice of the Learning Organization*. New York: Doubleday.

Sherman, A. (1994). *Wasting America's Future: The Children's Defense Fund Report on the Cost of Child Poverty*. Boston: Beacon Press.

Shiva, V. (1989). *Staying Alive: Women, Ecology, and Survival in India*. London: Zed Books, Ltd.

Shure, M. B., and G. Spivack (1974). *Interpersonal Cognitive Problem Solving (ICPS): The PIPS Manual*. Philadelphia: Hahnemann University, Department of Mental Health Sciences.

Shure, M. B., and G. Spivack (1978). *Problem Solving Techniques in Childrearing*. San Francisco: Jossey-Bass.

Shweder, R. A. (1991). *Thinking Through Cultures: Expeditions in Cultural Psychology*. Cambridge, MA: Harvard University Press.

Sidel, R. (1996). *Keeping Women and Children Last*. Boston: Beacon Press.

Slaughter, D. T. (1983). Early intervention and its effects on maternal and child development. *Monographs of the Society for Research in Child Development* 48 (4, Serial No. 202).

Smetana, J. G. (1994). Parenting styles and beliefs about parental authority. In J. G. Smetana (ed.), Beliefs about parenting: Origins and developmental implications. *New Directions for Child Development* 66: 21–36.

Smith, V. (1990). "Loopholes of retreat": Architecture and ideology in Harriet Jacob's *Incidents in the Life of a Slave Girl*. In H. L. Gates, Jr. (ed.), *Reading Black, Reading Feminist: A Critical Anthology*. New York: Meridian Books.

Spelman, E. (1989). Anger and insubordination. In A. Garry and M. Pearsall (eds.), *Women, Knowledge, and Reality: Explorations in Feminist Philosophy*. Boston: Unwin Hyman.

Sprinthall, N. A. (1980). Psychology for secondary schools: The saber-tooth curriculum revisited? *American Psychologist* 35: 336–347.

Sternberg, R. J., and W. M. Williams (1995). Parenting toward cognitive competence. In M. H. Bornstein (ed.), *Handbook of Parenting: Vol. 4. Applied and Practical Parenting*. Mahwah, NJ: Lawrence Erlbaum.

Stetson, E. (1984). Silence: Access and aspiration. In C. Ascher, L. DeSalvo, and S. Ruddick, S. (eds.), *Between Women: Biographers, Novelists, Critics, Teachers and Artists Write About Their Work on Women*. Boston: Beacon Press.

Tannen, D. (1990). *You Just Don't Understand: Women and Men in Conversation*. New York: William Morrow.

Tarule, J. M. (1996). Voices in dialogue: Collaborative ways of knowing. In N. R. Goldberger, J. M. Tarule, B. McV. Clinchy, and M. F. Belenky (eds.),

Knowledge, Difference, and Power: Essays Inspired by Women's Ways of Knowing. New York: Basic Books.

Taylor, C. (1992). *The Ethics of Authenticity*. Cambridge, MA: Harvard University Press.

Thorne, B. (1993). *Gender Play: Girls and Boys in School*. New Brunswick, NJ: Rutgers University Press.

Thurer, S. L. (1994). *The Myths of Motherhood: How Culture Reinvents the Good Mother*. New York: Houghton Mifflin.

Traub, J. (1996). Passing the baton: Workplace democracy in the Orpheus Chamber Orchestra. *The New Yorker*, August 26 and September 2, 1996.

Vermont State Office of Economic Opportunity (1983). *Vermont Profile of Poverty*. Montpelier, VT.

Vygotsky, L. S. (1978). *Mind in Society: The Development of Higher Psychological Processes*. Cambridge MA: Harvard University Press.

Wade-Gayles, G. (1980). She who is black and mother: In sociology and fiction, 1940–1970. In La Frances Rodgers-Rose (ed.), *The Black Woman*. Beverly Hills: Sage.

Walker, A. (1983). *In Search of Our Mothers' Gardens*. San Diego: Harcourt Brace Jovanovich.

Walker, A. (1984). Looking for Zora. In C. Ascher, L. DeSalvo, and S. Ruddick (eds.), *Between Women: Biographers, Novelists, Critics, Teachers, and Artists Write About Their Work on Women*. Boston: Beacon Press.

Walker, A. (1985). The democratic order: Such things in twenty years I understood. In U. Owen (ed.), *Fathers: Reflections by Daughters*. New York: Pantheon.

Wallace, M. (1979). *Black Macho and the Myth of the Superwoman*. New York: Dial Press.

Waring, M. (1988). *If Women Counted: A New Feminist Economics*. San Francisco: Harper & Row.

Washington, M. H. (1984). I sign my mother's name: Alice Walker, Dorothy West, Paule Marshall. In R. Perry and M. W. Brownley (eds.), *Mothering the Mind: Twelve Studies of Writers and Their Silent Partners*. New York: Homes and Meier.

Washington, M. H. (1990). The darkened eye restored. In H. L. Gates, Jr. (ed.), *Reading Black, Reading Feminist: A Critical Anthology*. New York: Meridian Books.

Weinstock, J. S. (1989). *Epistemological Expressions Among College Women in Two Contexts: Conflicts with Friends and Authorities*. Unpublished master's thesis. Burlington: University of Vermont.

Weinstock, J. S. (1993). *College Women's Conceptions of Close Friendship, Conceptions of Conflicts with Close Friends, and Epistemological Perspectives*. Unpublished doctoral dissertation. Burlington: University of Vermont.

Welch, S. (1990). *A Feminist Ethic of Risk*. Minneapolis: Fortress Press.

Woodson, C. G. (1930). The Negro washerwoman, A vanishing figure. *Journal of Negro History* 15: 269–277.

Woolf, V. (1929/1957). *A Room of One's Own*. New York: Harcourt, Brace & World.

Yellin, J. F. (ed.) (1987). Introduction. In H. A. Jacobs, *Incidents in the Life of a Slave Girl: Written by Herself*. Cambridge, MA: Harvard University Press.

Youniss, J. (1994). Rearing children for society. In J. G. Smetana (ed.), Beliefs about parenting: Origins and developmental implications. *New Directions for Child Development* 66: 37–50.

Zimmerman, H. (ed.) (1980). *Mothers' Center Manual*. Unpublished manuscript. Mothers' Center Development Project, 336 Fulton Ave., Hempstead, NY 11550.

Zinn, H. (1964). *SNCC: The New Abolitionists*. Boston: Beacon Press.

INDEX

Accounting systems (in ernational, economic), women as nonproductive versus men as productive in, 22–24

Action projects, developmental leaders and, 273–75

Activity. *See* Parent activity

Addams, Jane, 175–76, 206, 286–87

Adolescent girls, coming of age among black versus white, 25–26

Adorno, T. W., 42–44

AFI. *See* Authoritarian Family Ideology

African American women: autonomy and connection among, 25–30; coming of age among, 25–26; as cultural workers, 157 *see also* Center for Cultural and Community Development; Cultural work/cultural workers; as developmental leaders, 12–13, 169–74, 176–79; developmental leadership taught by, 295–307; emotions and, 19; procreation and creativity among, 30–37; public homeplaces and, 162; slavery and, 27–28, 29, 30, 176. *See also* Center for Cultural and Community Development

African Diaspora project 242–43

African Ensemble, 240

Anger, homeplace women handling injustice with, 278–87

Anti-Semite and Jew (Sartre), 35

Argentina, Mothers of the Plaza de Mayo in, 178

Aristotle, 277

Art: African American women and, 34–35; constructivists and, 63–64

Art-making. *See* Cultural work/cultural workers

Asante, Molefi Kete, 27

Authentic public spaces, 161. *See also* Public homeplaces

Authoritarian, mother-child communication as, 135

Authoritarian Family Ideology (AFI), 46

Authoritarian personality, research on, 42–44, 46–47; ego development and, 45–47; epistemological development and, 44–45

Authoritarian Personality, The (Adorno, Frenkel-Brunswik, and Levinson), 46, 47

Authoritarian Personality, The (Adorno, Frenkel-Brunswik, Levinson, and Sanford), 42–44

Autonomous Stage, of ego development, 46, 50

Autonomy, connection versus, 25–30

Awakening, The (Chopin), 28–29, 30

Bailey, Sister, 296–97, 298, 299–300, 303, 305

Baker, Ella: beloved community and, 162–63; developmental leadership and, 170–71, 174; In Friendship and, 170–71, 247; influence of, 12, 176–78, 295; Student Nonviolent Coordinating Committee and, 12, 162–63, 171, 176–77, 247; success of, 169

Barnwell, Ysaye, 287

B'BAC. *See* Black Belt Arts Center

Belenky, Mary F., 4, 9, 51, 55–66, 157–58, 230–33, 332n4